To:

....

From:

....

BEING STILL

GOD

WITH

A 366 DAILY DEVOTIONAL

HENRY & RICHARD
BLACKABY

COUNTRYMAN®

A Division of Thomas Nelson Publishers

THOMAS NELSON
Since 1798

NASHVILLE MEXICO CITY RIO DE JANEIRO

Being Still with God

© 2007 by Dr.'s Richard and Henry Blackaby

Published in Nashville, Tennessee, by Thomas Nelson, Inc.

ISBN 13: 978-0-5291-0556-1

Printed and bound in China

www.thomasnelson.com

15 16 17 18 19 DSC 6 5 4 3 2

"You shall love the LORD your God with all your heart, with all your soul, and with all your might."

DEUTERONOMY 6:5

JANUARY

He who keeps His commandments
abides in Him, and He in him.

1 JOHN 3:24

A Fresh Beginning

"Behold, I will do a new thing,
Now it shall spring forth . . .
I will even make a road in the wilderness
And rivers in the desert."

ISAIAH 43:19

God uses events in our lives to shape us, to teach us, to grow us—and some of the key events are those sparked by sin (our own or someone sinning against us), by our missteps, by our confusion. Memories of the past, therefore, can too easily feel like shackles holding us to failures, regrets, ignorance, foolishness, and sin.

However, God doesn't want us bound to our past. When God saves us from the death we deserve for our sin, He frees us from the guilt and shame of our former life as well. He gives us a fresh beginning. He frees us to receive every good thing He wants to give us.

If your past feels like a wilderness, know that God wants to make a road through it, perhaps to help you navigate the difficult years and salvage the good. If your past feels like a desertland of death, know that God will make rivers of redemption flow as He brings beauty out of ashes. Embrace the fresh beginning God wants to give you.

Now That's Power!

*"You shall receive power when the Holy Spirit
has come upon you; and you shall be witnesses
to Me . . . to the end of the earth."*

ACTS 1:8

Diesel. Electrical. Mechanical. Hydroelectric. Nuclear. Atomic. There are many forms of power, but none is equal to that of the Holy Spirit.

The Holy Spirit's power is described by the Greek word *dunamis*, the root for *dynamite* and *dynamic*. Whereas dynamite destroys, *dunamis* gives life. This word for an active, energizing power implies a miracle or divine influence—and that's exactly what we need as we obey the resurrected Lord's command to be His witnesses.

Just as the Holy Spirit empowered Christ to fulfill His earthly assignment, we too need the Spirit. The Holy Spirit's power is absolutely essential to kingdom work, which is why Jesus told His disciples to wait for it (Acts 1:4–5). Jesus knew that His disciples could do more in a day in the Spirit's power than they could do in a lifetime on their own.

Jesus ministered and served, preached and taught, lived and died by the Holy Spirit's power, and now He gives His power to all who believe. As we walk in the Spirit's power, He will greatly impact the world through us.

Making Choices

So Abram said to Lot . . . "Is not the whole land before you?
Please separate from me. If you take the left, then I will go to
the right; or, if you go to the right, then I will go to the left."

GENESIS 13:8—9

Lot faced a monumental decision. He had the opportunity to choose which land to settle—land that would support his family and his flocks now and in the future. It was a hugely important decision, so Lot looked around and surveyed the land carefully.

As Lot's uncle, Abraham could have pulled rank and had the first pick. But instead of carefully looking over the land, Abraham looked up to the Lord. Abraham's faith was in his unseen God. He did not make choices based on what looked most attractive to him, as Lot did. Instead Abraham acted with confidence that God would not only guide him but also accompany him in whatever direction He led him to go.

What is the basis for your decisions? Although we need to wisely consider the situation at hand, we must remember that appearances can be deceiving. When Lot chose the well-watered plain of Jordan, he also chose Sodom. So we must, like Abraham, look up to the Lord for His guidance when we need to make a choice.

Not My Will . . .

*[Jesus] said, "Abba, Father, all things are possible
for You. Take this cup away from Me; nevertheless,
not what I will, but what You will."*

MARK 14:36

Just because something is the right thing to do doesn't mean it will be easy. Just because we face problems and obstacles doesn't mean we have missed or misunderstood God's will for us. All of us have undoubtedly faced times when doing God's will demanded all of our strength and determination—and our Savior has walked that path.

It's hard to imagine doing anything more difficult than what Jesus chose in Gethsemane. He was given the most difficult assignment possible. Misunderstood by His closest followers . . . betrayed by one of the twelve He had poured His life into, denied by His most outspoken disciple, deserted by the rest . . . arrested, unfairly tried, cruelly beaten, dying a criminal's brutal death on a cross, then facing the righteous wrath of God for the sin of humanity. This was the cup Jesus accepted in Gethsemane. Jesus submitted to God's plan and walked the path that caused Him to feel the unimaginable weight of all humanity's sin.

At times you—like your Savior and Lord—must make the difficult choice to put aside your own wishes and submit to God's will. God's way is not always the easy path, but it is always the right one.

Called—and Enabled

I thank Christ Jesus our Lord who has enabled me, because
He counted me faithful, putting me into the ministry.

1 TIMOTHY 1:12

Those whom God calls to a specific task He always enables. When the Lord sees we have been faithful in a little, He gives us more—and His "more" will always stretch us. We would find it easier to continue being faithful where we already are than to go to the next level in our walk with God, but then we would stop growing. So God puts us in places of greater service where we will fail unless we develop a greater trust in Him than we have ever had before.

But along with every challenging call comes God's perfect enabling. He is prepared to meet every need we will face as we step out in obedience and faith. He will grant us the strength we require to match every demand. He will bestow the wisdom we require to navigate every decision.

It is an awesome experience to realize that Almighty God is personally equipping you to serve Him. So if God is calling you to a new assignment, be encouraged! You are about to experience God in ways you have never known before.

"I AM"

*God said to Moses, "I AM WHO I AM . . . . Say
to the children of Israel: 'The Lord God of your
fathers, the God of Abraham, the God of Isaac,
and the God of Jacob, has sent me to you.'"*

EXODUS 3:14–15

The Hebrew word for *Lord,* God's name, is *YHWH.*
Translated "I AM" and used about seven thousand times
in the Old Testament, this most sublime name of God was
whispered by the high priest in the Most Holy Place once a
year. Outside of that important occasion, the name was never
written or uttered.

YHWH, or *Yahweh,* speaks of God as "He that always was,
always is, and ever is to come." God revealed this name to
Moses, and it became the name associated with the covenant
between God and His people.

That Old Testament covenant has been fulfilled in the New
Testament, enabling you to find forgiveness for your sins and
to enjoy an intimate relationship with your heavenly Father. As
you live out your faith, you will come to know God as Healer,
Protector, Provider, Comforter, and Savior.

Your unique life experiences will reveal God's nature to you
in countless personal ways. Ask Him to help you see this very
day some of the ways He is revealing His character to you.

The Power of Scripture Beginning with Moses and All the Prophets

[Jesus] expounded to them in all the Scriptures the things concerning Himself.

LUKE 24:27

As the two travelers walked toward Emmaus, their minds were swirling. *How could Jesus have died? We were convinced He was the Messiah, but we saw Him nailed to the cross . . . And the Eleven have scattered . . . How could we have been so sure and so wrong about Jesus of Nazareth?*

In times of confusion or uncertainty, Jesus will open the Scriptures to us. That's exactly what He—the resurrected Lord—did for those two men who were hungry for truth. The Scriptures are words of life that hold God's answers to whatever problems we face; they give reason for peace and hope, and they remind us of God's love and faithfulness.

God's Word is clear and direct, yet we tend to complicate it by debating it, adding to it, or being selective about what we read and believe. Ask the Holy Spirit to grant you insight into God's Word. Ask Him to use His truth to teach you, reassure you, and equip you to live your life and to serve Him. He will also use His Word to strengthen you for life's challenges so you are fully equipped for what He knows is coming next.

Grace to All

The book of the genealogy of Jesus Christ, the
Son of David, the Son of Abraham . . .

MATTHEW 1:1

Genealogy in this context means "origin," and the origin of Jesus of Nazareth was very important to first-century Jews wondering if He was in fact the long-awaited Messiah. Significantly, Matthew traced Jesus' lineage back through King David to Abraham, two key Jewish patriarchs.

Further reading reveals that the list includes four women. This is unusual not just because females were typically excluded from such records, but because of who these women were. Tamar had a scandalous relationship with Judah (Genesis 38); Rahab was a Canaanite harlot from Jericho (Joshua 2); Ruth was a Moabite (Ruth 1:4); and Bathsheba committed adultery with David (2 Samuel 11:1–12:25). Their inclusion reflects God's forgiveness and grace to all people.

God offers the same clemency to all people. His mercy is available to you and, through you, to others. Thank God for His amazing grace. Praise Him for opening your eyes to the reality of your sin and the good news of His forgiveness. Then let Him know you are available for His purposes—just as He used Rahab and Ruth and many other sinners and outsiders— to further His kingdom and to proclaim His grace to others.

Finding Strength in God

The word of the LORD came expressly to Ezekiel the
priest . . . and the hand of the LORD was upon him there.

EZEKIEL 1:3

Ezekiel's name means "God will strengthen"—and God's strength is exactly what the prophet needed as he carried out his God-given assignment to proclaim judgment and restoration to the people of Judah during their Babylonian exile.

Ezekiel's ministry was marked by visions, prophecies, symbolic actions, and unpopular speeches. At times his actions appeared extreme: he set his face against a clay tablet (4:1–2), lay on one side for 390 days and on the other for 40 days (4:4–6), shaved off his hair (5:1–4), and spoke his many visions of judgment.

Under the triple burden of opposition, confusing circumstances, and an arduous assignment, Ezekiel remained faithful. He also knew that, in the midst of adversity, people do not need a better understanding of their plight; they need a fresh vision of God's majesty and the reminder that, no matter the crisis, God is sovereign.

Ezekiel's unique ministry exemplifies a life completely surrendered to God and committed to His purposes. The prophet serves as one of Scripture's most notable examples of being a living sacrifice in service to God. Ezekiel found his strength in the Lord, just as we must.

Life and Death

*For the wages of sin is death, but the gift of God
is eternal life in Christ Jesus our Lord.*

ROMANS 6:23

Every human being will die, and that death is a doorway into an eternity of either separation from God or joyful living in His presence. Which path will be yours?

All of us are born in sin. We all inherit Adam's sinful nature; we don't stand a chance of living a life without sin. But God has made a provision for sinners who turn to Him. God sent Jesus to die for repentant sinners. Christians are therefore alive by faith, and we will never die spiritually.

Spiritual death is what Paul was referring to in Romans 6:23. In that verse *death* means something beyond the mere termination of physical life. The apostle was referring to spiritual death, a state of utter darkness and absolute abandonment. In spiritual death, our souls are without hope. In spiritual death, our souls are forever separated from the God whom a person refused to acknowledge during life.

So which eternal path will be yours? And which will be the destination of your loved ones, dearest friends, neighbors, and co-workers? You have an extremely important message to share with them. Make sure each person clearly knows what is at stake.

Contending for the Faith

*I found it necessary to write to you exhorting
you to contend earnestly for the faith which
was once for all delivered to the saints.*

JUDE 3

The Greek behind our word *contend* means "to earnestly struggle for something." It suggests striving against opposition as if in a battle. It describes a contestant straining for victory against a foe. Jude exhorts Christians to "contend . . . for the faith" as combatants in a spiritual conflict.

Evil forces seek to rob us of our faith and disrupt our relationship with Jesus. Christ's adversary will do whatever is in his power to destroy the body of Christ—and this reality ought to keep us alert. We can't afford to treat our Christian faith casually. We need to guard it and nurture it. We need to fight for it. For what our enemy cannot do, our neglect and carelessness can.

In what ways is the Christian faith in general—and your faith in particular—being attacked today? More importantly, what are you doing to stand strong? Don't forget to put on the armor of God—the belt of truth, the breastplate of righteousness, the gospel of peace, the shield of faith, the helmet of salvation, and the sword of the Spirit (Ephesians 6:13–18). With prayer and the Holy Spirit, you are ready to do battle for your precious faith!

Always Within Us

He who keeps His commandments
abides in Him, and He in him.

1 JOHN 3:24

Many things in your life will change over time. But thankfully, by God's grace, when the Holy Spirit enters the life of a believer, He's there to stay.

That is the implication of the Greek word translated *abide*: "to remain or stay in one place; to take up residence and live somewhere." The word emphasizes the permanence and faithfulness of God as He dwells within us, as He maintains a relationship with us.

We learn from Jesus Himself that God makes a believer's life a temple in which He dwells through His Spirit (John 15:4–7). That truth has profound implications for how we live. We are, for instance, to be good stewards of our body, which is the temple of God's Holy Spirit (1 Corinthians 6:19–20).

Even as God abides in a believer's life, we are to abide in Him. To abide in God is to live in His presence and, as a result, to take on His characteristics. His life becomes our life as our life is hidden in Him.

We are therefore to face every situation and relate to every person with the distinct awareness that Jesus is always with us *and* within us. How is that affecting the way you are currently living?

Diligent Devotion

Be diligent to be found by Him in peace,
without spot and blameless.

2 PETER 3:14

Webster's defines *diligent* as "characterized by steady, earnest, and energetic effort; painstaking" and "earnest application to some specific object or pursuit."

What God is telling us through Peter, then, is that we believers must never treat our spiritual life casually. We are to pursue the Christian life with great effort, for we know the day of the Lord is fast approaching.

We believers must also endeavor to maintain unity (Ephesians 4:3); to persevere to present ourselves approved unto God (2 Timothy 2:15); to seek carefully to enter God's rest (Hebrews 4:11); and to work to be found blameless (2 Peter 3:14). Similarly, the apostle Paul urged believers to "work out your own salvation with fear and trembling" (Philippians 2:12).

What specific steps are you taking to "work out your salvation," to live a life that pleases your Lord? You'll be more successful if you have a specific plan—a program for reading the Bible, a person to pray with, a small group for Bible study and discussion, a church home in which to worship. As you invest time and effort in your relationship with God, you are investing in eternity. Be diligent in every area of your walk with Christ.

Riches Are for Sharing

You know the grace of our Lord Jesus Christ, that
though He was rich, yet for your sakes He became poor,
that you through His poverty might become rich.

2 CORINTHIANS 8:9

Human love typically expects something in return; divine love, however, is unselfishly given regardless of the response of the recipient. Whether we choose to love God or not, His love for us remains.

Jesus sacrificed that which was rightfully His (unbroken fellowship with His holy Father and the riches of His heavenly divinity) and endured suffering that was rightfully ours. Jesus has loved us unconditionally and blessed us with riches beyond imagining—forgiveness, cleansing, fellowship with Him, becoming fellow heirs in His kingdom, a personal relationship with God, the presence of the Spirit, and life everlasting in heaven.

Riches are for sharing. We can never adequately thank, much less repay, God for all that He has showered upon us. But we can give of our talents and energy, our time and our money as an expression of our devotion and love for Him.

Any and all giving we do is a humble response to God's unsurpassed generosity to us and to the "indescribable gift" of His Son Jesus (9:15). What does your generosity say about your love for Christ?

Pausing at the Cross

Let this mind be in you which was also in Christ Jesus.

PHILIPPIANS 2:5

Our thoughts are far from being God's thoughts. We strive to save our lives; God commands us to give our lives away. We want to exalt ourselves; God instructs us to humble ourselves. We aim to be first; God tells us to be last. We adamantly defend ourselves; Jesus asks us to turn the other cheek. We cannot think like the world does yet have the mind of Christ. We must allow the Holy Spirit to transform our carnal, self-centered, ungodly thinking.

Consider how far you presently are from having a mind like Christ—from His willingness to serve, His passion to be obedient to God to the point of death, His unblemished holiness.

Do you truly want to have the mind of Christ? Are you willing to abandon your current values, prejudices, resentments, jealousies, and unforgiveness? Are you prepared for the Holy Spirit to expose those areas of your thinking that are not in line with Christ's? Are you willing to fill your mind with God's thoughts found in Scripture?

May pausing at the cross remove the pride that defies God's right to your life and keeps Him from using you for His glory! It is incredibly freeing to think like Jesus.

Spiritual Powerlessness

The disciples came to Jesus privately and said,
"Why could we not cast [the demon] out?"

MATTHEW 17:19

The man's son had suffered severely from seizures. His father explained, "He often falls into the fire and often into the water" (v. 15). Desperately wanting his son cured, the father took him to the disciples—who were unable to help.

Why? That's what the disciples wanted to know. It may also be a good question for you to ask about your circumstances.

Spiritual powerlessness provides compelling evidence that something is wrong with our faith. At such times, though, we need not merely speculate about why God's power is absent from our lives. We can—and we should—do as the disciples did: go directly to God and ask Him.

Jesus rebuked the demon and healed the boy. Then, answering the disciples' question, He simply said, "Because of your unbelief" (v. 20). He went on to say that "this kind [of demon] does not go out except by prayer and fasting" (v. 21).

If you're experiencing spiritual powerlessness, perhaps prayer and fasting are in order. Or perhaps your faith must be strengthened. Your prayer may need to be that of the father in Mark's account: "Lord, I believe; help my unbelief!" (9:24).

God's Anointed

You have an anointing from the Holy One.

1 JOHN 2:20

We live in an evil age. Our world is filled with voices inviting us to turn away from Christ and to pursue the carnal world's values. We must constantly be alert in this kind of environment.

Thankfully, God has given us all we need to stand strong in His truth and His ways. He has given us His Word as our guidebook and our foundation. Scripture clearly sets forth God's truth, His commands, and His instruction. We do not have to be confused in this complicated and deceptive world.

God has also given us the church. Believers are not to stand alone. We are called to be iron sharpening iron, to bear one another's burdens, to hold one another accountable for decisions and choices, to go to one another for counsel and prayer. We don't have to face the enemy on our own.

We are further blessed to have the Holy Spirit. In Old Testament times, prophets and kings were anointed with oil to set them apart for a great task. In this epistle, the apostle John suggested that God has spiritually anointed believers for His work. So go forth into your world in that anointing, in God's power and presence. Be confident that when God anoints you, He stands ready to grant you success in what He has called you to do.

God's Surprising Servants

*"Nebuchadnezzar the king of Babylon, My servant . . . will
bring them against this land, against its inhabitants, and
against these nations all around, and will utterly destroy them."*

Read again God's pronouncement in Jeremiah 25:9. God is
speaking—and notice the "servant" He mentions!

Nebuchadnezzar was king of the Chaldeans, a nation that
campaigned against Judah between 605 and 586 BC. After
Nebuchadnezzar conquered the land, he chose to follow the
same fierce policies that his Assyrian predecessors had effectively used when they overtook Israel.

Nebuchadnezzar did not seek God, follow Him, honor Him,
or try to obey Him, but God is not confined to using only His
people for His purposes. His entire creation is at His disposal.

God will work with any instrument He chooses. Even God's
enemies can become His servants, carrying out judgment on
His people. That's exactly what Jeremiah was prophesying:
God will use Nebuchadnezzar as an agent of judgment against
His straying people.

When has God used one of His enemies as a servant—perhaps even as a servant of judgment—in your life? Be careful
and don't assume that every difficulty in your life is the result
of spiritual warfare. You may be encountering God's chastisement through an unknowing servant.

No Return

So [God] drove out the man; and He placed cherubim at the east of the garden of Eden, and a flaming sword which turned every way, to guard the way to the tree of life.

GENESIS 3:24

Why do you think you'll be going to heaven? Because of the good works you've done—given blood, worked at the soup kitchen, donated significant sums to a worthwhile charity, attended church regularly, and even taught Sunday school? Because of the bad things you've avoided—all those nasty things you *didn't* do?

What about the people you've murdered in your heart or those with whom you've committed adultery in your mind? What about the times you haven't turned the other cheek, loved your enemy, or blessed those who curse you? According to Jesus' teaching in Matthew 5, you have broken God's law.

Whether we're talking about the sin of Adam and Eve or our own, we need to realize that God's judgment of sin is thorough and absolute. Sin separates us from God, and there is nothing we can do to regain access to His holy presence. The most devastating consequence of sin is separation from God. Only God in His grace can enable us to return to Him: Jesus dying on the cross for our sin is the ultimate picture of grace and our only hope.

God's Sovereignty

The LORD carried Judah and Jerusalem into
captivity by the hand of Nebuchadnezzar.

1 CHRONICLES 6:15

It was a time in Israel's life when God seemed to no longer be in control. How could He allow the pagan enemy king to carry off His chosen people and destroy the holy temple? Were the Babylonian gods so much stronger? Or was God unaware that His people needed Him?

Sovereign God was totally aware of what Nebuchadnezzar was perpetuating against His people. Nebuchadnezzar, as powerful as he appeared, was not in control. God alone oversees people's destinies. Prominent leaders may boast of their accomplishments, but it is God who uses them to carry out His purposes in ways that He determines. Kingdoms conquer and leaders rule only within parameters set by God.

In addition to that encouraging truth, remember that God goes before you into battle and even into captivity. If you want to walk confidently as you face God's enemies in this world, make sure you have sought God's wisdom and are, in turn, following His commands. When you have done this, you can live with inner peace, confident that your Lord goes ahead of you to secure victory. Regardless of how your present circumstances may appear, God remains sovereign and He will accomplish His purposes in your life.

Yoked to Christ

*"Come to Me, all you who labor and are
heavy laden, and I will give you rest."*

MATTHEW 11:28

"Weary and burdened" may describe you.

Weariness comes with being human. We fill our schedule too full. We run out of energy. The demands on our time overwhelm us. We get a bad night's sleep. We succumb to the common cold germ. . . .

Burdens come with being alive. We have responsibilities. People make demands of us. We all have—to one degree or another—an awareness of our own sin, of the hurts of those around us, of the needs of the world . . .

But if you are weary and burdened because of what you're doing for the Lord, you are not yoked to Him. Those who walk in the Lord's strength as they serve Him do not complain. Because His yoke is light. Those who seek to produce for God by their own efforts will encounter frustration and disappointment. They will grow weary and feel burdened. God does not burn people out!

Are you serving where God wants you to serve? Remember that He does not reward our duty; He blesses our relationship with His Son. Keep that relationship with Jesus your priority as you serve God.

Unbelief Angers God

*[Moses] said, "O my Lord, please send by the
hand of whomever else You may send."
So the anger of the LORD was kindled against Moses.*

EXODUS 4:13–14

He was full of doubts: "What if they don't believe me?
What if they don't even listen to what I have to say?"

He had plenty of excuses: "I'm not eloquent. I'm slow of
speech."

And he had a Plan B: "Please send someone else."

Moses' response to God's command to lead the Israelite
people out of Egypt revealed his unbelief. No matter how difficult God's assignments appear, God desires obedience. He is
God. He owes us no explanation as to why He has chosen us or
about how He will use us to fulfill His plans.

God, however, gave the reluctant Moses a spokesperson
in his brother Aaron. But Moses' refusal to believe that God
could use him as His messenger meant that he missed out on
what God intended for him. God may accommodate our lack
of faith, but our unbelief always costs us and those around us.

What is God calling you to do? What are your doubts . . .
and your excuses? What help and power has He provided?
Step out in obedience and faith, avoid God's disapproval, and
enjoy His blessings that follow.

Sowing Bountifully

He who sows sparingly will also reap sparingly, and
he who sows bountifully will also reap bountifully.

2 CORINTHIANS 9:6

For every good work God lays before us and calls us to do, He is ready to provide all that we need to respond obediently and joyfully. God gives to us so we can give to Him and to His people. His provision is never short, and it is never late. He also gives in proportion to our faith. . . .

Rosalind Goforth and her husband, Jonathan, were missionaries to China in the late 1800s. Their early labors brought few results, and Rosalind grew discouraged by the apparent futility of their efforts.

One day, struggling with disappointment, she turned to 2 Corinthians 9:6. The words leaped out as God's clear answer to her situation. Greatly moved by God's truth, she wrote the words "HE WHO SOWS BOUNTIFULLY WILL ALSO REAP BOUNTIFULLY" on a blackboard. For the next two years, she kept that truth—written in bold black and white—before her. In due time, God used the Goforths in one of the greatest periods of revival in missionary history. . . .

Our generous God loves to bless those who have generous hearts for His kingdom work and His people. Therefore, sow seeds of His love bountifully in the lives of those around you.

Remember God's Glory

"And you shall tell your son in that day, saying,
'This is done because of what the LORD did
for me when I came up from Egypt.'"

EXODUS 13:8

What is your faith story? At what moments has God's grace been unmistakably at work in your life? What stories of His deliverance have you told your children or perhaps even your grandchildren?

What do you know about your parents' faith story? about your grandparents' journey with the Lord?

Knowing your Christian heritage can strengthen your trust in and devotion to God. Passing your faith on to your children is a privilege and a duty. God commands His people to remember His mighty deeds. The Israelites were to tell the next generation about the powerful works God did in delivering them from slavery in Egypt—the plagues, the angel of death, the parting of the Red Sea, and the destruction of the Egyptian army. Likewise, we are to tell the next generation about the wonders God did in delivering us from slavery to sin—Christ coming in human form, living a sinless life, His willingness to submit to death on a cross, the brutal Crucifixion, the glorious resurrection.

It is crucial that we pass our faith on to our children because unbelief is always just one generation away.

"Able to Keep You from Stumbling"

Now to Him who is able to keep you from stumbling,
And to present you faultless . . .
To God our Savior . . .
Be glory and majesty,
Dominion and power,
Both now and forever. Amen.

JUDE 24—25

In Jude's day, like today, wolves—heretics and hypocrites, imposters and idolaters—lived among the flocks of God's sheep. God's Spirit, however, enables those in a relationship with Him to recognize these predators. Relying on the Spirit, we won't be fooled by corrupt people seeking to destroy Christ's body and exploit the faith of believers.

The forces of evil that sought to undermine Christ's earthly ministry continue to assault His church today. But the almighty God, who empowered His Son to win the victory over Satan, continues to sustain believers. God warns that the end times will see an increase in adversity against His people, but He also promises that through His strength victory is assured.

Don't let your circumstances or spiritual failures discourage you. Your spiritual victory is not based on your wisdom, your strength, or your ingenuity. It depends entirely upon Christ and His ability to hold you in His hand. He is more than able; He can cleanse you from every impurity; and His forgiveness will allow you to one day stand faultless before Him. Amen!

Always Burning

"A fire shall always be burning on the
altar; it shall never go out."

LEVITICUS 6:13

F ive times God commanded the priests of Israel to keep the altar fire burning (Leviticus 6). The reason for this may have been that God Himself originally started the fire (Leviticus 9:24). Or maybe the fire was to symbolize Israel's perpetual worship of God. Or perhaps the constantly burning fire indicated that God's people continually needed to atone for their sin.

Figuratively speaking, the fire on God's altar is always burning today just as it was in Old Testament times. Atonement—once and for all—has been made through Christ. Now forgiveness of sin and the possibility of a restored relationship with God are, like the ever-burning flame, always available to those who seek it whenever they seek it.

What, if anything, is keeping you from asking for God's forgiveness and from restoring your relationship with Him? Or what is keeping you from fully embracing His forgiveness? His forgiveness is always available, and no confessed sin is too great for Him to pardon. Thinking otherwise ("How could God forgive me for . . . ?") is a form of pride the enemy will use to keep you from your heavenly Father's gracious and healing love. God is always ready for you to return to Him. The fire on the alter waits.

A Word of Warning

The LORD is righteous,
For I rebelled against His commandment.
Hear now, all peoples, and behold my sorrow;
My virgins and my young men have gone into captivity.

LAMENTATIONS 1:18

*R*ighteous. Webster's defines it as "morally right or justifiable; acting in accord with divine or moral law: free from guilt or sin."

In Lamentations 1:18 we see that God remains righteous regardless of what we choose to do. When we rebel, He will not be passive about our sin. To maintain His righteousness, He must punish our transgression.

But that doesn't come unannounced; His punishment shouldn't surprise us sinners. The destruction of Jerusalem should not have astonished the straying Hebrew children. After all, in Lamentations 2:17, we read this:

The LORD has done what He purposed;
He has fulfilled His word . . .
He has thrown down and has not pitied,
And He has caused an enemy to rejoice over you.

God had warned His people from the beginning that if they forsook Him and did "not obey the voice of the LORD your God, to observe carefully all His commandments and His statutes which I command you," (Deuteronomy 28:15–16). He would punish them. When God chooses to address our sin, nothing—not security, wealth, friends, position—can shield us from His discipline. We have been warned.

A Passage Read, a Life Changed

Let us walk properly, as in the day, not in revelry and
drunkenness, not in lewdness and lust, not in strife
and envy. But put on the Lord Jesus Christ, and make
no provision for the flesh, to fulfill its lusts.

ROMANS 13:13—14

Augustine was born in North Africa in AD 354. His mother, Monica, was a devout Christian, but his father was an unbeliever.

Brilliant but highly undisciplined, Augustine recklessly pursued carnal pleasures. When he went to Milan, Monica encouraged her son to attend church and listen to Bishop Ambrose preach. Although Augustine enjoyed listening to Ambrose, he wasn't ready to turn from his sinful lifestyle.

Then one day, while sitting in a friend's garden, Augustine heard a child saying, "Take up and read!" Seeing a collection of the apostle Paul's writings, Augustine began reading Romans 13:13–14. Later he recalled: "No further would I read; nor needed I: for instantly at the end of this sentence, by a light as it were of serenity infused into my heart, all darkness of doubt vanished away."

Augustine became one of the most influential thinkers in church history . . . because he took up God's Word, read it, and was convicted by the Holy Spirit. "Take up and read" God's Word—and see what He has to say to you!

Eternal Life . . . Now

*"This is eternal life, that they may know You, the only
true God, and Jesus Christ whom You have sent."*

JOHN 17:3

Eternal life doesn't merely mean going to heaven when you die and living forever, as amazing and wonderful as that promise is. Eternal life involves knowing Almighty God intimately. That began the moment you entered into a relationship with Christ, and it will extend throughout eternity.

Eternal life, however, is a quality of life more than a quantity. It's abundant life. It's security in the nurturing intimacy of your personal relationship with your heavenly Father, contentment in the joy of His presence with you, and radiantly hopeful because of His promises to you. To thoroughly experience eternal life in the present as well as in the future, you must continually strive to know God more intimately.

Some Christians seem to think that they have to wait until heaven to truly know and experience Christ, so they unwisely neglect their relationship with Christ in this life. Yet Scripture suggests that we take with us into eternity the relationship with God that we began on earth.

God invites us to experience and enjoy eternal life—by knowing and experiencing Him. Start enjoying eternal life . . . today.

Walking in the Spirit

Walk in the Spirit, and you shall not fulfill the lust of the flesh.

GALATIANS 5:16

Walking in the Spirit is a choice we make. It involves choosing—moment by moment—to live under the direction and in the power of the Holy Spirit.

Walking in the flesh will always produce sin. Walking in the Spirit will always result in righteousness. Life situations are opportunities for the Spirit residing in Christians to live out His life through them and to reveal to a watching world what God is like.

To open yourself to the work of the Spirit, linger before the cross of Jesus Christ. Gaze upon your crucified Savior until sin's grip is loosened and Christ's love takes hold of you. After all, the Crucifixion and resurrection were the pivotal events that ushered God's power into our lives.

The Holy Spirit will help you walk in God's ways. He will enable you to resist the temptations of the world, to keep your eyes on the Lord, to recognize the enemy's lies, and to stand strong in God's life-giving truth. In the Holy Spirit—by His power—you can experience His strength and you can reflect His divine character in any circumstance. Keep in step with the Holy Spirit daily.

Forgiveness—for Them?!?!

[Jonah] prayed to the LORD, and said, "Ah, LORD, was not this what I said when I was still in my country? Therefore I fled previously to Tarshish; for I know that You are a gracious and merciful God, slow to anger and abundant in lovingkindness, One who relents from doing harm."

JONAH 4:2

As the book of Jonah opens, we see that God wanted to send His word to the most vicious and debased people of that day, the inhabitants of Nineveh. But when He chose Jonah to do it, God's holy messenger fled in the opposite direction! His concern—as he confessed in his prayer above—was that God might actually forgive the Assyrians, a people whom Jonah despised.

Perhaps we, like Jonah, are reluctant to share God's message with those who have yet to hear the gospel. We may think more of our safety and comfort than of the multitudes who desperately need to learn about God's love. Or perhaps we, like Jonah, want to serve God on our own terms.

Where might God want you to share His love? With the office mate who never smiles? The new mom down the street? The grocery clerk who hasn't looked well recently? Your Nineveh may be closer than you think.

FEBRUARY

The LORD is my shepherd;
I shall not want.

PSALM 23:1

Holy God, Holy Followers

*"You shall offer of your own free will a male without
blemish from the cattle, from the sheep, or from the
goats. Whatever has a defect, you shall not offer,
for it shall not be acceptable on your behalf."*

LEVITICUS 22:19—20

To be holy is to be set apart for God, to be absolutely pure, without sin or fault. The central message of Leviticus is God's holiness and His desire that His people be holy, as He is. Although Christ's death on the cross superseded the animal sacrifices of the Old Testament, Leviticus reveals the gravity of encountering a holy God.

Holy God, for instance, demanded an animal "without blemish" to be sacrificed. God's people were tempted to give their lame, injured, less costly animals as a sacrifice, but God is not a beggar. He will not accept just any sacrifice. He is our Most Holy God, and He demands that we give Him our best. Anything less is an affront.

Quoting from Leviticus, Peter called New Testament believers to "be holy, for I am holy" (1 Peter 1:16). We must live pure lives because we belong to and serve a holy God. He sets the standard for holiness; we do not.

Are you giving God your best? Are you living according to His holy standards? Is your worship acceptable to almighty God?

Humble Strength

Let him who thinks he stands take heed lest he fall.

1 CORINTHIANS 10:12

Victory is indeed a fleeting experience—and that may be especially true of spiritual victories.

You may have held your tongue (victory), but it won't be long before another rude comment comes your way (temptation). Or you may have controlled your temper (victory), but the next spark could soon ignite an outburst (temptation). Thinking about how well you did in a given situation—as opposed to giving thanks for the Spirit's help—makes you prideful and an easy target for failure.

While you're busy celebrating a success, the enemy can catch you off guard and bring you plummeting down. So praise God for your success. Focusing on Him like that will keep you from letting pride suggest that you're invincible. You are always in critical need of God's strength and guidance—but especially right after a victory. Victory can make us far more vulnerable than can defeat.

Paul clearly taught that no sin is irresistible. God always makes provision for escape if we will choose to make use of it (v. 13). Opting for that escape route, though, calls for a humble awareness that our strength in the face of temptation comes from God alone. Turning to Him, especially after a victory, will keep us from falling.

Silence Before God

Do not be rash with your mouth,
And let not your heart utter anything hastily before God.
For God is in heaven, and you on earth;
Therefore let your words be few.

ECCLESIASTES 5:2

King Solomon, traditionally believed to be the author of Ecclesiastes, sought everything the world has to offer in his attempt to find fulfillment. Despite his wholehearted effort, he remained dissatisfied with life. He concluded that our search for significance and meaning is in vain until we seek God.

That shouldn't come as a surprise since our Creator God is also our Teacher. Only when we seek Him do we, His creatures, gain His wisdom. The results of all our attempts at enlightenment and our most industrious pursuits of knowledge fall far short of God's infinite wisdom.

So, humbled by our futile efforts, we are to enter God's presence to receive a word from Him, not to ask Him to do our bidding. We are to adjust to His will, not ask Him to bless ours. We are to seek His thoughts rather than merely inform Him of ours.

It is wonderful to offer God our praise and to express our needs, but to leave His presence before He speaks is a travesty. Waiting upon the Lord and listening to Him are foundational to our relationship with Him.

Calling on the Name of the Lord

Men began to call on the name of the LORD.

GENESIS 4:26

Their child died just ten days after she was born . . .

His crime landed him in prison for ten years . . .

The alcoholism led to the crumbling of her marriage and her family . . .

The peace they experienced during that
horrific time was palpable.
The Christian who visited him each
week never gave up on him.
When she reached her lowest point, she
found God waiting for her.

Sometimes the low points in life turn us to the Lord and compel us to call on His name. Sometimes the high points lead us to acknowledge the Giver of all good gifts—the gifts of love and life, of truth and hope.

Calling on the name of the Lord does not come naturally to people. It originates from a desire for God's holiness and love. It follows the recognition and acknowledgment of our own inability and God's all-sufficiency. The Holy Spirit works through events in our lives to arouse a desire for God, to prompt the recognition of our human limitations and sinful ways, and to bring about the acknowledgment of God's forgiving love and redeeming power.

When did you start calling on the name of the Lord? Thank God for bringing you to that point in your life.

The Divine in the Daily

*As He who called you is holy, you also
be holy in all your conduct.*

1 PETER 1:15

The word *holy* refers to separation, to being entirely different and apart from that which is common. It's no surprise, then, that *holy* is the word used most often in Scripture to describe God.

Holiness speaks of God's very nature; it is the elemental characteristic from which all His other qualities emanate. God's holiness embraces His eternity, His glory, and His power, and His holiness evokes awe, reverence, and fear. The word speaks to the majesty and mystery of God, who reigns totally above all creation. Holiness also speaks of God's perfection and His purity.

Believers are called to be holy, to belong entirely to God, and, through the power of the Holy Spirit, to reflect His nature. Holiness is the dynamic expression of the divine in our daily life. We fulfill God's command to be holy when we obey His will and live consecrated lives that reveal His moral character.

So never tolerate, justify, or excuse that which draws you away from God. After all, the Almighty did not send His beloved Son to die for your happiness, prosperity, or health, but for your holiness.

His Terms, Not Ours

"With their flocks and herds
They shall go to seek the LORD,
But they will not find Him;
He has withdrawn Himself from them."

HOSEA 5:6

When your heart is far from God, His ways will seem puzzling and His guidance unimportant.

When your heart is far from God, His voice will be muted, and His Word—if you even read it—will seem strange.

You might think, God is always there for me—but don't presume upon Him. Our sin distances us from holy God, and it may keep us from finding Him in times of distress. As the nation of Israel had to learn the hard way, God is available to us on His terms, not ours. We may presume on God's presence, but that does not mean He will "be there" for us like we thought. We may leave God on our terms, but we can return to Him only on His.

So go to Him on His terms. Return humbly and with a pure and contrite heart, with a willingness to both learn from Him and serve Him, with an openness to being filled by Him and used by Him. You'll see that the more you revere the Lord, the more Christlike you become, the more you will understand God's ways, and the more readily you will follow Him.

Broken Fellowship

"What the chewing locust left,
the swarming locust has eaten;
What the swarming locust left,
the crawling locust has eaten;
And what the crawling locust left,
the consuming locust has eaten."

JOEL 1:4

The book of Joel is dominated by a horrific natural disaster: the devastating visitation of locusts on the land. Female locusts lay eggs that lie just below the earth's surface for several months until moisture causes them to hatch. Locusts multiply to enormous numbers and then swarm upon a region's vegetation.

A devastating mass of locusts assaulted the land of Judah in several stages, devouring the vegetation so thoroughly that grain and drink offerings could not be made in the temple. Thus the people were unable to give their regular offerings to God in worship. Fellowship with Him was broken.

When Joel appeared with a divine interpretation of the circumstances, the people were dismayed to learn that God had sent the locusts as His instruments of judgment. However, God's message is that if His people turn from their sin, He will be gracious and compassionate toward them. He will restore His relationship with them and bless them.

Has God recently allowed a disaster to enter your world? Could it be God's unequivocal message for you to return to Him?

Mercy and Grace

*I was formerly a blasphemer, a persecutor, and an insolent man;
but I obtained mercy because I did it ignorantly in unbelief.
And the grace of our Lord was exceedingly abundant.*

1 TIMOTHY 1:13—14

Peanut butter and jelly. Forks and spoons. Mercy and grace. Some things just go together—and, thankfully, mercy and grace are such a pair in the kingdom of God.

To obtain mercy means "to receive exemption from the punishment that one deserves." And every one of us deserves punishment for our sins. Perhaps those sins aren't as dramatic as Paul's—or maybe they're every bit as intense or worse. But God doesn't rank sin. Sin is sin, and all who sin—and that's everyone—deserves the punishment of separation from God forever.

Now for mercy's theological partner . . . grace. Whereas mercy is deserved punishment withheld, grace is undeserved favor bestowed. Our loving God hasn't given us what we sinners rightly deserve. Instead He has freely offered salvation through Jesus, who took our sin upon Himself. The apostle Paul deserved punishment as a blasphemer and persecutor of the church, but God showed him mercy.

Cups and saucers. Salt and pepper. And, yes, mercy and grace. Some things go together perfectly.

Thank You, Lord!

Completing a Kingdom Task

The elders of the Jews . . . built and finished [the temple],
according to the commandment of the God of Israel.

EZRA 6:14

Anyone who has attempted to rebuild something knows that unexpected events happen along the way. That was true for the Israelites as they rebuilt the temple in Jerusalem . . .

The unexpected for them, however, involved extra blessings rather than difficulties with contractors, delays in getting city approval, or additional expenses. Hear what King Darius of Persia decreed: "Let the cost [for building this house of God] be paid at the king's expense" (v. 8). Darius added, "Whatever they need [for offering to God] . . . let it be given them day by day without fail" (v. 9).

Often God adds bonus delights and blessings when He answers our prayers. Perhaps He does so in response to our faithfulness or obedience. The fundamental reason, however, is that He loves us dearly.

God showed His love for Israel by providing for the construction effort through a pagan king and people, enabling His children to persevere and complete the temple. What a cause for celebration!

What God-given assignment are you carrying out? Persevere—and watch God provide for you. The celebration of completing your kingdom task is worth the effort!

In Times of Crisis

But You, O LORD, do not be far from Me;
O My Strength, hasten to help Me!

PSALM 22:19

P salm 22 immediately reveals that David was in trouble. "My God, My God, why have You forsaken Me?" the psalm opens. David boldly complained that God was not hearing his prayers. He told God—as if the Lord didn't already know—that "trouble is near" and added rather accusingly that "there is none to help [me]" (v. 11). The accusations continued: "You have brought Me to the dust of death" (v. 15). As his enemies surrounded him, the situation looked grim for David.

Maybe your circumstances don't look good right now. In times of crisis, however, what others are attempting is not as important as what God is doing. The advance of the enemy, their weapons, their proximity—none of these is as important as God's presence and activity. When we focus on God in even the worst of predicaments, we always discover that He is near and that His presence is our deliverance.

Right now, focus on God's presence right where you are. Ask Him to deliver you from what besets you—the enemies of doubt, fear, poverty, loneliness, broken relationships, illness, loss—and watch Him work His perfect plan in His perfect way in His perfect time.

Wholehearted Repentance

"Now, therefore," says the LORD,
"Turn to me with all your heart,
With fasting, with weeping, and with mourning." . . .
Then the LORD will be zealous for His land,
And pity His people.

JOEL 2:12, 18

True repentance is not a pleasant experience, at least not initially. It involves a broken heart and deep sorrow. In Joel 2:12, such wholehearted repentance is character-ized by fasting, weeping, and mourning. No, it's not pleasant to get a glimpse of our sin-stained self from our holy God's perspective. . . .

But, ideally, that accurate picture of who we are in all our sin compels us to cry out to God, and whenever we do so, He hears us. Whenever we are brokenhearted and genuinely humbled by the reality of our sin, God will have compassion on us and for-give us. Sometimes in our pride, though, we think that not even God can forgive us. Know that such thoughts are the enemy's lies, and counter them with the truth of Scripture. The truth of 1 John 1:8–9 is a powerful weapon when Satan whispers in your ear that you've committed the unforgivable.

Also know that, when you've repented of your sin and received God's gracious forgiveness, the outcome is a new beginning, a conspicuous change in the direction of your life, the Lord's blessing rather than His judgment, and joy. The result of repentance is always amazing!

Compelled to Speak

We cannot but speak the things which we have seen and heard.

ACTS 4:20

Good news is too good to keep to yourself. You can't tell the amazing story often enough! Who can you share it with next? Everyone needs to hear it!

Is that the kind of passion you have for sharing the story of Jesus' life, death, and resurrection? Anyone who has truly encountered Christ and received the Holy Spirit is a transformed person, and having a zeal for telling Jesus' story will be part of that change. Experiencing Christ in the fullness of all His love and majesty, His power and mercy, inspires evangelism.

The church of Acts was characterized by its passion for telling people about Jesus. Again and again Peter, John, Paul, and others got into trouble—even to the point of death—for relating His story. Significantly, when trouble and persecution came, these early Christians didn't pray for deliverance from their oppressors. Instead they asked for boldness to keep speaking, to continue witnessing in the face of persecution, even if for just one more time (v. 29).

May we who have the same story to tell be just as compelled to declare it! May we know Jesus so well that we cannot stop talking about Him.

Contamination—and Healing

"But if [the plague] appears again in the garment,
either in the warp or in the woof, or in anything
made of leather, it is a spreading plague; you shall
burn with fire that in which is the plague."

LEVITICUS 13:57

Contamination—whether from the plague or from sin—cannot be treated lightly, for infection—spiritual as well as physical—refuses to remain isolated. Like the plague discussed in Leviticus 13, sin spreads. It affects every part of a person's life as well as every aspect of that person's family and community that it touches. An entire home can be destroyed if prompt action is not taken to eradicate any evil that enters it.

When physical infection is caused by a virus, doctors treat symptoms. When the contamination is spiritual and the result of sin, God doesn't just deal with symptoms; He addresses the cause and brings healing. He expects us to eradicate sin and its causes from our lives.

So be proactive about sin. Because everything and everyone you touch becomes contaminated when sin renders you unclean, it is imperative that you guard your purity—with the protection of God's Word, the power of His Spirit, and fellowship with His people. Too much is at stake for you not to.

Free to Serve

"For the children of Israel are servants to Me;
they are My servants whom I brought out of the land of Egypt:
I am the LORD your God."

LEVITICUS 25:55

God led the children of Israel out of slavery in Egypt—and believers out of slavery to sin—for a specific purpose: we are to be His servants. We have the privilege of serving the almighty God, of being His light of truth and hope in a very dark world.

God therefore wants us to remain free to serve Him. Are you available to serve your Redeemer and Savior? Are you prepared to share with others the forgiving love that He has poured into your life? Are you willing to extend the gift of acceptance on behalf of the One who has graciously accepted you as His child?

If you entangle yourself in debts or unhealthy relationships, in busyness or sin, you may not be able to join God in His activity when He invites you to. You might want to but be unable to. So keep yourself free from any encumbrances that might restrict your service to God when His invitation comes. And then, when the Lord directs you, be open to serving Him in the manner He asks of you. Respond to His call to service with obedience and love.

Rules or Relationships?

*When the scribes and the Pharisees saw Him eating with the
tax collectors and sinners, they said to His disciples, "How is
it that He eats and drinks with tax collectors and sinners?"*

MARK 2:16

Pharisees were religious Jews who sought to live lives
untainted by the world's sins—and they were very proud of
their effort and strict adherence to their religious laws:

- They regularly fasted on Mondays and Thursdays.
- Concerned about violating the Lord's Day, these Jewish
  religious officials identified thirty-nine different
  categories of work that were forbidden on the Sabbath.
- The Pharisees practiced the ritualistic, ceremonial
  washing of their hands up to the wrist, an action that
  symbolized their desire to remain pure.
  And how did Jesus respond?
- The term *hypocrite* was originally used to describe
  actors who wore masks to identify themselves as a
  character in a play. Jesus charged the Pharisees with
  putting on a religious mask and pretending to be devout
  followers of God (Mark 7:6).
- Jesus viewed the Pharisees' religious practices and
  customs as coming from them, not God (v. 8).
- Jesus often condemned the Pharisees' self-
  righteousness and pride.

Jesus doesn't want mere rule-followers in His kingdom; He
wants relationships with His children. Have you been content
with rules? Move closer to Him today.

Called by God

We also pray always for you that our God would count
you worthy of this calling, and fulfill all the good pleasure
of His goodness and the work of faith with power.

2 THESSALONIANS 1:11

Outside of the New Testament, *calling* usually signifies vocation, position, or station in life. One's calling is law or medicine, education or business, family or perhaps the family business. But the idea of calling has even greater significance for Christians.

If you're a believer, your salvation is an act of God. By His mercy and grace, He called you out of darkness into an eternal love relationship that is completely undeserved.

But God's calling to His people is much more than a vocation; it is a divine invitation to participate in His will and the work of His kingdom. We should consider our calling the highest privilege life offers; it means we are chosen by God.

God initiates our calling and reveals it to us through His Holy Spirit. His Spirit then guides and empowers as we serve God not only in our vocation but also by participating in His kingdom work.

God has a purpose for your life, and it involves far more than earning a living.

Life-Changing Scriptures

*These are written that you may believe that
Jesus is the Christ, the Son of God, and that
believing you may have life in His name.*

JOHN 20:31

God gave us His Word not merely for our information, but rather for our transformation. Our faith in both the written Word of Scripture and the living Word of Jesus opens our hearts to the work of the Holy Spirit to teach us as well as transform us. Are you making time for the life-giving Word of God?

God gave us His Word to help us believe as well as to enable us—by the power of His Spirit—to become the Christlike people He wants us to be. As you respond positively to Scripture's truth, the Spirit uses that truth to make you more like Christ. Has God's Word been changing you?

One more question. If you are spending time studying Scripture, memorizing passages, and meditating on God's truth, what is your motive? Is it a duty? a ritual? an obligation? Or is it an act of love? Consider the most fundamental question Christ ever asks any one of us: "Do you love Me?" Everything in our relationship with Him stems from our honest answer to this one question. Think of that question the next time you open your Bible.

A Full-Time Job

The LORD is my shepherd;
I shall not want.

PSALM 23:1

Herding sheep in David's time was hard work. There was nothing romantic about the night shift; shepherds did not relax on balmy evenings under the twinkling stars. They braved numbingly cold nights and worked hard to protect their sheep from predators. Night and day, they were never passive toward their flock. Shepherds had to lead, tend, feed, protect, and nurture the animals in their care. They provided everything necessary for their sheep's safety and well-being.

To appreciate the size of this challenge, remember that sheep are fearful, defenseless animals. Moreover, they aren't the brightest of God's creatures. They'll drink from any body of water—dirty or clean—that they stumble upon. They will not lie down unless they feel entirely secure. They are prone to ear infections that require special attention. Yes, sheep need a lot of care.

We are like sheep, the Bible tells us. On our own, we are defenseless against the power of sin and death. Without guidance, we will drink from any source of information and entertainment. We look everywhere for security, and we're vulnerable to diseases of our spirit, our emotions, and our mind. We, too, need a lot of care. Thank God for appointing Jesus to be your Good Shepherd. Rest in Him today.

The Fallen

"In the day that you stood on the other side—
In the day that strangers carried captive his forces,
When foreigners entered his gates
And cast lots for Jerusalem—
Even you were as one of them."

OBADIAH 11

What is your reaction to newspaper headlines about the CEO whose empire has crumbled due to unethical accounting practices?

What about the athlete whose career ended abruptly due to a test that came back positive for steroids?

How about the family down the street whose teenage son—unsupervised by his parents for so many years—was just arrested?

Our own heart's condition is revealed by how we treat those who have fallen. A hardened heart is indifferent about, or even rejoices in, another's calamity. A contrite heart—a heart that knows its own sin, that knows that "there but for the grace of God go I," a heart filled with Christlike compassion and love—breaks for those who stumble.

How does one's heart become more like Christ's? God is the One who opens our eyes to our own sin and pride . . . by bringing us to the cross to ponder the price paid for our sins . . . and by washing us clean with His forgiving love. A heart humbled by its own sin extends grace and love rather than judgment to those who fall.

A Gauge of Love

"You shall love the LORD your God with all your heart,
with all your soul, and with all your strength."

DEUTERONOMY 6:5

What is it that God really wants from us?

We have a Bible filled with the Lord's commands, kingdom principles, and specific instructions for godly living. This job description can be daunting! It's a good thing that God summarized His law in a single verse: each of us is to love God with all our heart, all our soul, and all our might.

God wants far more than external conformity to His laws. He seeks enthusiastic obedience as a response of love for Him, not obedience stemming from a sense of duty or obligation.

So, as God's child, flee from anything that draws you away from loving your heavenly Father. Beware if your heart is comfortable with sin—and remember that the closer you are to God, the more detestable evil will be. Put yourself in places where you can know God better, because to know Him is to love Him.

Finally, realize that a love relationship with God truly is His desire for your life. Obedience to His law is simply a gauge of your love; obedience is not God's ultimate goal for you. He wants your heart, not obligatory submission. He wants you to enjoy your time with Him. He wants you to love Him.

Fickle Followers

*The LORD raised up judges who delivered them out
of the hand of those who plundered them.*

JUDGES 2:16

After the period of Joshua's leadership, judges led the people of Israel and often acted as mediators of disputes. Judges are known mostly for delivering the Israelites from military enemies. Although they had many shortcomings, God chose to place His Spirit upon them, thereby enduing them with power and wisdom to lead His people and enabling them to accomplish the unusual and achieve seemingly impossible victories.

The book of Judges portrays God's determination to bring His prodigal people back to Himself. We see how fickle and easily tempted God's people are. Most Israelites did not knowingly reject God; they simply wanted to indulge in idol worship too. Judges also reveals the futility of trying to please God while participating in sinful activity. Finally, this book exposes the absolute depravity of the human heart. We repeatedly read that the people "did evil in the sight of the Lord."

When are you especially tempted either to mix the world's religions of materialism or narcissism with Christianity or to try to please God and sinfully satisfy yourself at the same time? In what ways are you doing "evil in the sight of the Lord"?

The Gifts

There are diversities of gifts, but the same
Spirit . . . . The manifestation of the Spirit is
given to each one for the profit of all.

1 CORINTHIANS 12:4, 7

Of course the eye can't say to the hand, "I don't need you." Neither can the head say that to the foot. Every part of our physical body needs every other part. That's God's design for His spiritual body, the church, as well as for the human body.

Every person in the church needs the other members. There is great diversity among the gifts people have been given even as there is great diversity among the parts of the human body. And—as Paul addressed in 1 Corinthians 12—unity of the spiritual body is just as critical as unity of the physical body.

All spiritual gifts are divine in origin. The Holy Spirit, however, doesn't merely give us a talent or ability; He gives us Himself. Then He works through us to accomplish the Father's will.

When people observe a believer doing good works, they are actually seeing the manifestation of the Spirit through a human instrument. If we don't walk in the Spirit, however, we are merely exercising natural talent and serving God in our own strength. That will never be enough. Let God show the world what He can do through one ordinary life, like yours.

Living the Gospel

Let your conduct be worthy of the gospel of Christ, so that . . .
I may hear of your affairs, that you stand fast in one spirit,
with one mind striving together for the faith of the gospel.

PHILIPPIANS 1:27

Consider three aspects of living the gospel.

First, the gospel is a message of pure love, willing sacrifice, redemptive suffering, and the gracious offer of salvation. It is the visible expression of Christ's heart. To truly receive the gospel is to find yourself living the gospel. Can others see the gospel—can they perceive pure love and willing sacrifice—in you?

Second, the phrase *striving together* means "to engage in competition," suggesting the need for exertion and discipline. This call for teamwork exhorts believers to fight together side by side. The gospel serves to unite Jesus' followers for a common purpose, the cause of Christ.

Finally, living the gospel means suffering for the gospel (v. 29). The New Testament always presents suffering for the sake of Christ as a privilege, a blessing that brings glory to God and that results in eternal rewards.

The sacrifice, the striving, the suffering. The love, the joy, the hope. The gospel is all this—and more.

Filled, Led, and Protected

*Jesus, being filled with the Holy Spirit . . . was led by the Spirit
into the wilderness, being tempted for forty days by the devil.*

LUKE 4:1–2

People who are filled with the Spirit will also be led by the Spirit, although the journey may not be easy. That was as true for Jesus as it is for you and me . . .

It was an amazing moment when John the Baptist baptized Jesus. The Holy Spirit descended like a dove, and a voice from heaven declared, "You are My beloved Son; in You I am well pleased" (Luke 3:22). Although filled with the Spirit, Jesus did not begin His public ministry right away.

The Spirit immediately led Jesus into the wilderness where He was tempted for forty days. We only have a record of the last three temptations, but in that account we see Jesus standing strong because of His knowledge of God's truth.

Clearly, being led by the Spirit does not mean we will never face temptations. But it does mean we can be victorious over every one of them. Following God's will may even bring us new temptations we did not have before.

The Spirit may lead believers—just as He guided Jesus— to difficult or dangerous places, but the Spirit's presence with us assures us of His protection and provision in any circumstance.

Making Prayer a Priority

Now in the morning, having risen a long while
before daylight, He went out and departed to
a solitary place; and there He prayed.

MARK 1:35

Of all the lessons we can learn from Jesus, none is more practical than what we gain from His example in this verse.

- The tense of the Greek for *prayed* implies continuous action. Jesus didn't simply say a prayer, cross it off His to-do list, and go about His business. Instead, Jesus earnestly communed with His Father and enjoyed unbroken, two-way conversation with the Almighty.
- Jesus rose early. Before the noisy world awoke and people were gathering around Him, Jesus spent "a long while" with God the Father. Can we afford to do any less?
- A few verses later we see that God instructed Jesus during prayer to "go into the next towns, that I may preach there" (v. 38). We are not to determine the agenda for our lives; God is. Our world is filled with needs, and we are to help meet those needs by doing whatever God directs us to do.

Prayer allows us to discern God's will and to avoid distractions that divert us from His activity. Jesus Himself shows us the priority that prayer needs to be in our lives.

Dying to Self

*It pleased God . . . to reveal His Son in me, that
I might preach Him among the Gentiles.*

GALATIANS 1:15—16

God alone, through the Holy Spirit, reveals Christ to us, for none of us can discern spiritual truth unless the Spirit reveals it to us.

Then, once we realize the truth of who Jesus is, we have two options. We can either work hard for God and let our effort be a showcase for our talents, or we can die to self and make ourselves available for God to reveal Christ in and through our mortal bodies. God clearly desires the latter.

- The world doesn't need to see good people doing their best for God; the world needs to see God doing His work through His people. Who comes to mind when you read that phrase "God doing His work through His people"?
- Christianity is not about living our best for God. Christianity is about dying to self and about Christ living in us. Why do we balk at the thought of "dying to self"?
- Our great weakness in serving Christ is *self*-confidence. Why does self-confidence interfere with serving Christ?

Either we deny self or we deny Christ. Ask God to help you die to self.

Following Noah's Example

Noah found grace in the eyes of the LORD. . . . Noah was a just man, perfect in his generations. Noah walked with God.

GENESIS 6:8−9

Noah lived in an extremely wicked age when people's thoughts dwelled continually on evil. Despite the corruption of his day, Noah lived blamelessly before God and men.

When God gave this "just man" the enormous and unusual task of building an ark, Noah obeyed even though the assignment lasted for many years. The onerous job involved enormously difficult physical labor. After all, the ark was approximately 450 feet long, 75 feet wide, and 45 feet high. Undoubtedly there were scornful snickers behind his back. Onlookers would have understandably wondered what their crazy neighbor was doing—and why.

While Noah worked on the ark and was harassed by those who watched, he preached to his contemporaries. They didn't heed those words of truth and went to their death when the rains did come. Noah's obedience, however, saved him and his family and set a biblical example of faith for you and me.

May we follow Noah's example today as we live in a world of evil . . . among people who taunt us for following the Lord . . . and as we fulfill God's assignments of ministry and evangelism, devotion and moral living—undertakings that look foolish to our neighbors.

A Picture of Love

My beloved is mine, and I am his.

SONG OF SOLOMON 2:16

When we love someone, that relationship helps define who we are. As we reciprocate God's love for us, for instance, we gain an identity as His people. Furthermore, our love for God enables us to love others.

The Song of Solomon celebrates both our ability to love our spouse and the beautiful gift from God that marital love is. After all, God designed man and woman to enjoy a divinely created dimension of intimacy. When we experience romantic love as God intended, we find great joy.

Love—for spouse, children, or God—is meant to be given completely as well as thoroughly enjoyed. The speakers in the Song are celebrating each other's love. We also see in their song that love is not passive but tenaciously active and vigorous. Love is characterized by action more than by affection.

Love also sees others in the best possible light. How precious it is to be viewed by another through eyes of love! That is how we ought to view our spouse, and that is how God sees us. He looks upon us through the forgiving eyes of unfailing love. We too can say, "He is mine, and I am His!"

Truths That Bless

"Return to Me," says the LORD of hosts, "and I
will return to you," says the LORD of hosts.

ZECHARIAH 1:3

M uch of the book of Zechariah is apocalyptic in nature, and at times its imagery is challenging to understand. The following three points the prophet makes, however, are unmistakably clear:

- God's compelling invitation "Return to Me. . . . and I will return to you" (1:3) is a cry to His people's hearts; it is not a request to simply resume religious practices. Worship and a holy lifestyle are the outward expressions of our love for the Lord. God calls His people out of sinful rebellion back into relationship with Him. It begins with our conscious choice to move closer to Him. The rest will follow.
- The prophet reiterates a fundamental spiritual truth: we do not serve God in our own strength nor by our own righteousness, but in the power of the Holy Spirit (4:6).
- We are unable to save ourselves. God alone has the power to remove our sin (3:4). We cannot even turn from our sin or call out to God unless He, by the power of His Spirit, enables us to do so.

MARCH

Cast your burden on the LORD,
And He shall sustain you.

PSALM 55:22

Seeing One's True Self

*Peter remembered the word of Jesus who had said
to him, "Before the rooster crows, you will deny Me
three times." Then he went out and wept bitterly.*

MATTHEW 26:75

As Jesus and the Eleven walked to the Mount of Olives, Jesus told His disciples that this was the night the Shepherd would be struck down. He also spoke of meeting them in Galilee after the resurrection, but that comment seems muffled by Peter's bold assertion.

With great confidence Peter announced, "I will never be made to stumble" (v. 33). Then Jesus calmly reassured His well-intentioned friend that, as a matter of fact, before morning Peter would deny knowing Him—and would do so three times. With even greater conviction, Peter proclaimed, "Even if I have to die with You, I will not deny You!" (v. 35)

Jesus knows us better than we know ourselves. He understands our natural weaknesses, but He also recognizes where we can find strength: in Him—and Him alone.

Self-reliance will always get us into trouble, for we simply don't have the ability to do what we should. As a result, God will reveal our limitations so we learn to find our strength in Him. As long as our confidence is based on ourselves, we will inevitably fail. Our boldness must come from Christ.

Set Free

*"For I will acquit them of the guilt of bloodshed, whom
I had not acquitted; For the LORD dwells in Zion."*

JOEL 3:21

J ohn Bunyan, famed author of *Pilgrim's Progress*, was tormented in his soul. He desperately longed for peace with God . . .

One day he encountered a small group of impoverished women discussing spiritual matters. He was deeply convicted by their obvious love for God and their devotion to Him, yet doubts continued to assail him. Whenever Bunyan considered the sins of his youth, he could not understand how a holy God could forgive him. Bunyan continued to be troubled by this until God sent His answer through His Word.

Bunyan encountered Joel 3:21. The truth of God's cleansing forgiveness, as expressed in that verse, struck a chord with him. God *had* forgiven him. A fresh sense of God's presence in his life was proof that God's Word was setting him free.

Consider, for a moment, the difficulties and crises that God has allowed in your life. Could they be one way He is calling you to return to Him? Also ponder the condition of your own heart in light of God's call for genuine repentance. Examine your life to see if sin has quenched the Spirit's presence in you. God is fully prepared to set you free as well.

Living Out Our Theology

You tread down the poor
And take grain taxes from him. . . .
I know your manifold transgressions
And your mighty sins:
Afflicting the just and taking bribes;
Diverting the poor from justice at the gate.

AMOS 5:11—12

We see in these verses God's deep compassion for society's poor and helpless. According to Amos, our love for God should translate into concern for others. Theology is not meant to be abstract; it is intended to be lived out in specifics.

Amos prophesied at a time when some people in Israel were growing extravagantly wealthy, and others were falling into abject poverty and slavery. While the wealthy lavished riches on themselves, the disadvantaged struggled. So distracted by their riches and pleasurable lifestyles, the pampered minority were oblivious to the plight of their fellow citizens. Such callous disregard for others' needs clearly demonstrated the people's distance from God—and His judgment was inevitable.

Let God use these next few minutes to help you consider your own selfishness, especially in light of those who are less privileged—the physically or economically poor as well as the spiritually and emotionally needy—who are all around you. What specifics does your theology—your love for God—compel you to live out in the world around you this week?

Walking Blamelessly

*What you are doing is not good. Should you
not walk in the fear of our God?*

NEHEMIAH 5:9

Life offers many opportunities for sin—and the same was
true in Nehemiah's day.

- Though he was angry when he discovered the practice
  of usury among God's people, Nehemiah demonstrated
  wisdom and strong character. His anger did not lead
  to rash action, but to "serious thought," insight, and a
  godly plan of action (5:6–7).
- Nehemiah knew the importance of walking blamelessly
  (6:9), for God will call us to account for our actions. Our
  love for Him should motivate us to live upright lives, and
  the knowledge of our accountability to Him ought to help
  keep us on a blameless path.
- Nehemiah discovered that a priest had defiled the
  temple (13:7). Sin strikes even in the afterglow of great
  spiritual revival. Backsliding is the perpetual malady of
  God's people.
- Nehemiah saw people failing to keep the Sabbath holy
  (13:18). He understood the futility of obeying part of
  the law while neglecting the rest of it.

Nehemiah understood that sin should always be dealt with
immediately, thoroughly, and permanently. What sin in your
life do you need to deal with in that way?

Lessons from the Book of Job

But when I looked for good, evil came to me; And
when I waited for light, then came darkness.

JOB 30:26

Job was bewildered. He lived righteously and showed compassion, but he received God's apparent punishment rather than His blessing. Why do the wicked prosper and the good suffer? Few questions vex the thoughtful soul more than this one. Consider these truths:

- God is infinitely more righteous than we are. He is not obligated to justify His actions to us. His ways are perfect; ours are not (4:17).
- God targets the pride in our lives because pride convinces us that we don't need Him. Such thinking is not only false, it's dangerous, so God vigorously opposes it (10:16).
- Some wicked men live long, seemingly contented lives while some good men suffer misery and die young (21:25). There is clearly no set formula for the way God deals with people.
- God challenges Job's credentials for judging the way He is ruling the universe (40:2). We are no more qualified than Job to question God's ways.

The book of Job reveals that God will allow the righteous to endure affliction, but He will never forsake us (8:20; 19:25). God's redemptive purposes far exceed our desire for comfort.

Learning in Silence

Let a woman learn in silence with all submission.

1 TIMOTHY 2:11

With that word *submission* in it, this verse can turn heads in the twenty-first century. But twenty-one centuries ago it turned heads as well.

For Paul to say—speaking on behalf of God—"let a woman learn" was encouraging for women, but it was incredibly radical for the culture. Most females in Paul's day were not literate, and even fewer women were trained in philosophy, rhetoric, or Jewish law. Given their lack of training as well as the threat of false teachers in Ephesus, it was prudent for Paul to instruct the women as he did; he could not allow false teachers to exploit the women in the churches and spread error.

Now, whether you're male or female, are you "learn[ing] in silence with all submission"? The word *submission* can apply to both sexes, for all of us need to voluntarily submit to God in order to learn from Him. Whether we're reading His Word or listening to it preached, we need to cooperate with God's Spirit so He will teach us, train us, and transform us. Our talking and our pride would only interfere.

We learn far more when we speak less and, with humility, listen more.

"For Such a Time as This"

*Yet who knows whether you have come to
the kingdom for such a time as this?*

ESTHER 4:14

Esther lived in the center of a world superpower. The immense Persian Empire had conquered the seemingly invincible Babylonian Empire. And Esther—an orphan, a woman, an exile—could hardly have seemed more powerless. But our station in life is inconsequential as long as we are in God's hands. Where He puts us is His sovereign decision; it is not our position but our God who makes our lives effective.

God chose to give Esther significant and far-reaching influence as He turned ordinary events (King Ahasuerus looking for a bride) into extraordinary opportunities to achieve His purposes (saving the Jewish people from extermination). Because of Esther's virtue and courage, God used her to save the lives of thousands of her countrymen and to change the course of history.

Just as God prepared Esther, He is preparing you for His next assignment. Each step of faithfulness prepares you for what awaits. God will use your current circumstances for His next great work in and through your life. God can transform a seemingly ordinary task into an extraordinary accomplishment.

Has God placed you in a position of influence? If so, have you asked Him why?

God's Blessed Presence

*"The nations also will know that I, the LORD, sanctify
Israel, when My sanctuary is in their midst forevermore."*

EZEKIEL 37:28

The restoration of Israel had been foretold in Leviticus: "I will look on you favorably and make you fruitful, multiply you and confirm My covenant with you" (26:9). God echoed this covenant promise when He said through the prophet Ezekiel, "I will multiply upon you man and beast" (36:11). Once again the people would be able to cultivate the soil and enjoy the rewards of the Promised Land. God would remove His agents of judgment—famine, wild beasts, plague, bloodshed, and warfare—and He would bless His people with the prosperity and life He had promised.

Furthermore, God promised His people that His tabernacle would be with them (37:27). The tabernacle was portable, signifying that God would go with His people wherever they went. God's presence with His people—then and now—is the ultimate proof of His forgiveness of their sin, His acceptance of them, and His pleasure being upon them.

One name of Jesus, God's Son and our Savior, is Emmanuel, meaning "God with us." Taking on flesh and blood, God came to mankind, His appearance testifying to His love and concern. Then, as now, God delights in walking with His people.

The Rewards of Discipline

I discipline my body and bring it into subjection, lest, when I have preached to others, I myself should become disqualified.

1 CORINTHIANS 9:27

Only one team wins the championship. Only one swimmer wins the gold medal. In Paul's day, only one runner wore the laurel wreath. All of these accomplishments require intense training on the part of the competitors.

In contrast to rings, medals, and wreaths that are earned, God's salvation is a gracious gift. We can't earn salvation, and we don't compete for it. Yet the richness of our salvation does depend largely on our effort and discipline. Like an athlete's accomplishment, Christian maturity and spiritual power do not come automatically. They call for sustained, determined effort.

What does your spiritual training regimen look like? Athletes have their weight training, skill development sessions, and endurance workouts. What are you doing to nurture your relationship with God and to enhance your Bible study, worship, and prayer? What are you doing to be sure that you walk in God's ways and honor Him in all you do? Are you being casual or careless about your relationship with Jesus?

Spiritual disciplines will pay off in this life and in eternal rewards far greater than any ring or wreath. Keep your eyes on the goal!

The Author of Salvation

It was fitting for Him, for whom are all things and by whom are all things, in bringing many sons to glory, to make the captain of their salvation perfect through sufferings.

HEBREWS 2:10

God's plan of salvation has existed since time began. Only He—in His wisdom, love, power, and perfection—could have devised such a deeply compelling yet incredibly costly plan. Only a God as infinitely loving as our God would be willing to let His sinless Son serve as the perfect and acceptable sacrifice for the sin of the human race.

Jesus, our Servant King, submitted Himself to this eternal plan. He allowed Himself to be nailed to the cross and mocked by His creatures because of our sin. By doing this, Christ established a path to God for sinners; He blazed the trail of salvation that countless others could follow. Interestingly, the Greek translated as *author* in Hebrews 2:10 can also mean captain, pioneer, or pathfinder.

God gave authority over all creation, over every power and authority, to the Servant Messiah who, completely humbling Himself, died on the cross for the sins of mankind. Two thousand years ago with His own Son and today with His children, God exalts the lowly, strengthens the weak, and honors the humble.

Seeking the Lord

Seek the LORD while He may be found,
Call upon Him while He is near.

ISAIAH 55:6

You've probably spent time looking for something that you knew had to be in the house . . . or in the garage . . . maybe in the office. You know, for instance, that you used your keys to drive home, so they have to be around here somewhere! It is extremely frustrating to look for something that refuses to be found.

In today's verse, the word *seek* does not mean searching for something that is hidden or something that is lost. Instead, *seek* means "coming to something that is known." In your seeking of the Lord, you are coming to something—Someone—who is familiar to you and Someone who (this is important!) wants to be found by you.

Despite God's passionate desire that we come to Him and experience Him, we must approach Him on His terms (we must confess our sin before our holy God) and on His timetable (our time for divine searching is not unlimited).

We must not assume that God will come at our beck and call. We are His servant, He is not ours. So today seek the Lord with energy and enthusiasm, for you will find Him!

"Cast Your Burden"

Cast your burden on the LORD,
And He shall sustain you.

PSALM 55:22

Do-it-yourself hardware stores have become popular—but often weekend do-it-yourselfers make several trips to the store before that Saturday project is done right!

"Some assembly required" tends to mean more confusion and frustration than we bargained for—and it often includes knocking on our clever neighbor's door.

A popular mantra among toddlers is "do it myself"—often when that's not a wise or safe choice.

Do-it-yourself is not always the best option, yet often we must reach the point of desperation before we ask for help. Another road *is* available: humbly recognizing your limitations, going to your heavenly Father, and casting your cares on Him.

Why should you shoulder your burdens alone when Almighty God wants to carry them for you? Your choice to trust in God enables you to place your every care into His hands.

Centuries after the psalmist shared his wise words, Peter was still reminding believers to cast their cares upon God: "Humble yourselves under the mighty hand of God . . . casting all your care upon Him, for He cares for you" (1 Peter 5:7). Why carry the load of your burdens one more day? Christ stands ready to take them. What have you got to lose? Do it today!

"The Lord Is for Me"

The LORD is on my side;
I will not fear.
What can man do to me?
The LORD is for me among those who help me.

PSALM 118:6—7

You've probably noticed that the circumstances of life in this fallen world can bring us to the brink of collapse. But we read in the Bible—and you have probably experienced this truth in your own life—that God always provides the strength we need to continue on His path.

Sometimes, though, we are merely putting one foot forward at a time; sometimes that's all the light we can see on our path at the moment (119:105).

Sometimes others are believing in God—and in His goodness and His power—for us when we can't believe for ourselves.

Sometimes others are praying for us when we struggle to pray on our own.

When God brings us through seasons like that—and He does see us through them—we realize that He truly is the champion for His children. Then we can sing with the psalmist, "The LORD is my strength and song, and He has become my salvation" (118:14).

That song may not be on your lips right now, but it will be someday as it has been in the past . . . because the Lord is for you.

Entering the Priesthood

You are a chosen generation, a royal priesthood, a holy nation,
His own special people, that you may proclaim the praises of
Him who called you out of darkness into His marvelous light.

1 PETER 2:9

As a Christian, you have a few specific, God-assigned jobs to do. We'll look at one today . . .

When you acknowledged the reality of your sin, the separation from God that your unholiness causes, and Jesus' death on the cross as payment for your sin, you entered God's family. At the same time, you entered His priesthood.

All Christians, regardless of their chosen professions, have been called to serve as God's priests. As such, you are blessed with direct access to His presence. Furthermore, wherever God places you, you represent Him to people of the world. As God's priest, you are also privileged to intercede before Him on behalf of lost and hurting people. This calling to represent God to people and represent people to God supersedes your vocation.

So free yourself from the self-centered preoccupations of life. Serve according to your calling, "proclaim the praises of Him who called you out of darkness into His marvelous light," become involved in changing lives, and impact eternity. Begin to behave like the priest you are.

Amazing Grace

This grace was given, that I should preach among
the Gentiles the unsearchable riches of Christ.

EPHESIANS 3:8

When you received Christ into your life, you were introduced to Someone who is limitless in His wisdom,
power, and love. Eternity is not long enough for anyone to
grasp all there is to know of Christ.

In fact, all spiritual knowledge, including the "riches of
Christ," remains a mystery unless God, through the Holy
Spirit, reveals the truth. The mystery of God does not mean
that He hides Himself from people, but that people corrupted
by sin cannot see, hear, or understand Him. All people are
dead in sin and cannot know God unless He opens their eyes
to spiritual realities.

Paul, who described himself as chief among sinners
(1 Timothy 1:15) and "less than the least of all the saints"
(Ephesians 3:8), knew the grace of salvation, and he passion-
ately preached it to those who were as spiritually blind as he
had once been despite the fact that he had studied theology
most of his life. He wanted others to know Christ as he was
now experiencing Him. After all, he had once persecuted the
very people of the God whom he now served. What amazing
grace to be transformed from persecutor to preacher—and
Paul knew it! Can you fathom the amount of grace God has
dispensed on your behalf?

On Level Ground

There is no partiality with God.

ROMANS 2:11

Can gossip really be as serious as murder? Can anger be a sin on par with adultery? Do pride and foolishness really fall in the same category as fornication and theft?

Romans 1:29–32 contains the most extensive list of sins in the Bible. (Other lists appear in Mark 7:21–22; Galatians 5:19–21; and 2 Timothy 3:2–5.) Whereas society rationalizes and even rank orders different sins, God judges them all . . . as sin. Sin is sin, and the consequence is death, meaning separation from God.

In a world that classifies us according to social status, race, wealth, intelligence, and abilities, we need to remind ourselves that those divisions are arbitrary and irrelevant to God. The ground at the foot of the cross is level. We all will stand there and realize how far short we fall from living according to God's standards and loving Him with the devotion and respect He deserves.

The Lord, who is keenly aware of our every sin, will judge each of us according to the way we respond to Him and to the death of His Son on the cross. Every sin you've committed—as insignificant as you might have considered some of them to be—put Jesus there. Don't minimize the sin that killed your Savior.

God's Presence with Us

The woman bore a son and called his name Samson;
and the child grew, and the LORD blessed him.

JUDGES 13:24

Samson was born as a gift of God to Manoah and his wife. He was dedicated at birth as a lifelong Nazirite, which meant he could not cut his hair, drink strong wine, or touch a corpse. Ultimately Samson violated all three restrictions. But in Samson's youth, the Lord blessed him. God gave him amazing strength and unbelievable victories.

Samson knew God's great blessing on his life, but this man's susceptibility to sensual pleasures was his downfall. Samson was defeated, not by his enemies, but by his own lack of self-control. Sadly, he was unaware when the Lord departed from him (Judges 16:20). It is possible to be so preoccupied and distracted from God that we, like Samson, don't even notice the Lord's strength departing from us. God is under no obligation to save us from the adversity we consequently encounter, especially if we have brought it on ourselves.

Sadly, Samson ultimately forfeited God's blessing on his life and ended his days in humiliation and grievous bondage. Samson's life had held great promise, yet he presumed on God's blessing. As a result his downfall was great.

What lesson does Samson's life have for you today? Have you taken God's gifts to you for granted?

God at Work

[Naomi's sons] took wives of the women of Moab: the name of the one was Orpah, and the name of the other Ruth.

RUTH 1:4

The book of Ruth shows God's loving care for ordinary people who are facing crises. This Old Testament romance also demonstrates that when God encounters faith, He intervenes in people's lives to accomplish extraordinary things...

When the famine in Israel ended, the widowed Ruth accompanied her widowed mother-in-law, Naomi, as she returned from Moab to Bethlehem. Ruth's devotion to Naomi as well as her embracing of Israel's God soon earned her the respect of all who knew her. She selflessly did what she thought was right rather than pursuing her own self-interest. Her virtuous character won her the respect of the equally righteous Boaz. God rewarded Ruth for her faithfulness by giving her a husband and a child. Eventually King David as well as the Messiah Jesus were among her descendants.

Ruth's life shows us how God takes the ordinary events of life and uses them to bless us as well as those who come after us. Her life may also bring to mind God's loving provision for you during your own difficult times. Only God can take events from your everyday life and do the extraordinary.

Serving God

"I will raise up for Myself a faithful priest who shall do according to what is in My heart and in My mind."

1 SAMUEL 2:35

God's desire is for us to do what is on *His* heart and *His* mind, and Samuel did just that. Samuel chose to serve God, not himself.

Samuel's name, meaning "heard by God" or "appointed by God," signified his birth as a direct answer to prayer. For years his mother, Hannah, had longingly prayed for a child. Dedicated to the Lord before his birth, Samuel lived as a Nazirite, never forsaking his mother's vow that he would serve the Lord all his life. He functioned as a prophet, an intercessor, a priest, and the last of the judges. He helped Israel make the transition from a theocracy led by judges to a monarchy ruled by kings.

Clearly fearing God more than he feared men, Samuel often spoke stern and condemning words of truth about the actions of powerful leaders such as Saul and David. Samuel's life also exemplified the foundational teaching that "to obey is better than sacrifice" (15:22).

You cannot obey what you do not know. Seek to know what is on God's heart and mind. Then ask the Lord to give you a heart to obey Him . . . and the desire to do what is on His heart and His mind.

A Life Well Spent

Do not grow weary in doing good.

2 THESSALONIANS 3:13

How do you want to be remembered? How about for not "grow[ing] weary in doing good"? That would indeed be a life well spent.

Life on earth is short and eternity is long. So serve the Lord with all your heart and make your life count.

- LOVE GENEROUSLY. God designed love to have a powerful impact on human relationships. Whether it is expressed by forgiving, addressing a person's needs, sharing the Good News, or encouraging the weary, love can change a life forever.

- SHARE CHRISTIAN KINDNESS. Kindness has been defined as "God's love expressed in practical ways." It is intentionally sharing the love He has given us. The condition of our relationship with God is reflected in how compassionate, tender, generous, and forgiving we are.

- PRACTICE HOSPITALITY. The character of the Christian home can do much to prove the relevance and attractiveness of the Christian message.

- SERVE THE CHURCH. God's work in believers' lives is evident when they love the body of Christ.

God has given you life, so—by His grace and in His power—persevere and live it well.

"God with Us"

"Behold, the virgin shall be with child, and bear
a Son, and they shall call His name Immanuel,"
which is translated "God with us."

MATTHEW 1:23

You know the dark times—those moments when nothing anyone can say or do will change your circumstances or make everything better. Perhaps you've been blessed in troubled times to have someone come sit with you, just be with you. That person's presence was a source of solace, hope, and strength. Similarly, the risen Christ offers His comforting presence to you today.

The word *Immanuel* appears only once in the New Testament. No one on record ever called Jesus by this name, yet it is one of the most familiar and encouraging designations of our Lord. Quoting Isaiah 7:14, Matthew applied this title to Jesus as God in the flesh. This name affirms the deity of Jesus, and—as it does so—it clearly implies that God is not only present but also personal and approachable.

It has been said that God the Father is *for us*, God the Son is *with us*, and God the Spirit is *in us*. That being true, we can know the hopeful reassurance of God's strength however dark our days may be.

The High Cost of Sin

*"If a person sins, and commits any of these things
which are forbidden to be done by the commandments
of the LORD, though he does not know it, yet
he is guilty and shall bear his iniquity."*

LEVITICUS 5:17

Whether our sin is deliberate or unintentional, we are responsible for our actions. We may not be aware of every sin we have committed, but we all have sinned, we all will be held accountable, and we should never treat our sin casually or flippantly. Sin is enormously costly.

In Old Testament times, meat was a rare luxury for everyone but the rich. Offering an entire animal to be consumed by fire was therefore a costly sacrifice for the average Israelite. In the New Testament, we see in the Crucifixion and resurrection the priceless sacrifice of God's only Son because of our sin. Clearly, God takes sin seriously, and so should we.

Are you too comfortable with your sin? Are you blind to it? Imagine standing at the foot of the cross. Look at the blood flowing from the innocent Christ. Hear the crowd's taunts and the thief's jeers. Listen to Jesus gasp as He struggles to lift Himself up by nail-pierced hands and feet for a breath of air. Sin—yes, *your* sin—is costly.

The Suffering Servant

He was cut off from the land of the living; For the
transgressions of My people He was stricken.

ISAIAH 53:8

Look in reverence and awe at God's Servant who suffered on your behalf and because of your sin . . .

- He had "no form or comeliness," no regal bearing. Nothing notable about His physical appearance would draw crowds to Him (v. 2).
- The Servant was "despised and rejected by men, a man of sorrows" (v. 3) who was keenly aware of the devastation caused by sin and the desperate condition of people separated from God.
- "Smitten by God" indicates that the Romans were not the ultimate cause of Jesus' death; the heavenly Father was (v. 4).
- The Servant "opened not His mouth" (v. 7), indicating His serenity and submission to His Father's will. He did not argue with, condemn, or revile those who were brutally murdering Him.
- Christ "was stricken": He suffered death by crucifixion for our sin. Our sin cost Him His life. The cruel, despicable horror of the cross is a powerful reminder of sin's ugliness.

Spend time this Easter season meditating on Isaiah's moving description of the Suffering Servant who endured so much agony to atone for your sins (52:13–53:12).

A Clear Conscience

*I myself always strive to have a conscience
without offense toward God and men.*

ACTS 24:16

One wise saint made this observation with a smile: "It would be very humbling to realize how infrequently other people are thinking of you—because they're too busy thinking about what you may be thinking of them!"

You can't control what other people think of you, but you can live at peace whatever their thoughts might be. You can know peace because, no matter what happens *to* you, you have control over what happens *in* you.

What happens inside you is determined by the condition of your heart. A heart at peace is a clean heart, a repentant heart that has experienced God's forgiveness and been cleansed (1 John 1:8–9). A contentious spirit comes with not allowing the Holy Spirit to rule in one's life.

So, like Paul, prayerfully and carefully live so as not to offend God or people. Having had your heart cleansed, be willing to humble yourself before God, to ask forgiveness when necessary, and, if doing so will bring reconciliation with others, even to overlook transgressions. Strive to be at peace with everyone and choose not to take offense at others. Often, what seems an unbearable offense at the moment, gradually fades from our memory as too petty to remember. Don't forfeit your conscience. A clear conscience is priceless.

Offerings to God

*"You shall daily make a burnt offering to the
LORD of a lamb of the first year without blemish;
you shall prepare it every morning."*

EZEKIEL 46:13

Our sacrifices aren't goats, lambs, or bulls, but we New Testament believers do have specific sacrifices to make. We can, for instance, make spiritual sacrifices of praise and thanksgiving, of sharing all that God has given us, of loving those who are hard to love, of witnessing, of serving, of prayer. Sacrifices are a way of acknowledging that God is the Master of our lives.

Spiritual sacrifices like those listed above also keep us mindful of the Lord. After all, if we are to serve Him as He desires, we must be in close communication with Him. Sacrifices can facilitate that.

Living such a life of devotion can sometimes seem to be a thankless job. Don't be deterred when it appears no one else is faithful to God. The Lord sees your life and knows if you are true to Him. Be assured that if you continue in God's ways even when others fall away—if you live a life of sacrifice and devotion to your loving Master—He will acknowledge and reward your faithfulness.

What offering will you give to your Lord today?

Even-If-He-Doesn't Faith

*Our God whom we serve is able to deliver
us from the burning fiery furnace.*

DANIEL 3:17

Shadrach, Meshach, and Abed-Nego would not bow down before the golden statue of King Nebuchadnezzar, and that meant death. Before throwing them into the flames, the king gave them another chance to bow before him, and once again they refused. They didn't argue with Nebuchadnezzar, nor did they try to defend themselves. These men simply proclaimed their faith and put their lives in the hands of the one true God.

Shadrach, Meshach, and Abed-Nego were supremely confident that God could ably meet their need. They knew that nothing is impossible for God. He can intervene on someone's behalf at any moment. Acknowledging God's freedom to choose what He does, these faithful three said (paraphrased), "God can rescue us, but even if He doesn't—for whatever reason—He is still the Lord, and our faith will not have been in vain. We won't bow down to your gods." Totally trusting in their God, Shadrach, Meshach, and Abed-Nego honored Him as they walked toward the flames—and God delivered them.

These three men lived out their faith in the truths that nothing is impossible for God and that He can intervene at any moment. Do you?

Giving His Blessings Away

*Is there not still someone of the house of Saul, to
whom I may show the kindness of God?*

2 SAMUEL 9:3

Snapshots from King David's life give us clues about living a life that pleases God.

- David forgave his son Absalom for the murder of another son Amnon (14:33). Forgiveness is not determined by the offense, but by the heart of the offended. One who has been forgiven ought to extend forgiveness to others.

- People of Israel rebelled against King David; "men of Judah . . . remained loyal" (20:2). There will always be people who misunderstand and oppose God's work. Keep your eyes on the Lord and be faithful to the end.

- In a song of praise, David acknowledged that those who humbly yield to God's majesty will be lifted high by His hand (22:28). The arrogant who try to elevate themselves find His hand upon them too, but it is bringing them down.

- King David's question above calls us to seek God's goodness not only for ourselves; but also to share with others. When He pours His blessing upon your life, find ways to give it away.

To whom will you show mercy, loyalty, humility, or generosity today?

Strength in the Lord

Be strong, therefore, and prove yourself a man. And
keep the charge of the LORD your God: to walk in
His ways, to keep His statutes, His commandments,
His judgments, and His testimonies.

1 KINGS 2:2–3

David knew well what it was like to both walk obediently with God and also to fail to obey His commandments. When David trusted in God, giants fell, opposing armies were routed, and enemies were defeated. Many of David's psalms record his joy in God's love and protection on his life.

But David also grievously disobeyed his Lord and suffered the painful consequences. Some of David's most heart-wrenching psalms record his grief over the devastating consequences of his sin against God. David lived daily with those consequences. He therefore earnestly desired that his son Solomon not make the devastating mistakes he had made. David recognized that only by carefully keeping God's commandments could Solomon enjoy the abundant blessings God wanted to give him. The real test of Solomon's manhood would depend upon how closely he followed after the Lord.

Take time to search the Scriptures for God's commandments and instructions. They are far too important for you to remain unaware of any of them. Then, empowered by the Spirit, obey God's commands and enjoy His favor on your life.

Our Jealous and Gracious God

For the L ORD your God is a consuming fire, a jealous God.

M oses describes God as "a consuming fire," and what fuels that fire is His jealousy. But God's jealousy is entirely different from our human envy of who someone is or what someone has. In Old Testament references to God, *jealousy* means "a zest for something." To be specific, jealousy is God's active passion for righteousness that arises from His holiness. His zeal for the truth that He alone is God generates a fiery condemnation of those who worship false gods, of those who turn away from Him.

Too often God's own people—"stiff-necked people," as Moses described them—strayed from the Lord. They were constantly grumbling, often quite stubborn, and persistently disobedient, yet still God viewed them as His special treasure. But Moses did not want them to forget that only because of God's grace did they know His blessing. Like Israel, we must always remember that our good circumstances are nothing more than an undeserved gift from God.

Do you have a passion for God that in any way resembles His love for you? How vigorously do you protect your relationship with Him? No one else can adequately guard your relationship with your jealous and gracious God.

Are you as jealous for God as He is for you?

Inquire, Honor, and Thank

[Saul] did not inquire of the LORD; therefore He killed him, and turned the kingdom over to David.

1 CHRONICLES 10:14

Learn from Saul's grave mistake—as well as from other scenes in 1 Chronicles.

Failure to seek guidance from the Lord inevitably leads to catastrophe. God won't force His counsel upon us, even though hearing it and heeding it would be for our own good. Instead, we must desire God's will and obey it whenever He reveals it to us. Saul neither desired nor sought God's will, and his humiliating death was the result.

God had promised that death just as He had foretold the subsequent crowning of David. Sometimes God's promises take years to come to fruition. The intervening time can be a period of struggle, but if you're in such a season of life, never doubt a promise from God. If He said something will happen, it *will* happen.

When the good that God has promised does indeed occur, know that the glory belongs to Him—and see that He is honored. Too often we are quick to cry out to God for help, but slow to shout our thanks and praise after He gives us the victory. The best way to remain constantly in God's will is to be continually inquiring of the Lord.

Equipping the Saints

He Himself gave some to be apostles, some prophets,
some evangelists, and some pastors and teachers, for
the equipping of the saints for the work of ministry.

EPHESIANS 4:11–12

Jesus Christ is Head of the church as well as Lord of our lives. As Head of the church, Jesus called some believers to be apostles, and these commissioned messengers—who were eyewitnesses of the resurrected Christ—had special authority to establish the church. Jesus also appointed prophets to both proclaim what God had said and foretell what He would do; evangelists, to herald God's message of salvation; pastors, to nurture, care for, and protect local flocks of God's people; and teachers, to explain and apply the Scriptures for God's people.

Believers today are also to equip the body of Christ for ministry. The Greek behind the word *equipping* calls ministers to bring God's people to a place where they are lacking nothing they need in order to serve in Christ's body. Every believer has a significant role in the body; each one of us, therefore, must be prepared to serve.

What are you doing to build up other believers so they can more effectively serve Christ? Which of Christ's people are helping you become more spiritually mature?

APRIL

How much better to
get wisdom than gold!

PROVERBS 16:16

The Courage of Humility

By the grace of God I am what I am, and His grace toward
me was not in vain. But I labored more abundantly than
they all, yet not I, but the grace of God which was with me.

1 CORINTHIANS 15:10

Webster's defines *humility* as "the state of being humble" and *humble* as "not proud or haughty: not arrogant or assertive." That's a starting point, but Christians add this aspect of understanding: humility is a right evaluation of who you are in relation to the almighty and holy God.

Paul's statement in 1 Corinthians 15:10 is an expression of genuine humility. Paul knew that he was who he was—an apostle in God's church as opposed to its persecutor—only by "the grace of God." Paul was a living testimony to the supernatural miracle of redemption; his life illustrates what it is like to be a new creation in Christ, born again by the Spirit of God, and having Christ dwell within. Paul knew that his labor for God's church was fruitful only because of "the grace of God which was with me."

When we remember that the grace of God provides everything we need to lead a godly life, we can live with a true humility that is confident and courageous.

"In Your Likeness"

As for me, I will see Your face in righteousness;
I shall be satisfied when I awake in Your likeness.

PSALM 17:15

Satisfaction is a state of contentment; it's wanting and needing nothing more. It's knowing, after that last bite of Thanksgiving pie, that you have had enough. It's pulling both cars into the garage after spending the day cleaning and organizing it. It's having put in a hard day's work in the yard and seeing the weeds gone, the grass cut, the flowers pruned, the bushes trimmed, and the sidewalks swept.

According to this verse, what is it that will satisfy the psalmist? He told God, "I shall be satisfied when I awake in your likeness." For believers, all of life is a pilgrimage to this ultimate destination.

The psalmist's desire was not earthly pleasures; the destination of his lifelong journey was Christ—to be with Him and to be like Him. Is that your desire as well? Is being with Christ and being like Him the primary goal of your life? Perhaps you've seen fellow Christians who clearly do reflect the likeness of their Lord. Know that you can too. Don't be satisfied with anything less.

Obedience That Honors God

*[Daniel] knelt down on his knees three times
that day, and prayed and gave thanks before his
God, as was his custom since early days.*

DANIEL 6:10

The edict had been signed: Darius mandated that no one could pray to anyone except him for thirty days. Daniel knew the law of the land, and he knew the law of his Lord. Daniel's allegiance was to God.

Daniel faced a very real danger, yet he did not compromise or conceal his loyalty to God. He trusted his life to God's mercy and did not abandon his lifelong habit of regular prayer—which was exactly what his enemies had expected when they set their trap. Had Daniel forfeited his prayer life, he would have betrayed his faithful Lord, and his accusers would simply have devised another trap. Nothing would have been gained through Daniel's compromise, but he would have lost the opportunity to prove faithful to his God.

Whenever we step out in faith and obedience to God as Daniel did, the Lord has an opportunity to demonstrate His character to a watching world. Always be aware that people around you observe how you respond to a crisis. They will develop much of their understanding of God through the testimony of your life. Don't squander an opportunity, no matter how difficult it may be, to bring honor to your Lord.

A Pattern for Life

[Jesus] Himself often withdrew into the wilderness and prayed.

LUKE 5:16

Before we can move ahead for God, we must withdraw from the usual activities of life and be with Him. The more meaningful those times of retreat are, the more significant our times of spiritual advance will be.

This was clearly Jesus' pattern for life. Prayer was not incidental to His kingdom work; it was the foundation and the lifeblood of what He did during His ministry.

When Jesus prayed, He was not merely looking to have the Father endorse His plans; He was seeking His Father's will. We must do likewise, for there is too much at stake for us to miss God's will. We want to join God in the work that He is already doing in the world. It's too easy, in our zeal for God, to rush into plans and ministries for Him that actually oppose His purposes. God does not need our ideas, our initiative, or our imagination. He already has a plan. He is simply looking for our obedience.

We see in the Gospels that, throughout His life, Jesus prayed and received His Father's strength and direction for the ministry that lay ahead. There was too much at stake for Him to misunderstand God's will or to advance without heaven's power.

Hurriedly make your way into the wilderness, and spend time with your God.

God's Purposes Prevail

*This is the book of the genealogy of Adam . . . . Adam
lived one hundred and thirty years, and begot a son in his
own likeness, after his image, and named him Seth.*

GENESIS 5:1, 3

Genesis 5 traces the family line from Adam, the man whom God created in His likeness, to Noah and his sons Shem, Ham, and Japheth. When God created Adam and Eve, He was clear about His purposes: "Be fruitful and multiply; fill the earth and subdue it" (Genesis 1:28).

God intended for Adam and Eve to populate the earth with their offspring. Their children, however, soon committed deceit, treachery, and murder. Sin sought to destroy every plan God had for His people. Yet God's purposes prevailed over the worst that sin could do.

That truth applies in the personal sense as well as in the global, eternal sweep of God's story. What is the worst that the sin you've committed has done in your life? Confess that sin, repent of it, and watch God's purposes prevail. What is the worst that sin committed against you has done in your life? Again, God's purposes can and will prevail. Turn to Him in confidence that His forgiving love and redeeming power will triumph in your life as He continues to both grow your faith in Him and craft your likeness to Christ.

God's purposes will prevail!

An Example to Follow

Then the LORD said to Aaron: "You shall have no inheritance in their land, nor shall you have any portion among them; I am your portion and your inheritance among the children of Israel."

NUMBERS 18:20

When the children of Israel finally reached the Promised Land, the Lord divided it among every tribe except Levi, the tribe called to serve the Lord in His tabernacle. The Levites, who had God as their resource for everything they needed, would receive their livelihood from the Israelites' tithes and offerings.

But God's instruction to the Levites continued: "When you take from the children of Israel the tithes . . . you shall offer up a heave offering of it to the LORD, a tenth of the tithe" (v. 26). Like the rest of Israel, the Levites were required to give 10 percent to the Lord in remembrance that God was the source of all they had.

God also calls us to give back to Him the first portion of what He gives to us. Doing so reminds us that it came from His hand; it also helps us hold loosely the things of this world, possessions that can easily entrap, distract, and compel us to leave the Lord's narrow path.

Are you tithing? Make it a topic of discussion with your heavenly Father. Be generous with God, as He is with You.

"The Lord Will Provide"

Abraham lifted his eyes and looked, and there behind
him was a ram caught in a thicket by its horns. So
Abraham went and took the ram, and offered it up for
a burnt offering instead of his son. And Abraham called
the name of the place, The-Lord-Will-Provide.

GENESIS 22:13—14

The instruction was strange, unsettling, incredible. Abraham was to sacrifice his long-awaited and cherished son, the boy through whom the Lord was to fulfill His promise to bless the world (v. 2).

Abraham obeyed. He gathered the wood, picked up his knife, and carried fire with him for the sacrifice. He built the altar, lay his son on it, and lifted his knife . . . Then the angel of the Lord called to him, telling him not to lay his hand on Isaac. Abraham's actions up to this point had demonstrated the degree of his faith. God provided another offering for Abraham's sacrifice. Can you imagine the relief the patriarch felt when God provided him a different sacrifice?!

The Hebrew name *Jehovah Jireh* means "The Lord Will Provide." This name speaks of the completeness of God's care for Abraham in particular and for His people for eternity. Just as God provided a ram as a substitute for Isaac, He would provide a Savior as a substitute for all people.

Praise God for providing for you—day by day and for eternity.

Countercultural Living

How much better to get wisdom than gold!

PROVERBS 16:16

The book of Proverbs contains practical applications of various commandments and admonitions given to God's people through the centuries. It also compares the way of the righteous with the way of the wicked, the way of the wise with the way of the fool.

Consider the following life lessons from Proverbs:

- PROVERBS 3:5–6: Depending on your own wisdom obstructs God's better plans for your life.
- PROVERBS 4:23: Your heart's affections determine your life's direction. God's Word keeps your heart pure and safe.
- PROVERBS 5:1–23: Beware of pursuing a cheap alternative to the blessings a faithful marriage can bring. Evil always tempts us to settle for less than God's best.
- PROVERBS 13:7: Live by godly priorities. What seems worthless to fools is often valuable to the righteous; what fools pursue is often meaningless in God's eyes.
- PROVERBS 25:21–22: Honor God and show respect for those He created by returning evil with goodness.
- PROVERBS 31:30: Revered above all else—above beauty, charm, prudence, industry, profitability, and wisdom—is a close relationship with God.

Go against culture's grain—and glorify your Lord!

After the Grave

"Many of those who sleep in the dust
of the earth shall awake,
Some to everlasting life,
Some to shame and everlasting contempt."

DANIEL 12:2

During the normal course of our busy lives, it is all too easy to neglect God and His Word. However, life—with its dangers and unknowns, with the questions that continually arise and decisions to be made, and with the inevitable losses and hurts—can make us acknowledge our need for Almighty God and look beyond ourselves to Him.

Sadly, many people reach the end of their days having not done so. There is a hauntingly stark contrast between the passing of those who oppose God and those who trust in Him. The person who defies God can expect a lonely eternity of dark separation from the Giver of life and Forgiver of sins. God's faithful children, however, can look forward to the welcoming embrace of their loving Lord and heavenly Father.

Daniel 12:2 is the most unambiguous reference to the afterlife found in the Old Testament. (Isaiah 26:19 provides a less-specific example.) Scripture makes it clear: people who follow God are vindicated, and those who oppose Him are delivered into eternal punishment. What are you anticipating will happen at the end of your days?

God Speaks

"Stand still and consider the wondrous works of God."

JOB 37:14

Why do the wicked prosper and the righteous suffer? Sometimes we need to stop theorizing and pontificating and simply listen for a word from God. We learn new truths by listening to God.

Here are some truths from the book of Job we must hear:

- The Lord gives blessings and allows suffering. We aren't to base our relationship with the Lord on His gifts or His blessings, but on His character and His love for us (1:21).
- God is constantly at work all around us. Failing to recognize His activity does not negate this reality (9:10).
- Why should we even think we could grasp the full extent of God's wisdom? We are but creatures; He is the Creator (11:7).
- God's wisdom infinitely exceeds our own. It is ludicrous for us to debate Him or judge His actions (12:17).

We don't need all the answers about the wicked prospering and the righteous suffering when we know that God has them. After all, when God speaks, the power of His word puts our lives and our questions instantly into perspective. Our ultimate confidence comes from God's Word, not our understanding. He is God. We are not.

On Whose Authority?

"All authority has been given to Me in heaven and on earth."

MATTHEW 28:18

The New Testament term *authority* means "freedom of choice." The greater the authority, the more autonomy one has to choose and to act. God has absolute sovereignty and is therefore completely free to do as He pleases. Once a divine decision is made, He cannot be thwarted by any power in the universe.

God—who has the absolute power to do whatever He chooses to carry out His will—has given His Son *all* authority, and the Son in turn gives power to those He chooses to represent Him. As His ambassadors, we Christians have Jesus' backing for what we do for Him. This is a God-given privilege, not license to do as we please. We are free *not* to do as *we* want, but to act according to the Lord's will.

Furthermore, the work of God's kingdom rests on Christ's supremacy, not our ability. Do not grow discouraged if a situation exceeds your competence and resources. At issue is your belief. Do you trust that Christ is able and willing to use your life to accomplish His work? When God sets an assignment before you, what you do next reveals what you believe about Him.

A Picture of Betrayal

The word of the LORD that came to Hosea . . .

HOSEA 1:1

Hosea had an extremely difficult assignment. Not only was he to minister to the northern kingdom of Israel during its demise and fall, but he was also to manifest, through his personal life, the agony that Israel's betrayal caused God.

By marrying an immoral, unfaithful woman, Hosea graphically demonstrated God's view of His people's idolatry. Gomer would publicly humiliate and forsake Hosea, but he was to take her back and love her, just as God willingly forgives and receives His wayward people. Despite the enormity of the task, Hosea obeyed immediately. Although Hosea's personal story fades into the background after chapter 3, the love and grace he extended to Gomer pervade the entire book and reflect the love and grace God extends to His people.

Hosea's life likened the covenant between God and His people to that of a marriage in which sacred vows of loyalty are pledged. Despite Israel's horrific treachery toward God, He continually looked toward a renewed time of reconciliation and intimacy.

Hosea's name is a variant of the name *Joshua*, meaning "The Lord Saves." God saves through His persistent, redeeming love—a love Hosea lived out in his marriage to wayward Gomer. It is the same relentless love He expresses toward you.

From Pain to Praise

Blessed is he whose transgression is forgiven,
Whose sin is covered . . . .
You forgave the iniquity of my sin.

PSALM 32:1, 5

He had shirked his duty as his nation's military leader and stayed home from battle. Walking atop his palace, he had sighted a beautiful woman—the wife of another man, in fact, the wife of one of his officers. He chose to commit adultery with her. When he learned she was pregnant, he arranged an elaborate plan for having her husband killed. He had committed these sins months ago, yet King David kept quiet about it. He did not confess his sin until the prophet Nathan confronted him . . . almost nine months later.

During those nine months, David felt God's righteous hand weigh heavily upon him. "My bones grew old through my groaning all the day long," David reported. "My vitality was turned into the drought of summer" (vv. 3–4). Silence about his sin wrought pain and suffering in his life. Confession brought forgiveness, a renewal, joy, and praise.

In fact, *blessed* describes the joy of knowing your sins have been forgiven by Holy God. Follow David's example. Confess your sin, acknowledge your waywardness, admit how you've fallen short of God's standards—and don't delay a minute longer. Confess your sin, receive God's forgiveness, and let praise replace pain.

Resurrection Power and Love

*Now if Christ is preached that He has been raised
from the dead, how do some among you say
that there is no resurrection of the dead?*

1 CORINTHIANS 15:12

Elijah revived the widow's son . . . Elisha raised the Shunammite's son . . . Jesus brought Jairus's daughter back to life . . . Jesus called Lazarus forth from the tomb after he had been dead for four days . . .

Each of these incidents revealed God's power over death, but these miracles involved resuscitation, not resurrection. Resurrection was unique to Jesus, God's Son.

Jesus was resurrected—in a manner previously unknown to humanity—to everlasting life in a transformed state of being that passed beyond death and decay. Resurrection is proof of the gospel's power to redeem, and Jesus was the first of all those who will be raised up on the day of His return. All who have died must appear before God in judgment, but believers will experience resurrection as transformation. Resurrection is the state in which believers will enjoy their eternal destiny, a life beyond physical death. Because Jesus lives, we shall live with Him.

Death temporarily removes us from those we love, but it relocates us into the presence of the One who loves us most . . . for eternity.

Fish in Water

Who can understand his errors?
Cleanse me from secret faults . . . .
Let the words of my mouth and the meditation of my heart
Be acceptable in Your sight,
O LORD, my strength and my Redeemer.

PSALM 19:12, 14

We're like fish in water when it comes to our sins. Some of our sins are so much a part of us that we don't even recognize them as sin, just as a fish doesn't acknowledge the water that comprises its world. When our sin fades and blends in to the backdrop, it is all the more dangerous in its subtlety. Just because we have grown accustomed to our sin does not make it any less loathsome to God.

God sees our sin; He knows what lies within the innermost recesses of our hearts. He is aware of our every thought whether or not we verbalize it. The psalmist knew he must deal with these issues—with the thoughts of his heart as well as with the words of his mouth prompted by those thoughts. And the psalmist knew he needed the Lord's help to do so.

God's help is available to you too. Turn to Him. Let Him cleanse you from your "errors" and "secret faults" and make your words and thoughts acceptable in His sight. He already knows all about them. He stands ready to free you from them.

Pure and Unfailing Love

Then the LORD said to me, "Go again, love a woman who is loved by a lover and is committing adultery, just like the love of the LORD for the children of Israel, who look to other gods."

HOSEA 3:1

God views your rejection of Him as spiritual adultery, and your betrayal grieves Him.

We get a portrait of that harsh truth in the life of Hosea. In obedience to God, the prophet married a woman whose harlotry mocked true intimacy. We are to see in Hosea's heartbroken reaction to his wife's unfaithfulness how deeply we offend God when we reject the pure love He offers us.

This powerful picture challenges us, God's bride, to be faithful to our covenant love. Every time we turn away from Him, we commit spiritual adultery. But that's not the only lesson Hosea's life offers.

We also see in Hosea's experience that even at the worst points of estrangement between God and His people, there is always hope because of God's unfailing love. Despite our rejection and betrayal, despite our unfaithfulness and broken promises, God continues to love us. When we stray from Him, He lovingly and relentlessly pursues us. If not for His unfailing love, we would be victims of our own wickedness. How marvelous to know that, even though we may turn our backs on God, He never gives up on us!

"Walk Humbly"

What does the LORD require of you
But to do justly,
To love mercy,
And to walk humbly with your God?

MICAH 6:8

God's desires for us are not shrouded in mystery. He has made it crystal clear how we can please Him. In this single verse from Micah, God outlines the way we should act, what we should value, and how we should relate to Him. Knowing what God wants us to do, will we choose to obey?

If we choose to walk humbly with God, we'll begin seeing with His eyes, hearing with His ears, and loving with His love. We'll also be more aware of where He wants us to be involved in His kingdom work. Both His guidance and His power are available to us.

As we draw near to God and immerse our lives in His character, our relationships, our words, and our actions will come to reflect His holy nature. We'll find ourselves disturbed by flagrant injustice and idolatry, and we'll weep with compassion for the needy. We'll shudder at sin—and know that our Lord is more powerful than evil's most constricting stranglehold.

God has made it perfectly clear what He is looking for in us. Will He find it?

Return to God's Love

"I have loved you," says the LORD.

MALACHI 1:2

L ove motivates God's every encounter with you. In order to understand both His blessings and His discipline, you must accept this lavish love and, in return, give Him your best, not spiritual leftovers (vv. 7–8). That's what God was getting from His people when Malachi urged the children of Israel to renew their enthusiasm for God and His commandments. God's perfect love for us deserves our wholehearted devotion in response.

Returning to God's love would refuel a passion for worship, because our understanding of who God is inspires our adoration and obedience. If we don't see Him as the almighty Creator and eternal Judge, we may discount His commands and offend His holiness. But when we realize who He truly is ("My name is to be feared among the nations" [v. 14]) and how much He loves us, we will return to Him wholeheartedly. God has loved us. How can we not love Him in return?

Malachi urged people to return to the covenant love relationship with God that they once enjoyed (3:7). He reminded them of how much God loves them.

You know the ways you stray from God. Will you return to Him today?

"Blessed Are . . ."

"Blessed are the poor in spirit,
For theirs is the kingdom of heaven."

MATTHEW 5:3

The word *blessed* means "happy or fortunate as a result of divine favor." But there is more to blessedness than simply being happy. After all, happiness (from the word *hap*, meaning "chance") is usually dependent on circumstances. God's blessings, however, override our circumstances. In the Beatitudes, for instance, Jesus teaches the paradoxical truth that those who are blessed experience the kingdom's inner riches even as they face external poverty and very real distress.

Consider that those who mourn "shall be comforted." Those who hunger and thirst for righteousness (who feel distress over the current unrighteous state of affairs) "shall be filled." Those "who are persecuted for righteousness' sake" shall know the kingdom of heaven as theirs.

The kingdom of God with its tangible blessings for its citizens is already here, but not yet in its fullness. After all, to be blessed is to have a relationship with God, who both satisfies our soul in the midst of whatever we're experiencing in the present and promises future and eternal rewards.

Are you presently enjoying the blessings that come from a personal relationship with the King?

Scrupulous Integrity

A bishop must be blameless, as a steward of God . . .
hospitable, a lover of what is good, sober-minded, just,
holy, self-controlled, holding fast the faithful word as he
has been taught, that he may be able, by sound doctrine,
both to exhort and convict those who contradict.

TITUS 1:7–9

This is quite a list of prerequisites! Let's look at three of these traits Paul listed as necessary for church leaders (the meaning behind the word *bishop*).

- The Greek word translated *blameless* also means "irreproachable, not a target for censure." The word doesn't imply complete perfection or flawlessness. It does, however, call for a life of scrupulous integrity. Church leaders should not bring disrepute or shame to the church through sinful or even questionable activity.

- In Paul's day, *stewards* were household managers who cared for someone's property and were accountable to that person. Church leaders are to care for God's people—His household—and are accountable to Him.

- Before being appointed over a church, potential elders were taught the fundamental truths of their faith. *Sound doctrine* was—and is—crucial in the church.

We are Christ's ambassadors. As such He expects us to represent Him accurately. That begins with our integrity.

Fear or Faith?

He said to them, "Where is your faith?"

LUKE 8:25

We often begin the journey of faith serving God confidently and enthusiastically—and then troubles come and doubts arise. Sometimes our circumstances can look utterly hopeless, but we never know the reality of our situation until we have sought Jesus' perspective on it. He knows many things we don't, and He has power that we can't imagine.

Furthermore, it's foolish to be discouraged or afraid when Jesus is right next to us to calm, to reassure, to act, and to graciously remind us that, despite our circumstances, we are still in God's will. Difficulties don't necessarily mean that we have missed or misunderstood God's will, but if we need to make adjustments in our lives, He will let us know.

Remember the disciples being surprised by a storm as they sailed on the Sea of Galilee? Jesus told them to head across the lake (God's will)—and then came the storm (difficulties). But Jesus was in the boat right next to the disciples, and He exercised a power we can't imagine: Jesus rebuked the wind and waves . . .

The measure of your faith is revealed during life's storms. Establishing your life on God's Word and walking through life with Him bring a security nothing can shake.

Worship First

Every animal . . . went out of the ark. Then Noah built
an altar to the LORD . . . and offered burnt offerings on
the altar. And the LORD smelled a soothing aroma.

GENESIS 8:20-21

It had been a long project, building that ark . . . It had been a memorable boat ride, tending all those animals . . . Now a new and equally daunting task awaited: starting all over now that the waters had receded.

Despite this formidable undertaking, Noah's first act upon exiting the ark was to worship God. It wasn't looking for building materials or scouting out the best spot for a new home. It wasn't scanning the landscape to see where he could farm or where his boys might establish their new homes. The first thing Noah did was build an altar for worship—and his Lord was pleased.

God receives genuine pleasure from the sincere worship of His people. He delights in our reverence and adoration. Our heartfelt worship elicits God's blessings and favor.

Do you put worship first in your life? Is there time for worship before you consult the day's to-do list or check your messages? Making worship a priority not only pleases God; it also puts your life in its proper perspective. Always put God first in your life and see how He aligns every other detail.

Fleeing

But Jonah arose to flee to Tarshish from the presence of the
LORD. He went down to Joppa, and found a ship going to
Tarshish; so he paid the fare, and went down into it, to go
with them to Tarshish from the presence of the LORD.

JONAH 1:3

Joppa was a coastal city in the area of present-day Tel Aviv. It lay fifty miles south of Jonah's hometown, Gath Hepher. Tarshish is generally identified with Tartessus in Spain, roughly two thousand miles to the west. Nineveh lay five hundred miles to the northeast. God wanted Jonah to go northeast, but he headed west!

Can we blame Jonah? God commanded Jonah to call the people of Nineveh, in the land of Assyria, to repent of their sin and turn to God. The last thing Jonah wanted was for these wicked enemies of Israel to escape God's wrath. Jonah had no desire to travel to the epicenter of evil with a message of forgiveness and healing.

God's assignments are enormous, aren't they? God calls us to do things that seem impossible and—like in Jonah's case—make us uncomfortable. However, there is no escaping God's call. Once God speaks, all we can sensibly do is submit to His call. Jonah learned that lesson the hard way.

Where is God sending you? Is that the direction you're headed?

Victory over Sin

In all things [Jesus] had to be made like His brethren,
that He might be a merciful and faithful High
Priest . . . to make propitiation for the sins of the
people. For in that He Himself has suffered, being
tempted, He is able to aid those who are tempted.

HEBREWS 2:17–18

That God Almighty—the Alpha and the Omega, the Infinite, Omniscient, Omnipotent One—would choose to take on the limitations of being human is an amazing fact of our faith.

Jesus willingly assumed the limitations of being a man. While He walked the earth, He was tempted in every way that we are. He then suffered immeasurable pain as He hung on the cross, and He experienced unimaginable spiritual anguish when He found Himself bearing the weight of humanity's sin.

Having remained totally free of sin, though, Jesus could be the propitiation—the atoning sacrifice—for our sin. After all, it is completely impossible for us human beings to do anything to satisfy God's wrath. Sinful by nature, we cannot make atonement for ourselves. But Christ's death fully satisfies God's holiness, allowing us to be reconciled with Him.

Having consistently resisted sin, Jesus stands ready to give us victory over every temptation we face. Victory is possible. Turn to Him today.

Christian Koinonia

If we walk in the light as He is in the light,
we have fellowship with one another.

1 JOHN 1:7

The Greek word *koinonia*, translated "fellowship" in this verse, needs many English words to express its full meaning.

When used to describe a person's relationship with God, *fellowship* means that people can have an intimate relationship with Him that impacts every area of life. The term also implies partnership with Him in His work.

It also expresses the sense of mutual sharing between two parties, each one giving freely to the other. It implies the stewardship people have over that which God entrusts to them.

Koinonia is used specifically to describe the close relationship between God's people.

Koinonia, therefore, is the outflow of God's love in various practical expressions. The measure to which God has shared His life with us is the same standard by which we should love other people in the kingdom of God.

Ask God to love people through you . . . to show you practical ways to love the people He puts in your world . . . and to enable you to die to self so you can share with those around you the love you have personally experienced from Christ.

God's Purposes

"For the LORD of hosts has purposed,
And who will annul it?
His hand is stretched out,
And who will turn it back?"

ISAIAH 14:27

This world is diametrically opposed to God and His purposes. So are Satan's demonic forces. At times it can even appear that God's enemies have thwarted the outworking of His will upon the earth, but this is not so. The opponents of God do rage against Him, but God is unconcerned. He knows what their end will be. He is supremely confident that every intention of His heart will ultimately unfold exactly as He plans.

God knows this to be true. Satan's forces wish it weren't. What about you? Have you begun to doubt whether some of the promises God has made will ever occur? Or do you have absolute confidence that whatever God proposes will ultimately come to pass?

Now consider your present circumstances. Does it seem that evil forces and wicked people are prevailing over God's people? Don't lose heart. The enemy's efforts are futile. God's victory is already won. When God speaks, it is as good as done. If the world's loud boasting has caused you to waver in your confidence in God's promises, take heart: "For the LORD of hosts has purposed, and who will annul it?"

Opposition—and Prayer

When Sanballat heard that we were rebuilding the wall . . .
he was furious and very indignant, and mocked the Jews.

NEHEMIAH 4:1

It shouldn't surprise us that evil people get angry when their plans to hinder God's people do not succeed. As Sanballat and his cronies ridiculed the Jews' construction efforts, though, Nehemiah prayed (vv. 4–5)—and kept building the wall.

What you do right after you pray reveals what you truly believe about God. A word from God followed by faithful action demonstrates trust in God, and Nehemiah clearly trusted God: "So we built the wall" (v. 6).

The opposition escalated, this time with a conspiracy to "attack Jerusalem and create confusion" (v. 8). Nehemiah's response? "Nevertheless we made our prayer to our God" (v. 9). Still, the obstructions came, and yet the construction continued.

Opposition to God's work is inevitable. God's enemies are threatened by the growth of His kingdom, so they move swiftly and rigorously to stop it. Expect ridicule, injustice, and even threats when you labor for the Lord. But know that you work with Him at your side—and turn to Him in prayer as you work. Listen to Him, not your critics.

Inspired by God

All Scripture is given by inspiration of God,
and is profitable for doctrine, for reproof, for
correction, for instruction in righteousness.

2 TIMOTHY 3:16

Painters can be inspired by the sunset. Poets can be inspired by the person they love. Young people can be inspired by great athletes. But the inspiration God provided the writers of Scripture is quite different.

The Greek behind *inspiration* means "God-breathed." God didn't merely spark a good idea, fill a heart to overflowing, or fuel a writer's effort. Instead, God—through His Holy Spirit—influenced men's minds in a way that made them His agents for the infallible communication of God's revelation.

The Scriptures, although penned by the hands of men, are the very Word of God. To fully and accurately understand Scripture's truths, then, we must receive illumination or enlightenment by the Holy Spirit, the divine quickening of the human mind. Only the Holy Spirit can enable us to understand the truth that has been revealed and communicated by the power of God. Before you open the Bible, ask the Spirit to open your mind and heart to recognize and understand God's wisdom.

Also, always open your Bible with trembling for you are about to encounter God's holy, life-changing, inspired Word.

The Hidden Mover

Now in the first year of Cyrus king of Persia, that the word of the LORD spoken by the mouth of Jeremiah might be fulfilled, the LORD stirred up the spirit of Cyrus king of Persia.

EZRA 1:1

World events come as no surprise to God. He has foreseen them. At times He foretells them. He is always sovereign over them . . .

Founder of the Persian Empire, King Cyrus overthrew Babylon in 538 BC, a fulfillment of prophecy. Cyrus was more lenient toward conquered peoples than either the Assyrians or Babylonians were. In fact, Cyrus often encouraged the continuation of local religious practices in order to gain the loyalty of his new subjects. While adopting this apparently novel and effective foreign policy, Cyrus was fulfilling God's redemptive plan for His people.

God was working through this pagan king, He was also active in the hearts of His people: "all whose spirits God had moved, arose to go up and build the house of the LORD which is in Jerusalem" (v. 5).

God awakens in His people the desire to participate in His kingdom work. Our wish to serve God is a direct result of His stirring in our lives. Even when the nations make their declarations and mobilize their forces, God continues to accomplish His purposes.

Dear Timothy

To Timothy, a true son in the faith: Grace, mercy, and
peace from God our Father and Jesus Christ our Lord.

1 TIMOTHY 1:2

His name means "honored of God." He is primarily known as a young companion and co-laborer with Paul. Apparently an apostolic representative to the churches, he encouraged the persecuted church in Philippi, corrected false teaching in Corinth, traveled to Macedonia, and gave leadership to the church in Ephesus. He is Timothy, a godly man who followed the Lord from his youth.

His godly mother was one reason Timothy's faith began so early. His Greek father may have died while Timothy was young, but his mother Eunice and his grandmother Lois were Christians who taught him the Scriptures from his childhood, unknowingly laying the groundwork for his powerful future ministry.

A godly heritage is truly a gift from God, a strong foundation for future opportunities to serve Him. Timothy's humble and teachable spirit was fertile soil for God's Word to take root and to produce fruit.

Thank God for the godly heritage He blessed you with—and/or for the godly heritage He is enabling you to provide your children. Ask Him to make your spirit humble and teachable like Timothy's.

MAY

Whenever I am afraid,
I will trust in you.

PSALM 56:3

Incarnate Love

*We were well pleased to impart to you not
only the gospel of God, but also our own lives,
because you had become dear to us.*

1 THESSALONIANS 2:9

Roses and chocolates . . .
Birthday presents and balloons . . .
A new bike or the latest technological toy.

These things are wonderful and fun, and each of them can communicate love. But genuine love involves much more than giving things to the people we care about.

Jesus Himself—who is, in His essence, love personified—did not merely provide us the gift of salvation; He gave us Himself.

The gospel is not a prescription detachedly doled out to those in need; the gospel is a gift of love from God. We therefore must give ourselves away for the sake of the gospel—just as Jesus did—in order for the world to truly know and experience God's love.

Our talk about God and His sacrificial love is hollow if we're merely throwing words at people rather than loving them by giving ourselves—by giving our concern, our prayers, our compassion, our Christlike, sacrificial love. Divine love pays the price. It gets involved. Incarnate love isn't always convenient, but it changes lives.

Choose to Trust

Whenever I am afraid, I will trust in You.

PSALM 56:3

I t's not something you generate by gritting your teeth. It doesn't come by osmosis from sitting in a pew Sunday after Sunday. And it's not highly contagious—although spending time with God's people can and does help.

The *it* here is trust, and trust is a choice. When the psalmist-king declared, "I *will* trust," he was making a choice. Despite the circumstances—the fighting surrounding him, the enemies oppressing him, the adversaries twisting his words, and the tears that he was shedding—David chose to trust God.

Just as when he stood before Goliath (1 Samuel 17), David didn't give in to fear. After all, fear betrays a lack of trust in God. When we truly know the God who sustains us, we have no reason to fear. Apparently David knew this truth: "In God I have put my trust; I will not fear. What can flesh do to me?" (Psalm 56:4).

As the apostle Paul would say, since God is for us, who can be against us (Romans 8:31)?

What enemies are oppressing you? What adversaries are twisting your words? What is prompting your tears? What giant are you facing? Choose to trust God. He will help you fight the battle and fell the giant.

Courageous Faith

*Be of good courage, and let us be strong for our
people and for the cities of our God. And may
the LORD do what is good in His sight.*

1 CHRONICLES 19:13

Does this passage describe a pattern in your life? When God has called you to be courageous and you've stepped out in faith, have you seen Him protect you and provide for you?

Perhaps the step of faith that called for such courage meant quitting a comfortable job or attempting something you had never done before. Maybe that step of faith was teaching a Bible study or battling a disease. Whatever the opportunity that called for courage, ponder the ways God met you during that experience.

In the Scriptures, God's charge to His people to be courageous is almost always followed by His promise of divine help. When you've been faithful to the Lord and when you are seeking to obey and honor Him, you can face anything without fear because God is faithful to walk with you.

So, keeping in mind this pattern of your courageous steps of faith and God's faithful provision in response, pray about any current life situation that calls for courage—and know that God will go with you.

Doing Battle

Be strong in the Lord and in the power of His might. Put on the whole armor of God.

EPHESIANS 6:10—11

If you are a Christian, you are engaged in a spiritual battle of universal proportions. Evil, dangerous, and sinister forces are seeking to destroy you, your family, and your church. Your very soul is in a conflict against the forces of evil. As frightening as the powers of darkness may appear, though, you serve an unimaginably powerful God, and the victory is His.

Despite that glorious and certain truth, some Christians live in constant fear, intimidated by Satan and his forces, and thinking too much about the enemy. Spiritual warfare is a reality, but we should not live in fear because God has provided us with armor that can protect us from any blow we might receive.

This divine protection and power should enable us to live each day with courage and peace. As God's people, we are fully equipped to overcome sin when it enters the church and to stand strong when the world opposes us. God has made provision for any and every circumstance we may face. So "be strong in the Lord" and live with confidence in Him. Expect God to give you victory as you do battle with the armor He provides.

Faithful in Everything

"He who is faithful in what is least is faithful also in much;
and he who is unjust in what is least is unjust also in much."

LUKE 16:10

God will not entrust great responsibility to someone who has not been faithful with a little.

If you are frustrated that God is not doing more in your life, consider how you handled the last assignment He gave you. Were you as faithful as you should have been? Do you think God would agree with your assessment?

We tend to overestimate our ability and our faithfulness. But God keeps an accurate record of our obedience.

If you handled your last assignment well—whatever its relative size or significance—be careful to recognize the Source of your success and give the glory to God.

If you were not faithful in what God gave you, you obviously cannot rework the past. But you can repent of your unfaithfulness and invite God to increase your faith—and your faithfulness. God wants to do greater things in and through your life than He already is, but He does not skip steps in the process.

Do you want to experience more of God's power in your life? Then be faithful in every little (and big) thing God places in your life. Then watch to see what God does next!

Pure Grace

Not by works of righteousness which we have done,
but according to His mercy He saved us.

TITUS 3:5

Have you lost the wonder of what Christ did when He saved you?

As we read Paul's words to Titus, we are reminded that our salvation is a gift of grace, not anything we merit because of our works (2:11–14; 3:3–7). Good works must result from our salvation as evidence of God's grace being present and at work in our lives.

Rather than being earned by our good works, God's gift of salvation is an act of infinite kindness toward us (3:4). Even with an eternity stretching before us, we do not have time to adequately thank Him for all He has done for us—on the cross and in our day-to-day lives.

In this current age of entitlement and self-centeredness, we are never to take our salvation for granted. Again, salvation is the kindness of God revealed. Our salvation is unearned, undeserved, and uncommon; it is nothing less than an act of divine love.

Take time to reflect on how good and kind God has been toward you. Live your life as an expression of gratitude for all God has done for you.

All Is God's Work

*The LORD said to Moses, "When you go back to
Egypt, see that you do all those wonders before
Pharaoh which I have put in your hand."*

EXODUS 4:21

The Hebrew word translated "wonder" is somewhat different from our understanding of a miracle. Our word *miracle* implies the transcending of, or the suspension of, the natural order. The Hebrews, however, understood *wonders* to refer to the marvelous use of the natural order created by God. They did not distinguish between natural and supernatural, for all is God's work.

The Hebrews, for instance, saw God at work turning the water of the Nile into blood. Since the Nile with its water system was Egypt's sole source of prosperity, this wonder clearly demonstrated God's control over Egypt's destiny. God used the natural order He had created to reveal His power.

God is at work in the world around us today, too, both in nature and in daily events of our lives. What can appear to be a coincidence may well be God at work accomplishing His purposes in our lives. So always look for evidence of God's presence and activity in the seemingly ordinary events of your life. Always look for the ways He is revealing His power in the world around you.

Talk Is Cheap

Then God saw their works, that they turned from their evil way; and God relented from the disaster that He had said He would bring upon them, and He did not do it.

JONAH 3:10

Apologize to your sister."

"Tell your brother you're sorry."

What parent hasn't used these words to urge a child to do what is right? After all, when we blow it—when we sin—we need to apologize to the person we've hurt or offended. The important thing—for adults as well as toddlers—is meaning it when we say, "I'm sorry."

We also need to do what we can to make amends. It's one thing to say you're sorry; it's another to live out your repentance. The truest sign of genuine repentance is a changed life.

Jonah told God he was sorry he hadn't obeyed, but the prophet did more than just say the words. Once he was freed from the fish, he made his way to Nineveh. By his actions he validated his repentance.

What new direction do you need to head to show that you meant it, too, when you said to God, "I'm sorry for that sin"? What change in words, habits, and actions must occur if you are to follow through with what you've said to God.

Our Glorious Transformation

We all, with unveiled face, beholding as in a
mirror the glory of the Lord, are being transformed
into the same image from glory to glory.

2 CORINTHIANS 3:18

It was a divine encounter that Peter, James, and John never forgot. Jesus led them to a high mountaintop, and there the Lord was "transfigured before them. His face shone like the sun, and His clothes became as white as the light" (Matthew 17:2).

These three disciples were privileged to observe in a dramatic way that Jesus is "the glory of the Lord," the complete personal expression of God. This unfading, eternal glory radiates through believers who are transformed into God's image and who share in His glory.

The Greek word translated "transformed" or "transfigured" means "changed into another form either externally or internally," but this change is not self-generated. Our remodeling into Christlikeness is God's work in us. It begins at salvation, and it happens by the Spirit as we walk with and abide in Christ.

God, by His Spirit, gradually but assuredly conforms you into His image. So learn to live continuously in God's presence. Yield to every change the Spirit seeks to make. Never let a hurried lifestyle disrupt your abiding in Christ. Keep your eyes on Him as the Holy Spirit transforms you into Christ's likeness.

Unholy Relationships

Do not be unequally yoked together with unbelievers.
For what fellowship has righteousness with lawlessness?
And what communion has light with darkness?

2 C O R I N T H I A N S 6 : 14

We Christians are not always aware of how radically different our lives should be from the world around us. We are different, and we should be diligent to remain so. After all, darkness and light don't mix. Good cannot be combined with evil and still remain good. Righteousness and sin simply cannot coexist.

Paul's warning not to be "unequally yoked together with unbelievers" was his way of warning believers to not be too closely entwined with non-Christians. Many people affirm this truth when it comes to the matters of dating and marriage, but this principle applies equally to close friendships and business partnerships. People whose loyalties diametrically oppose ours cannot partner with us without the opportunity arising for us to compromise our faith and values. So be careful about whom you choose to get closest to and to whom you make yourself vulnerable.

Your relationship with God must be unrivaled, unequalled, and unadulterated. Beware of unholy allegiances that will draw you away from the Lord. Paul's warning is not a call to be isolated from the world, but to be consecrated unto God.

God's Good Purposes

But as for you, you meant evil against me; but
God meant it for good, in order to bring it about
as it is this day, to save many people alive.

GENESIS 50:20

Accused of attacking his boss's wife, Joseph could have expected the death penalty for such an offense (39:20). Yet his master, showing Joseph mercy, instead had him imprisoned. Thus Joseph was preserved for God's purposes.

In fact, God was with Joseph in prison, and "He gave him favor in the sight of the keeper of the prison" (v. 21). Clearly, Joseph's false accusation and unfair imprisonment did not thwart God's plan: His favor was still upon Joseph.

God tenaciously blesses those whom He chooses to bless. In fact, He overrides and even uses the evil intentions of people to accomplish His good purposes.

When have you seen this happen in your own life or in the life of someone you know? Praise God for His faithfulness and power—and let that difficult situation, like Joseph's, be a touchstone of faith for you.

When you are mistreated or wrongly accused, don't be discouraged. Instead, turn your situation over to God. Allow Him to take the painful events in your life and use them for your good and His glory. Expect God to work, even in the worst moments of your life.

"Peace, Be Still!"

A great windstorm arose, and the waves beat
into the boat, so that it was already filling.

MARK 4:37

The Sea of Galilee lay seven hundred feet below sea level with bordering mountains that rose several thousand feet high. Cool winds from the mountain peaks would sweep down onto the sea and stir up strong, violent winds. The disciples' boat was caught in just such a storm.

Jesus, however, was asleep in the stern—until His disciples frantically awakened Him with, "Teacher, do You not care that we are perishing?" (v. 38). Do you know that feeling when, overwhelmed by the circumstances of life, you cry out to God?

Undaunted by either their question or the storm, Jesus stood, rebuked the wind, and commanded the sea, "Peace, be still!" (v. 39). Calmness came immediately.

We human beings are limited by physical constraints and nature's laws, but God is not. In fact, what are obstacles to us are thoroughfares for God. The key is trusting God in spite of what appears to be imminent disaster.

So, whatever your senses are telling you about your current situation and however overwhelmed you may be feeling, know that God cares deeply about you and that He can calm any storm in your life, no matter how severe.

True Peace

I lay down and slept;
I awoke, for the LORD sustained me.

PSALM 3:5

This simple statement may not seem remarkable—until you examine its context. David began this psalm by crying out to the Lord: "How they have increased who trouble me! Many are they who rise up against me" (v. 1). The fact that—four verses later—David could lie down and sleep is worth considering.

Scholars date this psalm to the time when David was fleeing from his son Absalom. Not only was David running for his life, but the one who wanted to kill him and usurp the throne of Israel was his own son. In addition to physical danger, David experienced heartache that most parents can't even imagine.

True peace—that which we experience despite our circumstances—comes not from the absence of adversaries but from trusting God. Nothing can disrupt your sense of peace when you choose to focus on the reality of God's presence in your life.

What enemies are pursuing you? Turn to God as David himself did. Let his words be yours: "But You, O LORD, are a shield for me" (v. 3). And sleep well.

Does Jesus Know You?

"I will declare to them, 'I never knew you; depart from Me.'"

MATTHEW 7:23

Imagine prophesying in the name of Jesus, casting out demons in His name, and doing many other wonders as you invoked His powerful name—and Jesus not being pleased!

We see in Jesus' words that eternal life is not dependent on whether you know Christ, but on whether He knows you. If He has a relationship with you, then He has taken up residence in your life and you are filled with His Spirit. Your life reflects His holiness. When He speaks, you hear—and you respond to His will. Obedience, not activity, is the sign of a genuine and saving relationship with Jesus Christ.

Does Jesus know you? Do you truly belong to Him? Ask Him to help you see your life as He sees it, to discern whether you are relying on His Spirit, hearing His voice, responding to His will, and obeying His commands.

If there is anything in your life you must be certain of, it is that you are in an intimate, saving, personal relationship with Christ.

God Is at Work

I thank my God upon every remembrance of you . . .
being confident . . . that He who has begun a good work
in you will complete it until the day of Christ Jesus.

PHILIPPIANS 1:3,6

God loved you, chose you, drew you, enlightened you, and saved you—and He is not finished with you yet.

God desires that your foremost pursuit would be your deepening relationship with Jesus Christ. Purpose and passion, peace and contentment would then characterize your life. Consider that the Holy Spirit gave the apostle Paul joy even while he was in prison. The same joy is available to you whatever your present circumstances.

Another one of God's desires for you is to bring you into the center of His activity according to His kingdom purpose for your life. So stand before Him with a heart of ready obedience. After all, God alone knows what you will become as you serve Him according to His plan.

Finally, be encouraged to know that God will not give up until He has thoroughly completed everything He has initiated in your life. The challenge you face is to walk with Him and to completely release yourself to His will. You can trust your day-to-day life—as well as your eternal future—to Him.

Temptation and Sin

Her house is the way to hell,
Descending to the chambers of death.

PROVERBS 7:27

I t's ancient wisdom for an age-old problem. Hear what some of the proverbs teach about sin:

- PROVERBS 5:21: God is fully aware of the temptations you will face. He also knows the certain destruction that awaits you if you succumb to sin's entrapments. The same God who warns you of these dangers gives you the power to overcome them.
- PROVERBS 6:35: Some sins leave a lasting mark; no compensation or remorse will undo the damage done to ourselves and to others. God warns us about the devastating aftermath of sin. If we choose to sin anyway, we should be prepared for devestating consequences.
- PROVERBS 7:12: God protects His people when we stay on the right path. But when we choose to stray, we fall prey to the evil that is ready to lead us to destruction. Our protection is dependent on our proximity to the Protector.
- PROVERBS 7:27: Temptation and sin are ultimately from Satan, forged in deceit and designed for our demise. Our loving God therefore provides us with the truth in His Word to safeguard us.

What is God saying to you today about the temptation or sin you're facing? Will you listen to Him?

Judgment and Justice

"It is a righteous thing with God to repay with tribulation
those who trouble you, and to give you who are troubled
rest with us when the Lord Jesus is revealed."

2 THESSALONIANS 1:6—7

God is fully aware of every wicked person who opposes Him and who harms His people. The wicked may boast and taunt and blaspheme today, but one day they will stand mute before an awesome, holy, divine Judge and realize what fools they have been.

God is absolutely just. He hates sin, and no one will escape His judgment. No one defies Him without someday having to give Him a full accounting for their actions. Although God is incredibly patient, He will ultimately bring complete and total justice to both the oppressor and the oppressed.

God cares for the victim. In this evil age, the weak will always be injured by the strong, and there will always be those who grievously suffer injustice. But a day is coming soon when justice will prevail and those who have suffered will enter eternal, blissful rest.

God knows everything you are going through. He is prepared to give you His peace, comfort, and rest. Trust in His justice and His timing.

A New Perspective

Lead me to the rock that is higher than I.

PSALM 61:2

Are you a beach person or a mountain person? Do you like to stare at the stars or marvel at cloud formations? How do you react to satellite pictures of the earth—and of galaxies far, far away?

In these situations and others, we can be reminded how small we really are. The vastness of the ocean, the grandeur of the mountains, the distance of the stars, the movement of the clouds, the immeasurable nature of the universe—hints of these realities can help us put our lives and our concerns in perspective.

That is especially true when we let these amazing aspects of creation point us to the Creator, to the One behind the magnificence, the One who is Himself even more immeasurable and splendid.

After all—and though we don't like to think about it—we human beings are frail and weak. Life's pressures and pain can easily overwhelm us. Yet God is greater than our problems; He is undaunted by our worst trials. That's why, when he was feeling overwhelmed, David asked the Lord to "lead me to the rock that is higher than I." Follow that example and let God help you see things from His perspective, the perspective of your all-loving, all-wise, all-powerful heavenly Father.

Now!

*Now it is in my heart to make a covenant with the LORD God
of Israel, that His fierce wrath may turn away from us.*

2 CHRONICLES 29:10

When God puts a desire in your heart, *now* is the time to respond. The assignment may be huge or daunting, yet as you begin to obey Him, you will sense His presence, power, and pleasure in ways you would not otherwise know.

King Hezekiah, for instance, knew that *now* was the time he and the nation of Israel needed to get right with God. It was a sign of his spiritual maturity that he humbly and quickly obeyed once he knew that God wanted the temple cleansed, temple worship restored, the Passover kept, and other reforms instituted.

It is a sign of spiritual maturity when we, like Hezekiah, humbly and quickly obey when God speaks to us. Spiritual immaturity is slow to heed God's voice unless hardship comes. Spiritual deadness is revealed when no word from God can move us to action.

When you serve God wholeheartedly, when you hold nothing back, He withholds nothing from you. So if He's calling you to act now, do it now—and watch Him work!

The Bread of Life

*"I am the bread of life. He who comes to Me shall never
hunger, and he who believes in Me shall never thirst."*

JOHN 6:35

Jesus had just fed five thousand men plus their families. He
had only five barley loaves and two small fish to work with,
but the people ate "as much as they wanted" (v. 11)—and there
were leftovers (v. 13).

This miracle—the only one before Jesus' resurrection
recorded in all four Gospels—was met a few days later by
Jewish leaders asking for a sign of His divinity, specifically the
sign of manna from heaven. Clearly, a heart that is unwilling
to believe in miracles will not be convinced regardless of the
quantity or quality of proof provided!

Are we so different from those Jewish leaders? When we see
Jesus do a mighty work in our lives, do we soon turn around
and ask Him to prove that He really does love us and that He
really will provide for our needs? Has your loving God recently
provided for a need in your life but you find yourself already
worrying about another problem?

What would it take for you to trust your heavenly Father
completely?

Experiencing Salvation

Work out your own salvation with fear and trembling.

PHILIPPIANS 2:12

God's great salvation is not a one-time, once-and-for-all event for a believer. Experiencing God's salvation is actually a dynamic, lifelong process of implementing all the power, embracing all the love, and fulfilling all the plans He has for you.

"Work out your salvation" means to access all God has made available to you. It is not a command to work *for* your salvation. It is a call to enter into your relationship with Jesus with all that you are.

We who are privileged to be called the children of God have a choice. We can enjoy our status as adopted and beloved children of the King and know abundant life in Christ, or we can live as spiritual paupers and neglect all that is rightfully ours. It is not enough to know in our minds that we are God's children. That truth must move into our hearts and impact our lifestyles. Don't be like too many of the King's children who choose to live spiritually impoverished lives.

The process of salvation calls for us to apply energy and effort, focus and faith. The Holy Spirit empowers, Jesus embraces us, and God rewards us now and for eternity.

God's Ways

Teach me Your way, O LORD;
I will walk in Your truth;
Unite my heart to fear Your name.

PSALM 86:11

God's ways are not our ways, and a brief overview of the gospel offers a powerful case in point.

The Almighty's only Son left His throne and took on flesh. He came to serve—and He did so in a miraculous, humble way. He healed people of their infirmities: when He spoke the word or touched the broken body, the lame walked, the blind saw, and the deaf heard. He also forgave sins, taught people the fulfilled law of God ("I don't say an eye for an eye; I say turn the other cheek" [Matthew 5:38–39, paraphrased]), and—as He submitted to death on the cross after a completely illegal and unfair trial by both Romans and Jews—modeled sacrificial love in the ultimate way as He died to atone for our sins.

God's ways are not our ways, are they? Who would have imagined such a gift, such an act of amazing grace on our behalf? God is not a sinful, self-centered human being. We don't think like He does. God must open our hearts to receive His truth, and then He must teach us His ways if we are to live by them.

May the psalmist's prayer be ours: "Teach me Your way . . . Unite my heart to fear Your name."

Brokenhearted

"My heart will cry out for Moab."

ISAIAH 15:5

It is a terrifying thing to make God your enemy. After all, He stretches out His hand and commands the seas to do His bidding. He can devastate a nation at any moment (23:11), and He did so to the land of Moab. The water in the land dried up, "the green grass . . . withered away" (15:6), and the people were weeping. God exercised His righteous judgment, and the nation was destroyed.

And the prophet who foretold this righteous but nonetheless tragic event wept. Such grief for a sinful enemy nation's downfall was highly unusual for a Judean prophet, but Isaiah's grief was modeled after God's own. After all, a child of God cannot help but grieve for those who choose judgment over repentance. It is heartbreaking to see people reap the consequences of their sin, and Isaiah's heart was broken.

What in the world around you breaks your heart? Consider headline news, events in your community, or circumstances of people in your neighborhood. World Vision founder Bob Pierce prayed this: "May my heart be broken by the things that break the heart of God." Make that prayer your own this week and see how God uses your compassion and love in this hurting world.

"I Remembered"

When my soul fainted within me,
I remembered the LORD;
And my prayer went up to you,
Into Your holy temple.

JONAH 2:7

Bittersweet is a word that aptly describes the hard times when we turn to God and find Him to be all that we need.

Think about those times when you've had nowhere else to turn but the Lord—and you weren't even sure He was listening or if He even cared. That was a bitter starting point, but the sweetness came in time. Oh, the circumstances may not have changed—the marriage may not have been rehabilitated, the child may not yet be walking with the Lord again, the chemo may not have done what you'd hoped and prayed for—but everything was different because of the sweet presence of your heavenly Father.

It's all too easy to forget that we need Him, isn't it? It's generally during the crises more than in the peaceful times that we remember our dependence on God and prayerfully turn to Him. When it feels as if our soul faints within us—as Jonah's did—we remember our all-powerful, ever-faithful God and lift our prayers to Him.

Whether your current circumstances are sweet or bitter or somewhere in between, lift up your voice to God today.

Knowing Only Secondhand

The LORD came to Abram in a vision, saying,
"Do not be afraid, Abram. I am your shield,
your exceedingly great reward."

GENESIS 15:1

The crowd at Niagara Falls was amazed as the tightrope walker traversed the mighty waters without faltering. Then, on his return trip over the raging waters, he pushed a wheelbarrow. Astounding! Next the tightrope walker asked the onlookers if they believed he could carry someone on his back across the rope. Of course they believed! Then he asked for a volunteer—but he had no takers. After all, there's a vast difference between believing that someone can do something and putting your own life on the line as he proves it.

Likewise, it is one thing to believe that God will protect you and quite another to experience God's protection. You might easily say with confidence, "Of course God can protect me, provide for me, and guide me!" Yet finding yourself or allowing yourself to be put in a situation where you absolutely need God's protection, provision, or guidance is a much different matter. That's the step of faith.

We know much about God intellectually, but God wants us to also know Him experientially. What divine truths do you know only secondhand? Today take a step that will enable you to know God by experience.

Repentant—Or Not?

The LORD is good,
A stronghold in the day of trouble;
And He knows those who trust in Him.

NAHUM 1:7

One hundred years earlier Jonah spoke to Nineveh. Now it was Nahum's turn, and his message was quite different ...

The prophet Jonah spoke of imminent doom, and the Ninevites repented, saving themselves from God's certain judgment. By the time of Nahum, the Ninevites' sin had become so entrenched that there was no longer any hope of return—and no one to whom they could turn for help.

How terrifying to realize that God is against you! Our God is long-suffering, gracious, and merciful, but He is also thoroughly just. If we do not turn to Him in repentance, He will measure out His justice. He looks past our religious ritual and formulaic prayers and sees our hearts. He knows who genuinely trusts Him, and He will be their unassailable fortress in times of distress.

Jonah and Nahum had messages for Nineveh: Jonah indicated that God will show mercy to those who turn to Him; Nahum revealed that God's judgment must fall on the unrepentant.

Are you truly repentant? Guard your heart lest you become indifferent to God's grace and mercy.

He Wants You Back

"I blasted you with blight and mildew.
When your gardens increased,
Your vineyards, your fig trees, and your olive trees,
The locust devoured them;
Yet you have not returned to Me,"
Says the LORD.

AMOS 4:9

God blessed Israel with His tender love and faithful care, yet they turned away from Him . . .

God punished the Israel He loved, yet they did not return to Him . . .

Hear the heartbreak in the Lord's words above—and realize that God loves His people too much to let them go their own way, to let them stray into the pains of death.

Now personalize that truth: God loves you too much to let you go your own way. He will go to great lengths to gain your attention and make you aware of the peril of your defection. He wants you back.

Remember, too, that God sets the standards for our lives; we don't. We may insist that we haven't strayed from God, but there is no argument against God's measurement. He knows how far we have spiraled into sin.

If you're living in rebellion to God, you are only one heartfelt, repentant prayer away from the path of divine restoration. Repentance brings a return of God's favor and blessing.

The Choice to Rejoice

Yet I will rejoice in the LORD,
I will joy in the God of my salvation.

HABAKKUK 3:18

Life in this imperfect world, populated by fallen people, gives rise to lots of difficult questions. Consider these: Why does God seem to allow violence and injustice to go unpunished? Why does God use wicked people—like Babylon in Habakkuk's day—to be His instruments of justice? Why does it sometimes seem that God doesn't listen to our prayers?

We don't have to understand everything that is happening in the world around us as long as we trust in the One who is sovereign over history. We can choose, as Habakkuk did, to trust the Lord regardless of the trying circumstances we—or those we love—are dealing with. Nothing need prevent us from rejoicing in God. We can always choose to focus on the truth that God is on His throne and that His purposes continue to unfold exactly as He has planned.

Praising God and trusting Him should not, therefore, fluctuate with our situation. Conditions may change, but God remains steadfast. He may not remove your problems, but He will keep His hand on you. So choose to rejoice. After all, God is ever faithful.

A Picture of God

You come to me with a sword, with a spear, and with a javelin. But I come to you in the name of the LORD.

1 SAMUEL 17:45

Every part of God's Word can teach us about Him. In David's defeat of Goliath, for instance, we see that, no matter the circumstances, any number plus God is a majority. We also see that the source of genuine strength is not self-confidence, but trust in God.

Consider other truths about God revealed in 1 Samuel.

- At first the young boy didn't recognize God's voice when He called, "Samuel!" (3:6). The more frequent and intimate our times with Him, the easier it becomes to hear and identify His gentle voice.
- In 1 Samuel 9:21, Saul was surprised God called him to the throne. We don't always see the potential in ourselves that God sees. That's because the assignments God gives us aren't based on our ability, but on our obedience to Him.
- Samuel knew that neglecting to pray for others is to sin against God. God calls us to pray (12:23). Prayer is the greatest indicator of our relationship to God, revealing our faith in His ability to work in our world.

Which feature of this picture of God means the most to you today?

Simple, Not Easy

"Wash yourselves, make yourselves clean;
Put away the evil of your doings from before My eyes.
Cease to do evil, learn to do good;
Seek justice, reprove the oppressor;
Defend the fatherless, plead for the widow.
Come now, and let us reason together," says the LORD,
"Though your sins are like scarlet,
They shall be as white as snow."

ISAIAH 1:17–18

Our assignment is pretty straightforward—and it's consistent throughout Scripture. Here the prophet Isaiah makes clear what God calls His people to do in response to His love and grace. This calling comes as God condemns lifeless religious activity.

- God has made every provision so we can enjoy a close relationship with Him. Nothing is lacking. If you aren't experiencing an intimate walk with God, ask yourself why.
- Your heavenly Father longs for you to experience abiding joy, but are you pursuing worldly pleasures instead?
- They who view that which God despises as something good are desperately depraved. Do you love what God loves and hate what He hates?

Take time to reason together with your Lord. He will hear your cry, cleanse you from your sin, and lead you on the right path. Also, know that your simple-but-not-easy assignment is easier when you rely on the Holy Spirit for strength and guidance.

Choosing to Believe,
No Matter the Circumstances

*Be anxious for nothing, but in everything by
prayer and supplication, with thanksgiving, let
your requests be made known to God.*

PHILIPPIANS 4:6

God commands us not to worry. After all, anxiety demonstrates a lack of faith in Christ's promises to provide for every single one of our needs. We must choose to believe Him, no matter what our life circumstances might be.

One antidote to worry is meditating. In Philippians 4:8, Paul called us to consider or let our mind dwell on "whatever things are true . . . noble . . . just . . . pure . . . lovely . . . of good report . . . [of] virtue . . . [and] praiseworthy." When we contemplate such things, they are more than a worthwhile distraction from worry. The Holy Spirit works those values into our lives.

Another remedy to anxiety is pressing on "toward the goal for the prize of the upward call of God in Christ Jesus" (3:14). People can be preoccupied with and even controlled by their past, for they face an uncertain future. Believers, however, have dealt with their past and are inspired by a future hope.

So obey God's command to not worry. Thinking about the good He has called you to consider and focusing on the future He has for you will help.

JUNE

Faith is the substance of things hoped for,
the evidence of things not seen.

HEBREWS 11:1

A Dry, Thirsty Land

O God, You are my God;
Early will I seek you;
My soul thirsts for You;
My flesh longs for You
In a dry and thirsty land
Where there is no water.

PSALM 63:1

All of us have experienced physical thirst. We experience it regularly because the human body cannot go long without water. Our body craves liquid replenishing. But a deeper thirst plagues us—it is a spiritual, emotional thirst. It results from dwelling in a world that parches and depletes our soul. Being surrounded by worldly values, sin, conflict, and criticism, we often lose our spiritual vitality and begin to wither. In time we grow desperate for a refreshing, restorative drink from the Living Water. It matters not that we drank yesterday, or the day before. Today is a new day, and the hot, dry winds of this world have already begun to scorch our spirit and leave us depleted.

How good to know that we can cry not just to God, but to *my* God. The two-letter word *my* makes all the difference! He is my God. He is your God. And He will revive us. He has cool, clear, invigorating, living water in abundance that refreshes and restores. He can and will meet the deepest needs of our souls every day.

Are you thirsty? Has it been too long since you last drank from Christ's well? Make haste to draw near to Him and let Him satisfy the deepest thirsts of your life.

"All Have Sinned"

For all have sinned and fall short of the glory of God, being justified freely by His grace through the redemption that is in Christ Jesus.

ROMANS 3:23–24

As a member of Parliament, William Wilberforce worked for twenty-six years to abolish the British slave trade, a goal that was achieved in 1807. His Christian faith undoubtedly provided strength for the battle.

Wilberforce clearly understood the condition of the human heart:

> [Man] is indisposed toward the good, and disposed toward evil.... He is tainted with sin, not slightly and superficially, but radically, and to the very core of his being. Even though it may be humiliating to acknowledge these things, still this is the biblical account of man.

Sinners to the very core of our being, we are nevertheless justified—a legal term meaning "declared righteous." No one is declared righteous by the Law, for its purpose is to expose sin, not take it away. Instead, we are justified by faith in Christ, who perfectly and completely satisfied the Law's requirements.

Since every person is under the penalty of sin, we are all on equal footing to receive God's gift of grace. While some humbly accept it, others arrogantly reject it. Only when we become desperate and poor of heart can we receive the riches of salvation.

Wrath or Rejoicing?

The great day of the LORD is near;
It is near and hastens quickly . . . .
That day is a day of wrath.

ZEPHANIAH 1:14-15

As we see in the history of Israel and in our own life, our long-suffering God is merciful and patient despite His people's continual rebellion. God's love for His people, however, compels Him to hate that which destroys us, so He abhors sin. The reality is that those who reject His love and cling to their sin must face His overwhelming wrath.

"All the earth shall be devoured with the fire of My jealousy," God proclaims through Zephaniah (3:8). God's purposes require Him to discipline and even judge His people. Are you willing to undergo the disciplinary pruning process until God has purged you of your sin?

Remember that the purpose of God's discipline is to purify you so you can enjoy fellowship with Him who loves you dearly. He longs to care for you and comfort you, and He rejoices when you seek Him.

One more thing. You are not one of faceless, nameless millions. He knows you personally. He loves you and celebrates your love for Him. His wrath is simply the response of His holiness to lethal sin that will destroy you. He will do whatever it takes to draw you to Himself.

God's Wrath, God's Love

In this is love, not that we loved God, but that He loved
us and sent His Son to be the propitiation for our sins.

1 JOHN 4:10

David Brainerd was a missionary to the Indians of North America during the eighteenth century. In his early preaching, he focused on God's righteous wrath—and the people's response to his message was disappointing.

By God's grace, though, Brainerd discovered that when he spoke of God's love, the people were overcome with emotion and conviction. Once when he spoke on 1 John 4:10, the entire village was seized with sorrow over their previous indifference to such love. The people feared that they would somehow miss out on the divine compassion God was offering them.

Brainerd noted: "It was surprising to see how their hearts seemed to be pierced with the tender and melting invitations of the gospel, when there was not a word of terror spoken to them."

Before you were a believer, which topic did you hear more about—God's wrath or His love? Why is it important to hear about both? Which of those two topics most touched your heart?

What will you do today to share with others God's amazing love?

Do What I Say . . .

The fear of the LORD is the beginning of knowledge.

PROVERBS 1:7

Proverbs is a guidebook for successful living, and it makes no secret about what pleases God: caring for the needy, following God's law, acting with integrity, guarding our words, working diligently, and planning for the future. He wants us to lead holy, fruitful, and fulfilling lives.

- People who approach God humbly and reverently will see His character and learn His will (1:7).
- God provides for the poor through the generosity of others as they share the wealth He has given them (28:27).
- It was no small thing for a king to show compassion to the most needy in his kingdom (31:8–9). To God, caring for widows, orphans, and foreigners is true religion.
- God places high value on good character and personal integrity (19:1). Resist the temptation to compromise godly, moral values in the pursuit of worldly comforts.

The more we revere God, the more humble and teachable we will be and the wiser we will become. Ironically, the compiler of much of Proverbs—King Solomon—offers a tragic picture of what happens when one disregards God's truth. So do as Solomon said, not as he did . . .

The Heart Behind the Ministry

Our exhortation did not come from error or
uncleanness, nor was it in deceit.

1 THESSALONIANS 2:3

False teachers, inaccurate doctrine, heretical messages—none of this, sadly, is new to the church of Christ. Two thousand years ago Paul warned members of the early church to beware of people who preached for selfish gain, to please human beings rather than God, to gain some kind of status in the community.

Against this backdrop, Paul reminded his readers that he spoke God's truth. The word translated *deceit* is the same word used for a fishing lure, a metaphor that suggests pretense and trickery. The ancient Mediterranean region teemed with religious and philosophical charlatans.

Unlike others of his day, however, Paul backed up his message with his life. Behind his words and actions was an honest heart. He spoke God's truth, not just words that would gain him popularity. He encouraged people toward faith in Christ because he genuinely cared about them, not because he was seeking another convert or church plant to boast about. Perhaps Paul's heart is why he was so effective and why people are still reading his words and studying his life two thousand years later.

What is your heart like?

Flee—and Guard

*You were bought at a price; therefore glorify God in
your body and in your spirit, which are God's.*

1 CORINTHIANS 6:20

Paul had just explained that "your body is the temple of the
Holy Spirit" (v. 19). This is not merely a figure of speech.
It is reality: your body *is* the Spirit's temple. God's Spirit literally dwells within believers, and He uses our bodies for
kingdom purposes. Believers, therefore, must honor God with
their bodies.

That means we are to flee immorality, an infection that
spreads its deadly poison like a contagious disease. When we
reach out to sinners, we must beware of downplaying sin and
lowering God's standards of holiness. Both our spiritual health
and the condition of the church body are at stake. Don't be the
carrier who starts an epidemic infection of sin.

In addition, we are to avoid anything that can potentially
harm our relationship with Christ. Don't risk letting sin enter
your heart or your life. Once God has set you free by the blood
of Christ, don't walk back into bondage. Your salvation is too
precious to treat carelessly.

Diligently guard your relationship with God—and honor
Him with your body, a temple of the Spirit, so that your life
brings Him glory.

Testing the Righteous

The LORD tests the righteous.

PSALM 11:5

Remember those weekly spelling tests in elementary school? Every Friday you were to show that you'd learned the words you'd received on Monday. Then there were the verb tests in high school language class. The teacher wanted to see which conjugations you'd mastered since he first introduced you to the patterns. Tests give students a chance to show what they've learned.

Tests in life serve the same purpose. They provide the opportunity to show God, and ourselves, what we understand about Him—about trusting Him, about turning to Him when we're suffering, about finding joy in Him when life is tough, about loving the Giver more than the gifts, and so on.

While God sustains us on our journey through life, He also tests us. The way we respond to God's tests reveals our progress on our spiritual pilgrimage. But you can prepare for those tests beforehand by spending time with God in prayer and in His Word. Get to know Him better and better. Then when the tests come—when life situations prompt doubts about His goodness or power or love—you'll know better; you'll pass the test.

Righteous Prayer

Confess your trespasses to one another, and pray for
one another, that you may be healed. The effective,
fervent prayer of a righteous man avails much.

JAMES 5:16

I t's not difficult to see why these two statements are found side by side in Scripture . . .

First, we're called to confess our sin. We're to openly acknowledge our trespasses, fully agree with God that we've done wrong, and then accept what is to come as a result of our sins. Confessing in a public fashion—as James called us to do—provides an opportunity for personal cleansing as well as corporate instruction and accountability.

After hearing this call to confession, we read about the prayers of "a righteous man." When we confess our sin and ask forgiveness, we become holy due to Christ's death on the cross for that sin. Then, having been cleansed of our sin, we can pray effectively as we pray fervently.

You don't have to be a spiritual giant before God answers your prayer. But God does expect you to enter His presence with a keen sense of your need for His forgiveness and involvement in your life. The heartfelt prayers of a desperate sinner gain God's immediate attention.

So pray for forgiveness, pray fervently, and watch God work.

Love Whom?

Therefore "If your enemy is hungry, feed him;
If he is thirsty, give him a drink; For in so doing
you will heap coals of fire on his head."

ROMANS 12:20

One of the most difficult and unnatural ways to demonstrate our trust in God is to show love to our enemies—to those who oppose us, who have hurt us deeply, who are slandering us or making our lives miserable. Aren't we being sufficiently charitable if we simply ignore them and hope they go away? But to *love* them? For some of us, the very thought is revolting. We just don't think we can bring ourselves to do that. We have no desire to minister to someone who has opposed and perhaps even wounded us.

But God commands us to love our enemy. That kind of love shows the world the radical difference that Christ makes in our lives. Loving our enemies also drives us to depend on the Holy Spirit to a degree we would never have to if we were called to love only our friends and family. Finally, showing Christ's love to our enemies magnifies their guilt and guarantees their just punishment by God if they don't repent of their sin. When they reject Christ's love in you, they reject Christ and make their future judgment a certainty.

A Ministry of Encouragement

"Be strong, all you people of the land," says the LORD,
"and work; for I am with you," says the LORD of hosts.

HAGGAI 2:4

The unfinished temple lay in ruins until 520 BC when the prophet Haggai entered the scene and encouraged God's people to complete what they had begun. God's people had known for many years that they should rebuild the place of worship, but no one had yet been able to inspire them to complete the task. Then Haggai appeared and everything soon changed. The ministry of this faithful prophet, who was absolutely confident in the God whose message he spoke, resulted in the construction of a temple that would house the worship of God for nearly six hundred years.

Haggai's public ministry evidently lasted only four months. But his ministry was as effective as it was brief. Haggai knew there is no place for timidity in serving the Lord. He knew—and preached—that God's servants ought to have supreme confidence, not in themselves, but in the One they serve.

Clearly, Haggai inspired others to share his trust in God. Are any of God's people successfully serving Him as a result of your encouragement? What has been the enduring legacy of your life so far?

Afflictions—and Deliverance

Many are the afflictions of the righteous,
But the LORD delivers him out of them all.

PSALM 34:19

Why are we surprised when trials come, when disappointments mount, when unfortunate events snowball? Why are we caught off guard when health fails, when children stray, when friends betray?

Here in Psalm 34:19 we see the truth in black and white: God's people will not be spared hardships. Jesus Himself was very candid about this: "In the world you will have tribulation" (John 16:33).

But, thankfully, neither Psalm 34:19 nor John 16:33 ends there. The psalmist proclaimed that the Lord delivers the righteous from those inevitable afflictions. And Jesus reminded believers who are suffering that He has overcome the world.

Are you suffering right now? What pain and hardships beset you? Remember, in our times of trials, we believers experience God's provision. If you're skeptical, think about hard times in the past when God has delivered you. You know that God is the same yesterday, today, and tomorrow—He is faithful, powerful, loving, and wise. He is just as capable of rescuing you from your present circumstances as He has ever been before. Be ready to praise Him for the work of deliverance He has already begun.

Praying Through Life

[Jesus] said to [his disciples], "When you
pray, say: Our Father in heaven . . ."

LUKE 11:2

Prayer is not to be a ritual. Nor should it feel like a religious duty. According to Jesus' instruction on prayer and the model He provided, prayer is to be simply—and wonderfully—communing with our loving, all-powerful, and compassionate heavenly Father. No one could ever be as attentive or prepared to respond as He is. Why, then, do we find it so difficult to be faithful, focused, and passionate in prayer?

One reason is that the enemy likes nothing better than to interfere with our praying, for it is our lifeline to our Father. Sometimes we grow tired of praying when God's response doesn't match our timing. We can easily find ourselves distracted. After all, just living life—earning money, feeding families, maintaining a household, mowing lawns, attending meetings, and rearing children—takes time. Distractions can also come in the form of good things—of serving the Lord, for instance. But genuine service for God flows out of our devotion to Him. If you would rather work for Him than spend time with Him in prayer, your priorities are convoluted. The quality of your prayer life will determine the caliber of your life and service for God.

So pray—and keep praying—to your good and loving Father.

In Light of Eternity

Do not lose heart . . . . For our light affliction,
which is but for a moment, is working for us a far
more exceeding and eternal weight of glory.

2 CORINTHIANS 4:16—17

Are you living your life against the backdrop of eternity? That should be the setting for all that unfolds in the life of a believer and for our interactions with those we love.

After all, being God's children assures us of eternal life in Christ. That certain future helps us remember that everything physical is temporal, that all suffering is momentary. Ironically, however, adversity is what often enables the beauty of Christ's life to be displayed in our mortal bodies. The hard times testify of God's goodness as He walks us through them; these trials are also a testimony that this present world and our physical bodies are only temporary.

The pain, the struggles, the worries, the disappointments, the tragedies, the losses—all of this is very real. But this life lasts for but a blink of an eye, and then comes eternity. Step back for a moment and remind yourself that these temporary agonies fade in light of eternity's magnificence. It's a matter of perspective, so consider your life in light of eternity—and don't lose heart.

Don't Shoot the Messenger

"Stand in the court of the LORD's house, and speak to all the cities of Judah . . . all the words that I command you to speak to them. Do not diminish a word."

JEREMIAH 26:2

Each of us has a mission field: we have family members, neighbors, co-workers, and friends with whom we can share not only God's love but also His truth.

We run the risk of offending people, however, when we speak God's truth. After all, doing so can mean sharing a message that a person needs to hear but may not like. In fact, unregenerate people can be violently opposed to God and will sometimes slander and ridicule those He sends to them. (At times even God's people react the same way.)

Nevertheless, we—like Jeremiah—must communicate with absolute accuracy whatever truth God gives us to share. Though we may be tempted to adjust the message to make it more palatable, doing so might mean distorting the truth and misrepresenting God.

As you faithfully speak God's message, not diminishing a word, rest assured that God works in wondrous detail, tailoring His message precisely for those who need to hear it. Don't hesitate to accurately communicate that message—for the good of the person who needs to hear it.

Have Faith

Faith is the substance of things hoped for,
the evidence of things not seen.

HEBREWS 11:1

Read these restatements of Hebrews 11:1.

- Faith is the *essence* of things hoped for, the *proof* of things not seen.
- Faith is the *reality* of things hoped for, the *conviction* of things not seen.
- Faith acts as if that which is hoped for is already a reality.
- Faith is based on what we know, not on what we don't know.

Abraham demonstrated faith when, although he didn't know where he was going, he trusted the One who was telling him to go . . . By faith, Noah built the ark because of God's promise of rain, a natural phenomenon the world hadn't yet seen . . . And by faith in God that was greater than his fear of Pharaoh, Moses led the Israelites out of Egypt.

Faith is demonstrated through action. Sometimes faith results in incredible victory, dramatic healing, or miraculous deliverance. Other times faith is evident in confidence and peace despite continued pain, suffering, or rejection. Genuine faith perseveres in both trial and triumph.

Whatever you do for God, your life is not pleasing to Him if it is not characterized by faith. Be prepared for God to allow things in your life that provide you the opportunity for you to demonstrate your faith in Him.

Practical Love

Beloved, you do faithfully whatever you do
for the brethren and for strangers.

3 JOHN 5

True love is not sentimental. True love is practical; it is expressed in daily life. Consider this case in point from one of John's epistles: the fourteen verses of 3 John reveal how important hospitality is in the church. God wants believers to show kindness to everyone, "strangers" as well as "the brethren."

In the Greco-Roman world, travelers from place to place needed the practical support of hospitality. They were often solely dependent upon the goodwill of the people they encountered along the way. So hospitality became a wonderful opportunity for Christians to extend grace and love to others—to fellow believers as well as to nonbelievers. Meeting people's basic, practical needs for shelter and food became an occasion for a powerful ministry for Jesus' early followers.

Never minimize the powerful work you can do for God's kingdom through ordinary acts of service. Our world is filled with people with ordinary needs, and these needs are everyday opportunities to demonstrate Christ's love.

Why don't you ask the Holy Spirit to show you whom He would have you love today? Remember, genuine Christian love is practical. Don't just say you love people. Do something loving today!

A Heart in Tune with God's

Delight yourself also in the LORD,
And He shall give you the desires of your heart.

PSALM 37:4

This verse sounds too good to be true. The Lord will give us whatever we want?

But God is not a heavenly Santa Claus who always delivers everything on our wish list. Neither is He an indulgent grandparent who loves to spoil the grandkids by giving us all we want. Nor is God a weak parent who, annoyed by whining and tears, gives in to our wishes to keep the peace.

So what does this verse mean? God will give you the desires of your heart, but the prerequisite is setting your heart to delight in His ways. Are you able to do that, to rejoice in the things that give God joy? Is your heart broken by the agonies in the world, by the very things that break God's heart? Is regular time with your Lord nourishment for your soul? Do you love being in His presence in times of worship, both corporate and private?

As you delight yourself in the Lord in these and other ways, God adjusts your heart to be in tune with His. Then the longings that grow in your heart—the seeds of which are sown during your time with your Father—will be His desires for you. And of course He will satisfy that godly hunger. For God is always pleased to accomplish His will in your life.

Not Beyond His Reach

*Then the LORD will be known to Egypt, and
the Egyptians will know the LORD in that day,
and will make sacrifice and offering.*

ISAIAH 19:21

Who in your life could—like the land of Egypt long ago—win the not-to-be-coveted title "Least Likely to Be Saved"? Or would someone have ever awarded *you* that title? . . .

She lived the amoral, big-city lifestyle with gusto. She was single, a successful career woman living society's dream. She had the right clothes, the right address, and the right connections for the nighttime hotspots. A good person and a lot of fun, she served the god of self, yet would give whatever she had to a friend in need. She'd talked theology for years and concluded that "quaint Christian beliefs are fine for some." She was the last person anyone thought would become a Christ-follower . . . but she did. Now passionate about her Lord and articulate about her faith, she is God's ambassador among lost souls . . .

God is so powerful that even His most antagonistic enemies can be converted to belief and trust in Him. Those who appear farthest from God are not beyond His reach and may even be closer than you think.

Whom does this truth compel you to pray for or even reach out to . . . one more time?

Known by His Actions

*Now by this I know that you are a man of God, and that
the word of the LORD in your mouth is the truth.*

1 KINGS 17:24

As we—like Elijah—serve God, people will pay more attention to our actions than our words. They may listen to what we say, but most often it's what we *do* that convinces them that we are God's servants . . .

Elijah was God's spokesman during a dark time in Israel's history when the nation turned away from God. Many people claimed to be divine prophets, but God rejected them.

When a widow's only son died, she did not need a word from a false prophet, regardless of how reassuring it might be. She needed to hear from someone who knew and served the living God. Trusting in God, Elijah prayed over her dead son. When the Lord revived the child, the woman knew by the prophet's faithful and prayerful action that he was a man of God.

The Lord's powerful hand on Elijah was unmistakable. But it was not just Elijah's words that proved he served God; God's affirmation of Elijah's words proved the prophet's authenticity.

What do your actions reveal about whose servant you are? Is God presently affirming your words and actions? How is God's hand on your life evident to those who know you?

God Our Fortress

The name of the LORD is a strong tower;
The righteous run to it and are safe.

PROVERBS 18:10

Sometimes the righteous need protection; they must seek a place of safety from danger. In no time was that more clear than in the days of Nazi Germany...

Martin Niemöller was a pastor in Germany during Adolf Hitler's ruthless regime. When Niemöller refused to yield to Nazi demands, his church was bombed, and he was imprisoned. His trial began February 7, 1938.

As a guard led Niemöller from his dreary cell to the imposing courtroom, the pastor grew frightened. His church and his family were in danger, and unknown terrors awaited him. As he prepared to ascend the flight of stairs into the courtroom, Niemöller suddenly heard a whisper. It was his guard. This Nazi soldier was quoting Proverbs 18:10!

This word from God—through a highly unlikely channel—sustained Niemöller through his trial and the dreary years of imprisonment in Nazi concentration camps that followed... until he ministered in the church once again.

The Lord Himself is not intimidated by our greatest fears. He remains unshaken in our worst calamity. We experience incredible peace and security when we abide in His strength, for He alone is our refuge.

Don't Worry

*"Consider the ravens, for they neither sow nor reap, which
have neither storehouse nor barn; and God feeds them.
Of how much more value are you than the birds?"*

LUKE 12:24

Ravens were despised birds, considered unclean by the
Jews, yet—Jesus pointed out—God cared for them. So
of course Almighty God will surely care and provide for His
people, the ones He sent His Son to die for!

Yet we worry. Worry reflects a habitual lack of faith in the
Lord's willingness or ability to provide for us. Worry reveals
our hesitation to believe that God will meet our needs in practical ways, and our anxiety increases when we don't see how
we can provide for ourselves. Worry comes so easily, yet it
changes nothing about our circumstances.

Actually, worry is a much more accurate gauge of our faith
than any doctrinal statement we might utter. Instead of fret-
ting, we do better to remind ourselves that God has repeatedly
testified in His Word that He loves us. He has promised again
and again that He will provide for our every need, and He has
consistently declared His sovereignty over our future. If after
all these assurances we are still anxious, we must become better acquainted with our Lord.

God's Help, Not the World's

You may do nothing with us to build a house for our God;
but we alone will build to the LORD God of Israel.

EZRA 4:3

God prompted Cyrus, king of Persia, to allow His people back to Jerusalem to build His temple. At the same time, He gave His people the desire to do exactly that.

Only a small number of the Jewish exiles, however, responded to God's call. Most were unwilling to give up their Babylonian property or lifestyle to return to Jerusalem. It was a massive undertaking for so few in number.

When "adversaries of Judah and Benjamin" heard about the building project, they offered to help, although with mixed motives (v. 1), but the Hebrew leaders declined. Although assistance with construction would have been enormously helpful, it was wisely declined for three reasons: this task was given exclusively to God's people; accepting aid would obligate the Jewish people to Samaritan unbelievers; and the potential for corruption in worship was too great if Israel became allied with those who rejected the true God.

The surest way to accomplish a God-given task is to follow God's ways. You may encounter critics and opposition. However, success will not come from heeding your enemies but from obeying God's voice. Be careful not to include others in a task God gave solely to you.

Hope Remains

Take heart, men, for I believe God that
it will be just as it was told me.

ACTS 27:25

SCENE 1: The ship had sailed despite Paul's warning, and now the storm raged. God had assured Paul that none would die, but a shipwreck was inevitable . . .

No one looks forward to being on a boat as it is broken apart by violent seas, but Christians find real hope in the confident expectation that God will accomplish every promise He has ever made. Hope looks to the future and gives those who believe courage to remain faithful in the present.

SCENE 2: Being warned not to travel to Jerusalem, Paul declared his willingness to be bound and even killed "for the name of the Lord Jesus" (Acts 21:13).

Faith in God trusts, despite circumstances that suggest the contrary, that His will is best. Hope remains even when the comforts in life are removed, for God's love remains. Confidence holds strong in the knowledge that heaven waits for all who are faithful to the end.

Although the whole world may seem to be against you, fear not when God is for you. He will watch over you until His purposes are fulfilled. Nobody can thwart God's plans. Your hope in Him is always secure.

First or Last Resort?

Do not put your trust in princes,
Nor in a son of man, in whom there is no help. . . .
Happy is he who has the God of Jacob for his help,
Whose hope is in the LORD his God.

PSALM 146:3, 5

When the bottom falls out of the market, do you call your stockbroker right away? When the pink slip has your name on it, do you open the Yellow Pages for "headhunters" instead of opening Scripture? When you're in a jam, do you immediately call a friend? When heavy traffic is going to make you miss your flight, do you swear instead of pray?

Is God too often your last resort?

Our temptation and very human tendency is to turn to people in our time of need rather than to the One who is truly able to help us in any situation. Unlike human beings, God is not limited by time or space, power or knowledge, busyness or self-interest. The psalmist knew "there is no help" in princes and human beings. Ask God to do His work in your heart so you will turn first to Him in confidence and trust, ready to accept His solution, His timing, His love, and His perfect plan for you.

Where do you plan to turn next?

Relationship, Not Rules

Your ears shall hear a word behind you, saying,
"This is the way, walk in it,"
Whenever you turn to the right hand
Or whenever you turn to the left.

ISAIAH 30:21

For many people, rules may be easier than relationship. After all, rules are cut and dried; a relationship is much less predictable or controllable!

Rules give us a way to perform and therefore merit favor; a relationship is pure grace.

Rules offer a sense of power, accomplishment, and self-sufficiency; in a relationship we're vulnerable.

The Pharisees in Jesus' day liked rules—and they felt pretty good about themselves for meticulously following them. In a relationship with Jesus Christ, we can feel good only because He has called us—by name—to follow Him.

Many religions, however, are based on following laws, and people work hard to obey the rules. But the one true God doesn't intend His followers to take matters into their own hands like that. God wants a personal relationship with you.

To facilitate this relationship, God's Spirit resides within us; He is active in our lives. He knows which way we should go, and He wants to guide us. The obedience He looks for does not involve following laws; the obedience God insists upon is doing His will.

"Christ in You"

To them God willed to make known what are the
riches of the glory of this mystery among the Gentiles:
which is Christ in you, the hope of glory.

COLOSSIANS 1:27

Nothing else matters if your relationship with God is not as He intends it to be.

Think about that truth for a moment. Then ask yourself, "Is my relationship with God all that He wants it to be?"

Key to living out your relationship with God according to His will is that you understand the mystery of "Christ in you." Sanctification is not something Christ gives to us; it is Him dwelling in us. We do not imitate Him; He inhabits us.

This mystery of God is astounding: Christ dwells within us, and He has given us the hope of glory. In fact, because Christ lives in us, we bring hope to people who remain in darkness.

Ask the Holy Spirit to open your heart so you can better understand this mystery of God, this mystery of "Christ in you." That one truth will transform you—and as it does so, be prepared for "the hope of glory" to permeate your life and impact the lives of others. We cannot fully understand how a holy God could inhabit our body of dust. But we don't have to comprehend it. We must only surrender to it.

Power for Ministry

Him we preach . . . that we may present every man
perfect in Christ Jesus. To this end I also labor, striving
according to His working which works in me mightily.

COLOSSIANS 1:28—29

What kingdom goal are you working toward?

Any goal for God's kingdom—like any ambition you have for your life—requires effort. Note, however, that the energy fueling Paul's kingdom work was—in his words— "[God's] working which works in me mightily."

The Greek behind *working* also means "energy" or "power." It describes both physical and cosmic forces, but in the New Testament it refers primarily to the activity of either divine or evil powers. Paul used this word to identify the source of his strength for ministry: God's power that raised Jesus from the dead empowered Paul for ministry. The apostle labored and strived in the power of his Lord, accomplishing things he could never have done in his own strength.

The same power is available today to all who are in Christ. It is accessible to you. Are you "striving according to His working"? Are you laboring in the Lord's power? When you do, you'll be able to achieve kingdom accomplishments you never dreamed possible.

Our Heritage

Now this is the genealogy of the sons of Noah: Shem, Ham, and Japheth. And sons were born to them after the flood.

GENESIS 10:1

Yes, here's another list of who begat whom, the kind of list that peppers these Old Testament history books as well as the New Testament Gospels. Genealogies help us ground our spiritual history in the tangible history of the world. We can, for example, see that Jesus is in fact a son of Abraham, the Son through whom all the earth is blessed. We can see the Lord's faithfulness to generation after generation of His people even when those people stray. We can see His hand in the unfolding of history.

These genealogies also suggest something important about your own family tree and family history. They remind you that God is intimately familiar with your background. That can be truly comforting when you realize that your heavenly Father knows everything that has gone in to shaping you; He understands how you came to be who you are, why you've made certain choices, what you fear, and what your hurts are. God knows all your ancestors, and He understands the challenges you face because of those who preceded you. God always relates to you with your history in view. That's one more reason why you can trust Him fully as He leads you forward.

Hope in Christ

I do not want you to be ignorant, brethren,
concerning those who have fallen asleep, lest
you sorrow as others who have no hope.

1 THESSALONIANS 4:13

All around us are people who vainly place their hope in their money, their strength, their power, or their good health—but death reaches us all. It makes no exceptions. It is no respecter of persons. And nothing is more hopeless than the funeral of someone who did not place his or her hope in Christ. At such funerals the grim reality of the brevity of life—and of the futility of life without the Lord—is apparent, and it strips away every hint of strength and invincibility.

Yet people who have placed their trust in Christ need not sorrow like those who have rejected Him. Not even death can rob us of our joy or hope. For humanity's greatest foe—inevitable death—merely ushers us into our heavenly Father's glorious presence where we will enjoy fellowship with Him and our fellow saints for eternity.

Christians have no reason to fear death. Jesus has already overcome it. So live your life on earth well, but always with a view to the spectacular and eternal reward that awaits.

JULY

God has not given us a spirit of fear,
but of power and of love and of a sound mind.

2 TIMOTHY 1:7

"Be Still"

Be still, and know that I am God.

PSALM 46:10

Stop reading for a minute and listen. Just listen—and then list the noises you're hearing. Are there sounds from outside the house? Do you hear traffic? kids playing? dogs barking? people talking? airplanes flying?

Now identify noises from within the room where you sit. Is the television or radio on? Are you listening to music? Did the phone just ring? Are there clocks ticking? motors humming?

What about the noise in your head? What responsibilities, chores, or worries do you find preoccupying you and interrupting these few minutes with the Lord? What song is stuck in your mind? What item do you need to mention to your administrator or add to your to-do list?

Speaking of your to-do list, what does this week's calendar look like? What downtime, if any, do you have scheduled?

We fill our lives with incessant noise, commotion, and busyness—and then we wonder why we don't hear God's voice. As the psalmist knew long ago and believers have discovered again and again since then, it is in the stillness that we find God. So right now—for just a few minutes—be still, and know that He is God.

Labor of Love

Whatever you do, do it heartily, as to the Lord and not to men.

COLOSSIANS 3:23

Yes, God really does mean "whatever." He means anything and everything. All. No exceptions, no fine print. We are to do all that we do as if we are performing the task directly for God.

Imagine entering the workplace, the school campus, the neighborhood, or the church ready and willing to do whatever you went there to do "heartily, as to the Lord." Do you realize that the mundane tasks of life as well as your greatest challenges are ways to serve the Lord? They are!

As you think about this approach to life, consider Jesus' words from His parable of the sheep and the goats: "Inasmuch as you did it to one of the least of these My brethren, you did it to Me" (Matthew 25:40). We are to serve heartily—with energy and enthusiasm, with a willing heart and even with joy—whatever we are doing.

There is no place for mediocrity and laziness in God's service. If you are a child of the King, everything you do is for His glory. Your labor is an expression of your love for God.

Consider the effort and attitude you are demonstrating as you perform your tasks. Do they bring glory to God?

Which Path?

Fear God and keep His commandments,
For this is man's all.

ECCLESIASTES 12:13

Skepticism and pessimism are prevalent in the book of Ecclesiastes. Not until the end is it evident that this book is an apologetic discourse defending faith in God and describing the futility of life without Him. The argument is made that wisdom, resources, and plans apart from God lead to a meaningless existence. The fear of God is the only true key to happiness, fulfillment, and meaning. Is that the path you are choosing?

Life is brief and, apart from God, filled with such mundane activity as the pursuit of food, shelter, comfort, and safety. What, then, is the significance of human effort, sorrow, and joy? Only our relationship with God gives us an eternal perspective and divine purpose for life.

Earthly comforts are gifts from the Lord. Laughter, friendship, family, and marriage—as wonderful as they are—are all temporary. God created us for eternity, yet He puts rich blessings and profound joy in our path to remind us that He loves us. Apart from His grace, life would indeed be dreary and meaningless. Do you have a proper perspective on the life God has graciously given you?

Sharing God's Love

"You shall love the LORD your God with all your heart,
with all your soul, with all your mind, and with all your
strength . . . . You shall love your neighbor as yourself."

MARK 12:30−31

When the religious leaders of the day asked Jesus which was the most important commandment, Jesus answered right away. Their trick question wasn't at all difficult for Him!

Jesus summarized God's Law—the Ten Commandments and all of Leviticus—with these two commands: "love God" and "love your neighbor."

God is love. Only amazing love could have prompted Him to release His Son to die for us, the sinful rabble populating this earth!

As One whose essence is love, then, God is delighted when we share His love with the people around us. After all, His love first drew each one of us to Him. As we love God and His people in response to the compassion and love we have received from Him, His love works through us to draw others to Him.

God's love is not for hoarding, but for spreading. With whom will you share God's love today—and whom will you thank for being a channel of His love in your life?

Truth Offered

Peter said, "Not so, Lord! For I have never eaten anything
common or unclean." And a voice spoke to him . . .
"What God has cleansed you must not call common."

ACTS 10:14—15

D id God really expect Peter to eat "all kinds of four-footed
animals of the earth, wild beasts, creeping things, and
birds of the air" (v. 12)? That sure seemed to be the meaning of
the vision—and Peter had to object. This Jewish man had been
taught since childhood to refuse unclean foods. God's command to "kill and eat" (v. 13) signified a major shift away from
the law he had been taught. Of course Peter objected! So God—
our standard for truth and holiness—repeated the vision and its
message three times.

Learn from Peter's experience that tradition can hinder
obedience when God prepares to do something new—and
note that people react differently to truth. Some people hear
God's Word and receive truth that sets them free. Others hear
the same message and adamantly reject it, never experiencing
its inherent blessing. Others are reluctant, putting off any commitment to some future time. Only the Holy Spirit can give
spiritual insight, so ask Him to guide you into truth and abundant life—and then obey. And don't wait until God tells you
three times before you do!

Pride—Individual and National

He will lift up a banner to the nations from afar,
And will whistle to them from the end of the earth;
Surely they shall come with speed, swiftly.

ISAIAH 5:26

A major theme in the book of Isaiah is the truth that the world's nations are but God's instruments for His purposes—and the superpowers of Isaiah's day, Assyria and Persia (like the superpowers of our day), were unaware of that fact. How prideful these nations were as they strutted audaciously across the international stage completely unaware that they were wholly under the direction of Almighty God!

We human beings can also prance across the stages of our lives. Such pride is an affront to God. God will inevitably bring low those who exalt themselves with self-sufficiency and independence from their Creator; He will deflate those who puff themselves up.

After all, pride is the root of our sin. Adam and Eve's sin made them want to be like God. Likewise, pride makes us—nations as well as individuals—overestimate our position in God's creation. God will quell such pride in due time.

The antidote to pride? Look at your holy and almighty God and you will find yourself asking with the psalmist, "What is man that You are mindful of him?" (8:4).

Truth About Treasure

*Command those who are rich in this present age not to
be haughty, nor to trust in uncertain riches but in the
living God, who gives us richly all things to enjoy.*

1 TIMOTHY 6:17

God truly is the Giver of all good gifts—the gifts of family
and friends, of home and health, of laughter and love, of
hope and peace, of freedom and responsibility, of rest and work,
of music and color. The list goes on and on . . . God is also the
Giver of the good gift of treasure—of money, of worldly riches.

All that we have, we have received from His hand. As a
reminder of the truth that He owns it all, God calls us to invest
back into His kingdom what He has entrusted to us. In God's
economy, this kind of investing produces dividends both now
and for eternity. His kingdom is the only eternally secure place
to invest our treasure.

People who recognize that God is the source of their prosperity generously share with others their financial and material
wealth. Those people, however, who jealously hoard their possessions, demonstrate their ignorance of the eternity they are
facing—and they miss the joy of giving while they have the
opportunity.

It is pleasant to be rich in this life. It will be breathtaking to
be rich in the next.

Foolhardy Followers

*"Son of man, these men have set up their idols in their hearts,
and put before them that which causes them to stumble into
iniquity. Should I let Myself be inquired of at all by them?"*

EZEKIEL 14:3

Why does the Lord even put up with us?

The nation of Israel and the leaders themselves had clearly set their hearts on foreign gods. They broke God's Law; they rejected His standards; they strayed far off His path. Yet they still considered themselves God's people, and they assumed they could approach Him on their own terms. That was a further affront to their holy God! The total lack of repentance and humility reflected in their petition was also a further invitation to God's judgment.

Our God is a just God, and He will not overlook sin. He may, in His mercy, delay His punishment, but punishment will come. Whenever God punishes the sins of His people, His actions are absolutely just. In His words, "I have done nothing without cause" (v. 23). God never acts randomly or without reason. If He disciplines you, you can be certain it is deserved.

If God does not answer your entreaties, it would behoove you to make sure your life is pleasing to Him.

Alas for the Day!

*"For the day of the LORD is at hand; It shall
come as destruction from the Almighty."*

JOEL 1:15

The Israelites originally understood the "day of the LORD" to be a time when God would enable His people to triumph over their enemies. It apparently never dawned on them that their conduct—their faithfulness or lack of faithfulness to God's Law—would be addressed on that significant day.

The prophet Amos taught, however, that the day of the Lord would actually be a day of judgment first for God's people and then for others (Amos 5:18). On the day of the Lord, God will both demonstrate His sovereignty over all nations and execute His judgment on sinners. (The New Testament identifies this day with the second coming of Christ.)

We all have to face the dreadful reality of the day of the Lord. We must not assume that whenever God approaches us, it is always for blessing. Are you prepared for that day of awesome accountability? Perhaps you need to return to the Lord as did the people in Joel's day.

Although God loves us, He will satisfy His righteousness. When He relates to us, it is always in holiness, and it always involves thorough accountability for our sin.

Total Healing

Jesus, moved with compassion, stretched out His hand and touched him, and said to him, "I am willing; be cleansed."

MARK 1:41

Rarely do we human beings need healing on only a single level. Physical hurt tends to have its emotional and perhaps even spiritual components. Emotional wounds can manifest themselves in physical ailments. When injuries have caused isolation, we may also need relational healing. Jesus understands all this . . .

In Mark 1:40, a leper—who apparently recognized the power of the One to whom he was speaking—said to Jesus, "If You are willing, You can make me clean."

Jesus responded, "I am willing; be cleansed"—but healing came in another way as well. The fact that Jesus touched the man is significant. Such personal contact would have been immeasurably meaningful for a person who had been walking through life forced to yell, "Unclean!" so people could avoid him and his contagion. We don't know how long it had been since this man had experienced a human touch, but Jesus did. Jesus met the leper's deepest needs. How wonderfully encouraging and healing that touch must have been!

Two thousand years later Jesus still personalizes His encounters with people as He meets their deepest needs.

Love That Convicts

Godly sorrow produces repentance leading to salvation, not to be regretted; but the sorrow of the world produces death.

2 CORINTHIANS 7:10

Feeling sad for what you've done is definitely a step toward repentance, but it's only a step. It's not the same as repentance. Grief over what you've done can be little more than regretting that you got caught, that you disappointed someone or even yourself, or that you now have to deal with the consequences of your actions.

A step beyond sadness is acknowledging that what you've done is wrong, that it is a violation of God's commands, a failure to love Him with all your being or to love others as you love yourself. This step involves conviction about your sin and recognizing your sinfulness.

Conviction of sin is both good and godly. It means God cares about your life: He wants to remove that which will ultimately hurt you. Conviction will be an irritation to a defiant heart, but to the receptive heart it will bring sorrow leading to repentance and a renewed relationship with God.

True repentance is a gift of the Spirit, as He alone can convict of sin. When He does, respond humbly and immediately, not just with regret but with genuine repentance.

"I Must Decrease"

He must increase, but I must decrease.

JOHN 3:30

John the Baptist's assignment wasn't an easy one. After all, who wants to hear the call to repent? That's a message about sinfulness—but it's the God-given word John delivered in order to prepare the way for the coming Messiah.

This bold preacher—who greeted the influential Pharisees and Sadducees by calling them a "brood of vipers!" (Matthew 3:7)—was a humble servant who knew his role in the kingdom. So, when John learned of Jesus baptizing people, he did not become jealous or guard his turf; instead, he joyfully exalted Christ. John knew that the One whose way he was preparing had come to set people free from the separation from God caused by sin. John responded by declaring, "He must increase, but I must decrease."

The challenge of every Christian is to—like John—magnify Christ in whatever way God calls us to do it. We naturally tend to focus on self rather than on God; we crave acknowledgment and affirmation rather than self-denial. We gravitate toward activities that bring us praise and affirmation. But if Christ is to have His rightful place in our lives, we must set aside self—and selfishness—so He can be glorified. We must decrease.

When people encounter us, do they go away impressed with us or with Christ?

Commanded to Love

[It's] not as though I wrote a new commandment
to you, but that which we have had from the
beginning: that we love one another. This is love,
that we walk according to His commandments.

2 JOHN 5–6

God's commandment to love first appears in Leviticus. There we read, "You shall not take vengeance, nor bear any grudge against the children of your people, but you shall love your neighbor as yourself: I am the LORD" (19:18). Not much about human nature has changed through the millennia: vengeance and grudges come easily, and we still have to be commanded to love.

Jesus—who died on the cross as evidence of God's great love for sinners—echoes this command to love: "As I have loved you, that you also love one another" (John 13:34). Established eternally for every generation and culture on earth, God's commandments don't change. True devotion obeys these commandments, and His greatest commandment is to love. In fact, the most loving thing you can do for others is to obey everything God tells you to do about loving Him with all you are and loving others as yourself.

Ask the Lord whom you need to love with Christ's love—and then do so. What God is asking of you is nothing new.

The Living Word, an Open Heart

*The word of God is living and powerful, and sharper
than any two-edged sword, piercing even to the division
of soul and spirit, and of joints and marrow, and is a
discerner of the thoughts and intents of the heart.*

HEBREWS 4:12

God's Word, the Bible, is not merely a work of religious literature. It is living and powerful; its truth becomes active in people's lives.

- When have you experienced the living power of God's Word?
- When has the Word of God pierced your heart?
- When has a passage of Scripture spoken directly to you?
- When have you revisited a familiar section only to find fresh significance you had never noticed before?
- When has God used His Word to reveal your sin to you?

If you haven't experienced any of these things recently, remember that hearing God's voice is directly dependent on the condition of your heart. A pure and open heart will be ready to receive whatever God has to say. A hardened, distracted person will not recognize, let alone accept, God's Word.

So, whenever you prepare to open the Bible, first ask God to open your heart. Then be prepared for God's Word to powerfully and accurately address your life.

A Glorious Revelation

In these last days [God has] spoken to us by His
Son, whom He has appointed heir of all things,
through whom also He made the worlds.

HEBREWS 1:2

The covenants with Noah, Abraham, and Moses . . . The renewal of the covenants through the generations . . . The giving of the Law at Sinai . . . The establishment of the Passover and other feasts . . . The clearly defined sacrificial system and detailed instruction about temple worship . . . The calling of specific people for particular kingdom tasks . . . The words of the prophets and the psalmists . . .

Throughout history God has spoken to His people, but His greatest revelation to us has been through His Son. Now Christ is our great High Priest and Advocate who sympathizes with us in our weaknesses and who helps us overcome every trial and temptation.

Jesus is the High Priest who made the perfect, once-and-for-all sacrifice for our sin. Jesus is superior to the Law, the prophets, sacrifices, and any priesthood. All these are deficient in comparison to Christ, the perfect Sacrifice, the holy High Priest, the only Savior, the Word of truth, and the one and only Son of God.

Praise God for revealing Himself in His Son—and praise Him specifically for revealing Himself to you!

Miracles

*Joshua said to the people, "Sanctify yourselves, for
tomorrow the LORD will do wonders among you."*

JOSHUA 3:5

God's prerequisite for working mightily in and through
you is your sanctification. That sanctification or consecration happens—by the power of the Holy Spirit—as you
separate yourself from anything unclean. God's great work in
and through your life awaits your willingness to be made holy
and set apart for Him and His kingdom purposes.

God works His wonders and miracles for people of faith.
Realize that your faith in God is not something you declare;
faith is what God grants you, and faith is brought to life through
action. Saying you believe is commendable, but the people who
step out in faith are the ones who see miracles.

The miracle the children of Israel experienced was crossing
the Jordan on dry ground. We read, "The Jordan overflows all
its banks during the whole time of harvest" (v. 15). This was,
therefore, no small miracle. God stopped the Jordan's flow at
its peak level.

The Lord delights to do wonders through a consecrated
people. He wants to demonstrate His power to an unbelieving
world, but He wants sanctified instruments. Are you prepared
to be cleansed in order to be acceptable to God as His holy
servant? Consecration is a choice you make.

Joy in God

Let all those rejoice who put their trust in You;
Let them ever shout for joy, because You defend them;
Let those also who love Your name
Be joyful in You.

PSALM 5:11

Happiness and *joy*—these two words are not as synonymous as they might seem at first glance. Oh, they may feel a lot alike, but that's where the similarity ends.

Consider that the root of the word *happiness* is *hap*. And that simple word refers to luck, chance, fate; to circumstances that come our way. We can be happy when we get the job. We can be happy when the news from the doctor is good. And we can be happy when our team wins.

But joy frees us from sadness when we *don't* get the job, when the news from the doctor is *not* good, and when our team *loses*. That's because pure joy comes not from circumstances but from our love relationship with God. Our choice to trust in His sovereign, gracious plan for our lives sustains our hope in hard times, and that gives us joy.

One more thing. The greater our love *for* God, the greater will be our joy *in* Him. Grow your love for God through Bible study and prayer, worship and confession, praise and fellowship—and see if your joy doesn't increase. Life is too brief and harsh to squander even one day of it joylessly.

God's Transforming Power

God has not given us a spirit of fear, but of
power and of love and of a sound mind.

2 TIMOTHY 1:7

Second Timothy offers insight into the heart of an older, wiser Paul, whose life was characterized by a peace and depth of faith for which every believer should strive.

Yet this godly apostle was once a young, fervent persecutor of God's people. Only God's grace could have transformed that misguided murderer into the beloved saint who poured out his life for the church.

Hear Paul's hard-won wisdom: Don't give up. Press on. Be bold in your faith. Be diligent to learn the Scriptures. Above all, trust God to guide you so one day you, too, can say, "I have fought the good fight . . . I have kept the faith" (4:7).

Key to fighting that good fight is fearing God, not people. Most fear comes from the unknown, but a love relationship with God produces in us a sound mind that enables us to see our circumstances from His perspective. Fear of people paralyzes, but reverent fear of God empowers. If you currently are afraid of something, be certain of this: God is not the author of it! Paul and Timothy knew God's gifts of love, power, and a sound mind—and they used those gifts in God's service. You can too.

A Touch of Faith

*Jesus said, "Who touched Me?" When all denied it, Peter
and those with him said, "Master, the multitudes throng
and press You, and You say, 'Who touched Me?'"*

LUKE 8:45

The crowds pressed in on Him. Not only was Jesus surrounded by people needing His help and wanting His healing power, but He was on His way to the home of Jairus whose sick daughter languished near death. The fact that Jesus sensed someone touching Him is quite remarkable, and it reveals His sensitivity to every person who reaches out to Him in faith.

Someone had indeed reached out to the Lord and touched Him—actually, touched the hem of His robe—in faith that He could and would heal her of twelve years of bleeding. Luke the physician reported the woman's declaration: "she had touched Him and . . . she was healed immediately" (v. 47).

If you feel overwhelmed by what God has called you to do or, like the hemorrhaging woman, by the circumstances of your life, be encouraged. God will respond as you reach out in faith to touch Him. He will empower you and heal you, and you will see miracles happen in your life.

You cannot control the power God will use in your life. However, you decide whether you will reach out to Christ or not.

Almost a Stumble

My feet had almost stumbled;
My steps had nearly slipped.
For I was envious of the boastful,
When I saw the prosperity of the wicked.

PSALM 73:2—3

W atch where you're going!" We've all heard that warning, and we've probably all offered that advice to someone just learning to walk, to ride a bike, or to drive. It's also an important caution for our spiritual lives. Busyness, the cares of the world, the enticements of our culture, sin—all these can keep our focus off our Lord and even cause us to shift in our commitment to Him.

The psalm writer Asaph, for instance, almost stumbled in his faith when he shifted his attention away from God's goodness and began to envy the apparent pleasure and prosperity of the wicked. He even wondered aloud whether keeping himself pure and upholding God's standards were worth the effort since the wicked appear to act with impunity (v. 13).

He said he wrestled with these thoughts "until I went into the sanctuary of God" (v. 17). There Asaph realized that the wicked may appear to be sinning without consequence, but that they will pay the full price for their rebellion against God.

When the ways of the world get you down, follow Asaph's example and enter God's sanctuary. Spending time in worship and praise will help you keep your footing and reassure you of the rightness of God's ways.

An Exchanged Life

*I know that in me (that is, in my flesh) nothing
good dwells; for to will is present with me, but
how to perform what is good I do not find.*

ROMANS 7:18

It's not good enough to simply recognize your sin and confess it. It's not adequate to desperately desire a godly life. It isn't sufficient to work hard to change how you think or act. Nothing within us can defeat sin. We can't change our lives—but we can *ex*change our lives: when Christ lives within us, we die to sin and become alive to righteousness. The transformation of our character that is impossible for us is possible with God.

Then, transformed by God and no longer gripped by sin, we are free to follow Christ in the power of the Holy Spirit. Only with His guidance and empowering can we live the Christian life. The Holy Spirit, for instance, elevates our self-centered prayers and leads us to ask for the very things God wants to accomplish in our lives, in the lives of those for whom we're praying, and in the world around us.

So now that you're following Christ, rely on His Spirit to make you alive to righteousness and to guide your prayers so you can serve Him well. Let Christ elevate your prayers and your service to a level that honors Him.

A Divine Audience

*[Stephen], being full of the Holy Spirit, gazed
into heaven and saw the glory of God, and
Jesus standing at the right hand of God.*

ACTS 7:55

In the course of our hectic existence, we can easily forget that we live every moment before a divine audience. During life's mundane activities, our weak moments, our failures, and our victories, God is watching. That fact means that He is keenly aware of what we are enduring—for His sake.

When we are suffering, we can sometimes begin to wonder whether God is aware of what we are going through. Be assured that He is. While He may not directly intervene or remove the challenging circumstances, He is prepared to walk with us, and He is determined to comfort and bless us along the way.

Do you ever sense you are facing hardship alone? Do you ever think no one knows or cares about the sacrifices you are making? Do you feel that the trials you are suffering are unfair? Remember, God is taking note; He misses nothing.

One day Almighty God will welcome you—as He greeted Stephen—into your heavenly home and reward you according to your faithfulness, which He has observed each step of the way.

As you go about your day today, be confident of this: God is watching.

"Building a Temple"

I am building a temple for the name of the LORD my God.

2 CHRONICLES 2:4

At the beginning of Solomon's reign, Israel was an agricultural society that did not have the craftsmen needed to build the temple. Therefore, Solomon traded grain, wine, and oil for skilled labor from Tyre.

When requesting craftsmen and materials, though, Solomon made sure that Hiram, king of Tyre, understood that the structure was not being built to enhance his reputation as king of Israel. The structure would instead glorify the God of Israel and provide a place where His people could worship Him.

Solomon worked hard to offer God the best available skills, resources, and talents—and we should do the same today. The reason is not to impress God or gain His favor. We offer our best because He is God and He deserves nothing less.

So the Lord's house—Solomon's temple—would be spectacular, but even in its magnificence it could not contain our God. Nothing can.

Solomon built a breathtaking temple that caused people to worship God enthusiastically and reverently. Today our lives are being invested in the tasks God has given us. What type of monument will we leave in God's honor when we have completed our work?

Spiritual Examinations

Examine yourself as to whether you are in the faith.

2 CORINTHIANS 13:5

We shouldn't judge a book by its cover, but we should be able to determine whether people are followers of Christ by looking at them in action. Likewise, people ought to look at us and know that we are following the Lord instead of the world's ways. Of course it's always easier for us to come to a conclusion (right or wrong) about someone else than to look honestly at ourselves, isn't it?

Paul urged believers to scrutinize their own lives because God wants us to live according to the faith we profess. Our primary focus ought always to be on living our own lives in a Christlike manner rather than on critiquing those around us.

Jesus Christ abides in every believer, and His presence in our lives ought to make a difference that is obvious to all who know us. If there is no discernible difference between a person still living in spiritual darkness and a person who claims to live in the light of Christ, something is desperately wrong.

Our self-examination is therefore an opportunity to seek the Lord. Simply ask Him to help you see yourself as He sees you and to help you live so that the world knows you're His.

Life is too important to base it on assumptions. Examine your life so you know its true condition.

A Request for Wisdom

Give to Your servant an understanding heart to judge
Your people, that I may discern between good and evil.

1 KINGS 3:9

What would you say if God asked you, "What shall I give you?" as He asked Solomon early in his reign (v. 5)?

The Lord was pleased when King Solomon requested wisdom. What better tool for God's servant than an "understanding heart"! Solomon wanted to not only understand but also follow God's instructions. This willingness to hear God's voice and obey His instructions is the basis of godly wisdom and the foundation for discerning right from wrong. Such wisdom results in a life that pleases God.

God grants wisdom to those who earnestly desire it. He blessed Solomon with "wisdom and exceedingly great understanding, and largeness of heart like the sand on the seashore" (4:29)—and that "largeness of heart" refers to Solomon's ability to understand and respond to God and His ways. Seek to honor God and let His wisdom permeate every aspect of your life.

After all, God's wisdom is extremely practical and able to enrich all your relationships with understanding and insight. Basing your life on God's wisdom will enable you to live in a way He is pleased to bless.

For or Against?

To Titus, a true son in our common faith . . .

TITUS 1:4

Do your actions build up and strengthen? Do your words encourage and edify? Do your efforts gather and draw others to Christ? There is no neutral stance when we walk with the Lord. If we are not effective servants for Him, we are hurting His work.

Titus was very much a positive influence for the Lord and an encouragement to the apostle Paul (2 Corinthians 7:6, 13). Paul took Titus with him to evangelize Crete and left him there to establish the church. In the first century, Cretans as a whole were notoriously immoral people, known for their deception and evil practices (Titus 1:12). It would take a strong leader to help them anchor their faith and guide them in establishing church leadership.

Although a leader in his own right, Titus is best known for undergirding and supporting the apostle Paul and the work God had given him. Titus was a team player who honored God by giving his life for others. He was humble, strong in faith, and gentle of heart.

What will you do today to be a friend like Titus—or what encourager in your life will you thank? Being an encourager is a blessed way to live your life!

Rise Up

Jesus said to him, "Rise, take up your bed and walk."

JOHN 5:8

L egend had it that the first person into the pool at Bethesda whenever the water moved—supposedly stirred up by an angel—would be healed. A crowd of desperate, hurting, needy people huddled around the pool vainly hoping for a miracle.

Jesus encountered a man who had been lame for thirty-eight years. The man explained his predicament: "No one can help me into the pool, so someone always beats me into the water." Having no one to help him meant he was also friend-less, alone, abandoned.

When Jesus worked in this man's life, though, this once-lame man took a step of faith and turned to God. He didn't have all the theological answers yet, but he could not mistake his encounter with the Divine.

Note that after the man was healed, Jesus instructed him to "sin no more" (v. 14). Previously the man had exercised little control over what happened to him. But now that he had met Jesus, he could—out of gratitude—choose not to sin; he could decide to follow Jesus.

In what ways has God blessed you? protected you? guided you? What has your response been? You are no longer merely a helpless victim! Jesus has set you free!

Knowing God

*You are complete in Him, who is the head
of all principality and power.*

COLOSSIANS 2:10

What does it mean to be "complete in [Christ]"?

- To have a relationship with Christ is to know God in His fullness. After all, Christ was not *given* a divine nature; He *is* deity. To be complete in Christ is an incomprehensible truth beyond the scope of human intelligence. It is a mystery that only the Holy Spirit can translate into your life—but that is His assignment.

- To be complete means we lack nothing. In Christ, God gives us everything we need to be fulfilled, joyful, and pleasing to Him. Feeling dissatisfied, inadequate, or joyless reveals much about our relationship with God. Are we turning to Christ? He wants to be the answer for our every need.

- Also, since Christ is the head of every spiritual and earthly power, we Christians should know peace; we should not be frightened by or preoccupied with the enemy whom Jesus defeated and disarmed (v. 15). The vanquished foe, however, is the father of lies, and he tries to lure us into a phantom battle that Christ has already won. Trust God's promises, not Satan's lies.

Knowing Christ—knowing God—means having everything we need to experience a joyful, fulfilled, and abundant life.

Sharing God's Truth

*Be diligent to present yourself approved to God, a worker who
does not need to be ashamed, rightly dividing the word of truth.*

2 TIMOTHY 2:15

First of all, does God approve of you? Are you sure? Never assume God's satisfaction with your life and your service for Him. Strive to please Him, and one way is by immersing yourself in His Word, learning to live by it, and teaching it accurately and faithfully to others.

The importance of God's Word cannot be overstated. If you are to serve the Lord in any capacity, you must know Scripture thoroughly. You must study it, meditate on it, and obey it completely. God isn't satisfied with mere belief; He wants your obedience—and He knows that truth has moved from your head to your heart when He sees you living out His truth before others.

Scripture can be a mighty, awesome weapon in the hands of someone who knows how to use it. Discouraged people can find hope. Broken people can receive healing. Fearful people can gain courage. There is too much at stake for us to be careless or ineffective in the way we handle God's Word.

Consequences Are Your Friends

*"But where are your gods that you have made for yourselves?
Let them arise, if they can save you in the time of your trouble."*

JEREMIAH 2:28

Some actions that result from poor decisions naturally have consequences that reveal the foolishness of the decision: not thinking before speaking, for instance, inevitably leads to wounded relationships. At other times parents establish logical consequences that match the infraction: when a child has been told not to throw the ball in the house and does so anyway, resulting in a broken vase, that child pays for a replacement. Natural consequences and logical consequences can teach important lessons.

Perhaps that's one reason why God—who always forgives our sins when we confess them—doesn't always rescue us from the consequences of those sinful decisions. He knows the value of letting us experience the full effects of our poor choices.

In the verse above, God asks His people who have turned from Him where their false gods are now. Perhaps experiencing the impotence of their idols will keep God's people from turning to them next time.

What consequences has God allowed you—or is He allowing you—to face because of your sin? Those consequences can transform you if you will learn from them. Though certain lessons are painful, they may save us enormous grief in the years to come.

Marvelous Faith

*[Jesus] marveled, and said to those who followed,
"Assuredly, I say to you, I have not found
such great faith, not even in Israel!"*

MATTHEW 8:10

It was an amazing demonstration of faith, but the Roman centurion understood genuine authority. He knew that when a higher-ranking official issued a command, his soldiers obeyed. With his soldier's keen eye for recognizing authority, the centurion also knew that Jesus was Someone whose word had power and influence.

With His keen eye for recognizing faith, Jesus recognized someone who believed in Him. The centurion didn't demand a sign or answers to all his questions. He got right to the point.

And Jesus marveled at his faith . . .

Although it might seem difficult to impress the Creator of the universe, our faith in Him truly delights Him. Faith is the chief evidence that we genuinely know Christ—that we recognize Him to be loving, powerful, forgiving, present, healing, and so much more.

Conversely—and this should come as no surprise—a lack of faith is a jail, leaving us prisoners to our own resources and doubts.

In what situation today do you need to take the freeing step of faith? Don't stay limited by your own resources when the all-sufficient God is your heavenly Father.

August

Jesus Christ is the same yesterday, today, and forever.

Hebrews 13:8

Doctrine for Life

Whoever transgresses and does not abide in the doctrine
of Christ does not have God. He who abides in the
doctrine of Christ has both the Father and the Son.

2 JOHN 9

D o you think of doctrine as being for those in graduate school or the ministry? That's not the case at all. The word simply means "teaching or instruction," with the emphasis being not on one specific truth but on a teacher's entire line of thought.

When applied to Jesus, *doctrine* refers to His whole teaching, not just parts of it. The apostle John urged people to be faithful to all Christ taught. By knowing His message and choosing to obey it, his readers would prove to be Jesus' disciples, and they would be abiding in God.

How familiar are you with the Teacher's entire message? It's too easy to pick and choose from among Jesus' many teachings. We may inadvertently gravitate toward what is familiar or easy to understand and obey. We may avoid—consciously or not—the hard sayings that call us to make changes.

Regularly immerse yourself in Jesus' teachings. Carefully examine His life message. Then be diligent to practice all He taught.

Learning Obedience

[Jesus] learned obedience by the things which He suffered. And having been perfected, He became the author of eternal salvation to all who obey Him.

HEBREWS 5:8—9

What did Jesus—who is fully God as well as completely man—need to *learn*? What aspect of His character did this Holy Son of God need to have *perfected*?

Being "perfected" doesn't mean that Jesus improved or became more complete than He was before. Being perfected does mean that Jesus completed His earthly assignment and became fully qualified to be our eternal High Priest.

The matter of learning is related to this issue of completing His assignment. Jesus had never been called on to obey to the extent demanded by the cross. In that sense, Jesus in His humanness needed to face the ultimate temptation to choose a different path than the path to Calvary God had chosen for Him. Jesus walked to the cross.

The will of God inevitably leads each one of us to our own cross, because there are some things we can learn only through suffering. The Lord will grow our character and strengthen our walk with Him if we will obediently trust Him—as Jesus did—with the process and the suffering it involves.

How much are you willing to learn?

Israel's Pattern—and Yours?

The children of Israel did evil in the sight of the LORD,
and served the Baals;
and they forsook the LORD God of their fathers . . .
and they followed other gods . . .
and they provoked the LORD to anger.

JUDGES 2:11–12

Throughout history, God's people have lived out a perpetual fourfold cycle of apostasy: rebellion, punishment, repentance, and deliverance. The book of Judges testifies to this continual pattern.

Whenever the children of Israel finally realized their need for God, they would "[cry] out to the Lord" (3:9): God's people pleaded for Him to rescue them. This deliverance generally involved liberation from their enemies, but it might also be escape from the consequences of their sin. In the book of Judges, though, the people's pleas increasingly become nothing more than cries of distress under persecution, with no corresponding remorse for the sin that had brought about God's judgment.

This cycle of turning away from God throughout Judges may mirror a pattern in your life. Do you tend to stray from an intimate walk with God and then cry out for His deliverance as you face the consequences of your own sin? How genuine and lasting are your repentance and grief over your sin? How soon do you, like Israel, forget your total dependence on God?

Christ's Love

Though I bestow all my goods to feed the poor,
and though I give my body to be burned, but
have not love, it profits me nothing.

1 CORINTHIANS 13:3

We can do all the right things—we can have faith that moves mountains, we can give to the poor, we can even die a martyr's death—but unless these actions emanate from the love of Christ, they are dead works. We are to do all that we do—be a spouse or a parent, serve in the workplace or at home, be involved in the church and the community—in the name of Christ, and we are to do all these things with His love.

Love is not a gift that some people have and others do not. God calls everyone to love as He loves. There is no acceptable excuse for a child of God to be unloving.

To be a Christian is to live a life that is controlled by and motivated by God's love. Whether it comes naturally to you or not, the Holy Spirit will help you to love people in ways that reflect the heart of God.

It is good to serve God, to believe God, and to trust God. But in addition to all of these, God still calls us to love.

The Reliable One

Woe to those who go down to Egypt for help,
And rely on horses,
Who trust in chariots because they are many,
And in horsemen because they are very strong,
But who do not look to the Holy One of Israel,
Nor seek the LORD!

ISAIAH 31:1

Where do you turn in a crisis? That is your god. Whom do you immediately think of when you receive bad news? Is it God?

Israel thought of Egypt, and our world today offers many Egypts . . . We can go to medical doctors and accountants—and, at times, we should. We can go to the self-help, do-it-yourself section of the bookstore—and often we do need information from experts. We can hire someone to fix what broke, anything from a computer to a car to a refrigerator—and certainly that's prudent.

But getting help isn't the same as fully relying on that help. Getting help can even be an obedient response to the Lord's guidance.

So don't go to God only as a last resort, only after the world's suggested remedies or solutions have failed. Go first to the one true God for He—and He alone—can supply your every need, protect you from every enemy, and guide you to make wise decisions. Let seeking God always be the default for your life.

Ambassadors of Mercy

I appeal to you for my son Onesimus.

PHILEMON 10

Onesimus was a runaway slave whose name meant "useful," once useful to his master Philemon and then useful to Paul. Today his story helps us learn about being agents of reconciliation . . .

Scripture is silent about why Onesimus fled from his master, although it is generally assumed he absconded with some of his master's funds or property. However, after Onesimus became a believer, he was extremely helpful to Paul (v. 11). In fact, this slave's life was so transformed by God's love that he was willing to return to Philemon to face the consequences of his past sins.

Although the acceptable punishment for Onesimus's offense was death, Paul exhorted Philemon to see Onesimus not as an unworthy slave but as a spiritual brother. Paul's personal intervention in the life of a new convert is exemplary for all believers.

Every Christian is God's ambassador for reconciliation, forgiveness, and new hope in Christ. We must look at the heart of a person rather than the outward appearance or circumstances. God demonstrated through Paul's appeal that mercy is always preferable to harsh legalism.

You yourself have received mercy from the Lord. To whom can you extend that same mercy today?

Good News!

The beginning of the gospel of Jesus Christ, the Son of God.

MARK 1:1

Gospel means "good news." Heralds used this term to celebrate the pivotal moments in the lives of Roman Caesars. In the Christian era, *gospel* came to be identified with the good news of the life, death, resurrection, and second coming of Jesus Christ.

In sharing this good news, Mark painted a picture of Christ in action, of Jesus busy doing the will of the Father. No time is spent on the frivolous: this simple book focuses on the most basic elements of how God demonstrated His love for us in sending His Son to die as a sacrifice for humanity's sin. Mark brought us face-to-face with the gospel message as quickly as possible, and he urged the reader to waste no time believing and joining Christ in His mission to bring salvation to others.

It seems inconceivable that today you and I could withhold the good news of Christ from people who haven't yet recognized Him as God's Son and their Savior. After all, their eternal destiny is at stake.

Ask God to help you know whom you can talk to today about His Son. Join the ongoing story of God's redemptive work among the prophets of the earth.

Preserving Unity

Reject a divisive man after the first and second admonition, knowing that such a person is warped and sinning, being self-condemned.

TITUS 3:10–11

One reason God's people can be His light in this world is the remarkable love the Holy Spirit enables us to show one another. The unity of a wide variety of individuals—people from various cultural, educational, social, racial, economic, and even religious backgrounds—is a noteworthy manifestation of that love.

That's why Paul strongly warned about tolerating troublemakers in the church. People who consistently bring division are not walking in the Spirit no matter what they claim. A disruptive person is in bondage to sin and is therefore an enemy to God and His people.

To "reject" a divisive person was to condemn that behavior and to exclude that person from the religious community. Religious law provided many opportunities for that person to repent (the "first and second admonition," for instance); exclusion was a last resort. In our generation characterized by indiscriminant tolerance, exclusion sounds almost un-Christian, but bringing discord into the body of Christ is a serious offense that profoundly harms God's people. It therefore had to be taken seriously and dealt with decisively.

What are you doing to contribute to the unity—or disunity—of Christ's body?

The Race of Faith

*Since we are surrounded by so great a cloud of witnesses, let us
lay aside every weight, and the sin which so easily ensnares us,
and let us run with endurance the race that is set before us.*

HEBREWS 12:1

At times, living the Christian life can seem impossible, but a host of saints from throughout history provide powerful testimony to God's faithfulness as well as to the wisdom of staying true to Him. People have faced every manner of persecution, opposition, tragedy, crisis, temptation, and disappointment, yet remained loyal to their Lord. You can do the same.

Life is a journey. Every person is moving toward a final destination. However, there are sins and weights that can encumber us and trip us up. We must be ever diligent so that we do not become so entangled in worldly cares that we are no longer advancing with Christ.

One of the purposes of Scripture is to encourage us, and the examples of those who have gone before us do exactly that. The Bible provides concrete evidence that God strengthens, comforts, and guides His people during hard times. In its pages the lives of believers shout out, "God is faithful! Stay true to Him and you will experience His gift of abundant life."

Tough Love

If you endure chastening, God deals with you as with sons;
for what son is there whom a father does not chasten?

HEBREWS 12:7

It's a fundamental truth, not a throwaway cliché, that God loves you too much to leave you as you are. He will therefore work in your life and in your heart to make you more like Christ.

Don't misunderstand God's discipline in your life. It is not spiritual warfare and an attack from the enemy. It is not a sign that God does not love you or has abandoned you. It is instead an indication that God loves you deeply and is determined that you experience His very best.

The word *chastening* reflects this truth. The Greek means "correction, discipline, training, and nurturing, with the goal of improving one's character." Just as our human parents corrected us because they loved us, our heavenly Father will reprove and discipline us because He loves us. When He sees us straying from His path, He will not sit by idly and watch. When He sees us falling into sin, He will not ignore it. When He sees us getting lazy in our devotion, He will allow us to suffer the consequences. He will love us with persistent and transforming love. That's what a loving Parent does. He will bring to bear on our lives whatever is needed so our lives become like Christ's and bring honor to Him.

Our Perfect Parent's Instructions

He who loves [his son] disciplines him promptly.

PROVERBS 13:24

Proverbs offers practical guidelines for living a life that honors God.

- PROVERBS 13:24: Discipline carries the positive and negative meanings of reproof, correction, instruction, admonition, and training. God will not hesitate to intervene in our lives when He sees us, His children, straying into danger, and we should raise our children with that same diligent love.

- PROVERBS 17:6: Offspring are a divine gift, and with that blessing comes responsibility. The parents' character and choices have a tremendous impact on their children's future.

- PROVERBS 19:18: If we teach our children to fear the Lord while they are young, and if we model loving Him with all our heart, soul, and mind, we can help them avoid much suffering and disappointment down the road.

- PROVERBS 20:7: Our actions have a greater impact than we realize, and our children are directly affected by our choices. That truth should motivate us to approach parenting prayerfully.

- PROVERBS 22:6: As God leads and guides His children according to His ways, so parents should be intentionally involved in directing their children.

Look to your perfect heavenly Father as you rear the children He has entrusted to you.

Spiritual Perception

*"It has been given to you to know the mysteries of the
kingdom of heaven, but to them it has not been given."*

MATTHEW 13:11

This was Jesus' answer when His disciples asked Him why He spoke in parables when He taught.

Jesus explained that not everyone is privileged to understand His teachings and the truths of His kingdom. We can't know spiritual realities through mere physical senses. In fact, there is a profound difference between knowing through our own perception and understanding reality through spiritual eyes and ears.

Sin doesn't impede our ability to taste a meal or hear the doorbell. Sin, however, does dull our capacity to hear God's voice and recognize His activity. Sin dulls our spiritual senses.

There were many people in Jesus' day who saw Jesus but who did not recognize the Son of God. Their physical sense of sight worked fine; their spiritual sight was blinded by sin.

How are your spiritual senses? Could Jesus be working in and around your life but you're not recognizing His activity? Could God be trying to get your attention but you're not noticing? Could God be seeking to teach you a heavenly mystery yet you are not grasping it? Ask God to remove anything that is keeping you from recognizing all He is doing in your life today.

Our Unchanging God

Jesus Christ is the same yesterday, today, and forever.

HEBREWS 13:8

That simple, straightforward statement holds great riches to be uncovered.

To begin with, consider the qualities of God that are especially meaningful to you during this season of your life. Perhaps you think of His presence with you, His faithfulness, or His goodness. Maybe you focus on His holiness, justice, and perfection. You may think of His redemptive power and His ability to bring beauty out of ashes. Or you are clinging to the fact that He is all-powerful, all-knowing, and sovereign over the unfolding history of this world as well as your own personal pilgrimage. Whatever divine characteristics come to mind, know that God has always been that way and will always remain that way. Find comfort and peace in that assurance.

Now consider some implications of God's unchanging nature. The way Jesus led His twelve disciples is the same way He will lead you . . . The love Jesus expressed on the cross is the same compassion He extends to you . . . The power that raised Jesus from the dead is the same power available to you today . . . The same discipline He used on others will be meted out to you if necessary . . . Count on the certainty that Christ will not change and then live boldly in light of that wonderful truth.

Lifelong Faith

I your servant have feared the LORD from my youth.

1 KINGS 18:12

So declared the faithful prophet Elijah. We find in 1 Kings tips for living a life of faith just as he did.

- If we don't diligently follow God's commands, we—like Ahab—can too easily trivialize sin, become comfortable with it, and no longer see it as offensive to God (16:31).
- A lifetime of following God prepares us for times of crisis and uncertainty. Though we may not always understand our situation, experience tells us God is trustworthy. We can find comfort in a proven relationship with our God even when, like Elijah's, our faith is shaken (19:1–18).
- The world gives its counsel, and the Bible states its truth. We must choose between the two. We can't live in two worlds, as the people of Israel tried to do when they worshiped Baal as well as God. If we truly believe Jesus is Lord, our lives will verify our faith.
- Often we expect God to visit us in spectacular ways. We must learn to also recognize God when He speaks in a still, small voice (19:12). God's Word is no less powerful when He whispers.

As you walk with your Lord, listen, trust, and obey.

Desperately Discouraged

Cursed be the day in which I was born! Let the day not
be blessed in which my mother bore me! . . . Why did I
come forth from the womb to see labor and sorrow?

JEREMIAH 20:14, 18

The prophet Jeremiah didn't sugarcoat his feelings, did he? For more than forty years, Jeremiah faithfully ministered despite overwhelming opposition. This "weeping prophet," as he came to be known, found his heart breaking over the sins of his people and the difficult circumstances he endured. As a man of God, Jeremiah was constantly at odds with the authorities, both political and religious. An angry King Jehoiakim, for instance, burned the prophet's scroll piece by piece as each section was read publicly.

As if witnessing that were not painful enough for Jeremiah, the people of Israel whom he loved hated him. Despite his patriotism, he was branded a traitor as he prophesied judgment upon Judah and Jerusalem. He praised God, yet complained about the miserable conditions of his role as prophet.

It's not unusual for people encountering weighty spiritual battles to experience discouragement and to temporarily lose perspective. But God is faithful. He will uphold His servants and renew their strength as they turn to Him for comfort. God did that for Jeremiah; He'll do that for you.

"Doers of the Word"

Be doers of the word, and not hearers
only, deceiving yourselves.

JAMES 1:22

It's been pointed out that just as sitting in a garage doesn't make you a car, sitting in church doesn't make you a Christian. In the same vein, listening to solidly biblical sermons doesn't make you a follower of Jesus. Neither does reading God's Word religiously.

After all, as James pointed out, knowledge without action is useless. Knowing who God is and how much He loves you without loving Him and obeying Him in return is empty. Knowing what God demands and desires from His people but not doing any of those things is meaningless. Knowing calls for a practical response. The person who truly believes God's Word is not the one who studies it the longest or who argues most eloquently on its behalf. The person who truly believes God's Word is the one who incorporates it into his or her life.

We are to do what God's Word tells us to do, and we are to shun all that His Word designates as sin. That is how we express our faith. We deceive ourselves when we merely nod along in agreement with God's truth but do nothing in response.

Delighting in God

O Lord, our Lord,
How excellent is Your name in all the earth,
Who have set Your glory above the heavens!

PSALM 8:1

Key to understanding the psalmist's words of praise is knowing that God's name reflects His character. For instance, the name *El Shaddai* means "All-sufficient or Almighty One." *El Elyon* means "the Most High God" and refers to God's supremacy and sovereignty. The names of God reveal who He is.

Here the psalmist was truly delighting in who God is and what He is like. Look at the picture of God's amazing creation that the psalmist painted—"When I consider Your heavens, the work of Your fingers, the moon and the stars, which You have ordained"—and hear how he was humbled and awed by what he saw: "What is man that You are mindful of him, and the son of man that You visit him?" (vv. 3–4).

Within the majestic expanse of the universe, we are insignificant specks. Yet our infinite God sees us, knows us intimately, and loves us ceaselessly. Such divine consideration is truly beyond our comprehension.

O Lord, our Lord, Your love for me is truly amazing! Teach me to delight in You.

Faith

[Abraham] did not waver at the promise of God through unbelief, but was strengthened in faith, giving glory to God.

ROMANS 4:20

Abraham was one hundred years old and Sarah was ninety when God gave them Isaac, the son through whom all the earth would be blessed. His parents waited many years for his birth, and because they were human, some seasons of their waiting were characterized by faith more than others were. Here in Romans 4:20, Abraham is praised for his faith.

The Greek word *pistis*, translated "faith," means trust or confidence with the important nuance of obedience. Faith is belief in action. In the Bible, faith is belief in and commitment to God. Faith obeys God's commands no matter the circumstances. Faith in Christ—believing that His death and resurrection covered our sin and gave us access to a holy God—is necessary for salvation. Inherent in that belief is repentance from sin and the willful decision to follow Christ as Lord.

The sure evidence of a relationship with God is faith. Only those who know God will trust Him. So, if you struggle to have faith in God, spend more time getting to know Him. God wants to grow your faith so that it does not waiver. The greater your faith, the more you will glorify Him. Let Him strengthen your faith today.

Keep Your Eyes on God

We have no power . . . nor do we know what
to do, but our eyes are upon You.

2 CHRONICLES 20:12

In times of tranquility and prosperity, we face the constant danger of turning away from God to pursue our own goals and desires. In those good times we must diligently guard our hearts by remembering that our peace and prosperity are always gifts from Him.

When we are in the midst of trouble and pain, however, we more easily acknowledge our helplessness and dependence on God. But we may also ask hard questions about His love and power. In those times we may be tempted to doubt God or even abandon our faith. We must remember that no crisis is beyond God's control and that nothing can separate us from His love.

In good times or bad, it is always right to keep your eyes on God and trust in His wisdom. Be assured that no situation taxes His sovereign power.

Then, when God does deliver you, be sure to tell others of His mercy. People are watching your life. Your friends, your colleagues, your children, and even your enemies can learn about trusting God when they see you turn to Him in periods of ease and seasons of strife.

Where is your life focus right now?

Seeing Salvation

*Exhort bondservants to be obedient to their own
masters . . . showing all good fidelity, that they may
adorn the doctrine of God our Savior in all things.*

TITUS 2:9—10

The culture Paul addressed here was different from our own, yet the point he made here to servants is equally valid for those of us who are servants of the Lord today. Consider Paul's message . . .

Working people spend a great percentage of time at their jobs. Their most important mission field may be their colleagues and customers. Christian workers approach each day as an undeserved opportunity to share Christ with others through their words and actions.

If you are going to be an effective witness for Christ, don't be lazy! Don't be a complainer. Don't do substandard work. Don't put in minimal effort. You represent Christ! Honor Him with your labor.

Be Bold

Let us therefore come boldly to the throne of grace, that we may obtain mercy and find grace to help in time of need.

HEBREWS 4:16

The safest place to go when we have sinned is the throne of grace.

In Hebrews 4:15 we read that Jesus Christ can commiserate with our human weaknesses. *Sympathize* means "to suffer with," and even though Christ did not sin, He is able to sympathize with our struggles. The pressure to sin is intense and the temptations we face are powerful, yet Jesus understands what we are going through. He knows well the spiritual battle we are engaged in.

Therefore—because Jesus knows what the contest against sin is like—we are able to go before Him. Our confident approach is unlike an Old Testament high priest who always feared that his sacrifice might not be acceptable to the Lord. The consequence for that would be his life, taken in judgment.

We have the resurrected Lord as our High Priest. He was the perfect sacrifice for our sin, so we can—and we should—purposefully and boldly approach His throne of grace. The One seated upon that throne has mercy and grace in abundance for the humbled sinner.

He knows what we are going through; He knows what we need, and He can give us that which we seek. Go to Him today!

Being Watched

*[Ahaz] did not do what was right in the
sight of the LORD his God.*

2 KINGS 16:2

W ouldn't yesterday have gone better had you checked
in with the Lord more often? Don't you wish you'd
stopped and asked God for direction before making that decision? Wouldn't it be great if calling on the Spirit to give you
self-control were a way of life?

It's a sobering truth that all our deeds—good and bad—are
done in God's sight. The Lord watches our busy days, quick
decisions, and unplanned reactions and knows whether or not
our lives honor Him.

God wants you to honor Him with all you say and do; He
wants your life to radiate your love for Him; and He wants
the next generation to remember you as a person of faith. His
Spirit is at work in your life to make all this happen.

Furthermore, God is not the only One watching your life.
When you cry out to God, the world sees God's goodness to
you and watches how God responds to someone who trusts
Him and who turns to Him. They learn that trust in God
brings deliverance.

So, as God blesses you and people watch Him work in your
life, keep your eyes on Him. And remember, everything you
do, absolutely everything, is done in the sight of God.

Fallow Ground, Hardened Hearts

For thus says the LORD . . .
"Break up your fallow ground,
And do not sow among thorns."

JEREMIAH 4:3

Gardeners know what happens when soil is left alone for too long.

Like land that has never once been cultivated, soil that hasn't been tilled for lengthy periods becomes hard, full of weeds, and difficult to work with. Yet, according to God's law, farmers were to leave their fields uncultivated every seventh year. Obedience to that command meant rejuvenated, productive soil, not barren farmland, a sharp contrast to long-ignored and unprepared soil that is not welcoming to seeds that could bring new life.

Today's verse in Jeremiah is not a farming tip from the Lord, though. It is a call to His people whose hearts have become hardened like an irresponsible farmer's fallow soil. Hearts that have not been tilled with God's Word for some time become hard, full of weeds, and unresponsive to God's activity. Such unprepared hearts do not welcome seeds of God's truth that could bring new life.

A heart left untended can harden and become impervious to God's Word. There is too much at stake for you to be unprepared to respond to God's next word to you. What will you do today to keep your heart tender and receptive to God?

Who, Me?

*Adulterers and adulteresses! Do you not know that friendship
with the world is enmity with God? Whoever therefore wants
to be a friend of the world makes himself an enemy of God.*

JAMES 4:4

Adulterers and adulteresses? James couldn't be addressing
you—or could he? . . .

God wants us to love Him with all of our being. He is a jealous God who will not share His rightful place in our hearts
with anyone or anything. But we human beings are easily distracted by the world with its immoral, self-indulgent outlook
on life. James boldly declared that if we love either the sinful
pleasures of the world or the good things of the world more
than we love God, then we have committed spiritual adultery.

The world, which can indeed be alluring, sees God's wisdom
as foolishness. Yet, to God, the world's wisdom is folly and its
values lead to death. So will you look for joy in the pleasures the
world offers or in God and His will for your life? Your choice
reveals who is Lord in your life, and the results confirm the differences between God's ways and the world's.

Following the wisdom of the world—like committing adultery—leads to destruction. Don't deceive yourself: you are not
immune to such unfaithfulness.

Receiving and Giving Comfort

*Blessed be the God and Father of our Lord Jesus Christ,
the Father of mercies and God of all comfort, who
comforts us in all our tribulation, that we may be able to
comfort those who are in any trouble, with the comfort
with which we ourselves are comforted by God.*

2 CORINTHIANS 1:3—4

When has the companionship of a Christian friend been a source of comfort to you? When, by simply being next to you, has a fellow believer given you hope and eased your pain? In those times you have been "comforted by God" through His people.

Think about the times when God has used you—and your experience of being strengthened with His comfort—to console others. Consider what you were able to offer because you yourself had known not only pain but the Lord's peace as well.

Jesus' death on the cross for our sin opened the way for us to enter God's presence and enjoy fellowship with Him. Abiding in His presence, we can draw on His strength and know His comfort in any trial, and we are to share that strength and comfort with fellow believers.

God allows people to experience pain but He also provides heavenly comfort. Were it not for our suffering, we would have no need of the Comforter.

Let God bring specific, thorough, lasting comfort to you today.

Called to Serve

"The Son of Man did not come to be served, but to serve, and to give His life a ransom for many."

MATTHEW 20:28

Like any proud parent, Salome wanted her sons to have seats of honor in the kingdom Jesus was establishing. So she went to Jesus, knelt before Him, and made her request.

Jesus recognized that this misguided follower was blinded by the values and ways of the world. He gently responded: "You do not know what you ask." Then He asked the sons a question: "Are you able to drink the cup that I am about to drink?"—a cryptic reference to the cup of His imminent crucifixion and the baptism of His sacrificial death (v. 22).

At issue was the radical difference between the kingdom of God and the systems of this world. The world tells us to look out for ourselves; God tells us to give ourselves away. The world tells us to rule; God tells us to serve. The world tells us to be first; God tells us to put others ahead of ourselves. The King of kings came to serve. The world will see Jesus in us when they see us serve.

You cannot build God's kingdom using the worlds methods and values. Let Christ show you where the world has crept in to your thinking, and your heart.

The Wait of Faith

Those who wait on the LORD
Shall renew their strength;
They shall mount up with wings like eagles,
They shall run and not be weary,
They shall walk and not faint.

ISAIAH 40:31

The Hebrew slaves waited for generations for deliverance from their Egyptian taskmasters . . . The faithful children of Israel waited even longer for the Messiah . . . You are undoubtedly waiting on the Lord to answer a yet-unanswered prayer . . . And all of us are waiting for Jesus' second coming as the glorious Victor over sin and death . . .

Waiting on the Lord is an act of faith. After all, when circumstances bear down on us, we're tempted to grow impatient and orchestrate our own relief effort. Yet sometimes there really is nothing we can do.

But God is at work in us as well as in our circumstances as we wait. He is concerned about the people we become as we wait on Him.

If you tenaciously trust the Lord, He will renew your spirit and strengthen you for any challenge.

This comforting truth God shared with the children of Israel is for you as well . . . because their God is your God.

So wait in peace.

Signs of His Glory

This beginning of signs Jesus did in Cana of Galilee, and manifested His glory; and His disciples believed in Him.

JOHN 2:11

In his Gospel, John didn't set out to provide an exhaustive chronicle of Jesus' life (21:25). Instead, this apostle's goal was to present Jesus in a way that convinces readers of His deity, so John included seven specific signs that clearly prove this. Signs were divine acts that pointed directly to God.

John knew that Jesus' miracles served as a witness to His divinity and testified that He was the Messiah. For those with spiritual eyes to see, Jesus' actions were proof that He was God's Son and the fulfillment of prophecy.

At the wedding in Cana (2:1–11), for instance, Jesus did the miraculous in the most ordinary circumstances. Through His divine activity people saw God's glory revealed, and they chose whether to believe in Jesus or to reject Him.

In what ordinary—or maybe not so ordinary—circumstances did God accomplish the miraculous and help you see that you are a sinner in need of a Savior? How has God been demonstrating to you, even through ordinary events, that He is the Son of God and that He loves you? Thank God for that miraculous work in your life and thank Him that He cares enough about you to convince you of who He is.

Taming the Tongue

No man can tame the tongue. It is an
unruly evil, full of deadly poison.

JAMES 3:8

We've all been victims of that poison, haven't we? Many of us can still remember evil words spoken to us years ago; emotional, psychological, and relational scars may remain. Sadly, many of us can also recall poisonous words that we have uttered unthinkingly, spoken in anger, or spoken because . . . Who really knows why?

Curbing our tongue is a choice we make. But the fact that no person can tame the tongue means that only the Holy Spirit can free us from sinful talk, so we have to invite Him to do exactly that. We must acknowledge both our limitations and the fact that we need His help. Otherwise we will continue to start forest fires with our words.

James was not overstating the damage we do with our tongue. Bridling such a strong force calls for the power of the Holy Spirit, a power that is much stronger than our mere will-power. So invite Him—right now—to teach you to think before you speak, to call on Him when self-control seems out of reach, and to enable you to forgive those who, like you, struggle to sub-due the poisonous tongue.

Surrender your words to the Holy Spirit and let Him trans-form them into instruments of grace.

Appreciating Godly Leaders

Be an example to the believers in word, in conduct,
in love, in spirit, in faith, in purity.

1 TIMOTHY 4:12

When God chooses a spiritual leader, it's definitely a tall order to fill—from a human perspective.

When God appoints a spiritual leader, character—not age—is the determining factor.

When God calls a spiritual leader for His people, that person will be effective only to the degree that he or she is in a solid, life-changing, life-giving relationship with the Father.

Serving God calls for godly people, but even for the most saintly among us, service is not a right. Rather, service in God's kingdom is a privilege given to those who walk with God and who reflect His character.

If you are blessed to be in a position of leadership, ask God regularly to help you serve Him with a humble awareness of the privilege He has granted you. Ask God to make your life a godly example that others can emulate for their good.

If you are blessed to be led by godly leaders, pray regularly for them, thank God for them, and express your appreciation to the leaders themselves. Humble servants who faithfully handle the Word of God are a rare and precious gift to the church and ought to be treated as such.

In God's Sight

Do not enter into judgment with Your servant,
For in Your sight no one living is righteous.

PSALM 143:2

Any one of us can feel good about our righteousness if we compare ourselves to someone else. There is always someone less spiritual, more selfish, and prouder than we are. After encountering someone like that, we can piously mutter to ourselves, "Well, I may not be perfect, but I'm sure a lot better than . . ."

Then we encounter God. In His holy presence we become keenly, awkwardly, ashamedly aware of our sin. Before His righteous gaze we are embarrassed by our flimsy and inadequate excuses for our failings. When we stand before God and His radiant holiness, every sin in every corner of our lives is revealed in all of its hideous wickedness.

And that is often why we avoid entering His presence. The penetrating light of His holiness is far too invasive for those of us who will not relinquish our sin. If we want to reside in God's presence, though, we must see our sin as He views it. We must confess and turn from it so that when God looks upon us, He sees not our sin but the glorious shed blood of our Savior who has made us pleasing in God's sight.

SEPTEMBER

Open my eyes, that I may see
Wondrous things from Your law.

PSALM 119:18

Enduring Mercy

Oh, give thanks to the LORD, for He is good!
For His mercy endures forever.

PSALM 136:1

Mercy always precedes grace, but they always go hand in hand.

Before God gives us what we do not deserve (grace), He first withholds from us the judgment we have coming (mercy). God is, by nature, merciful: He does not treat us as we rightfully deserve. Rather, in loving grace, He pours out His forgiveness over us. For such mercy and grace we can never praise Him enough.

Imagine if God's mercy were to somehow expire, though. What if one day He'd had enough of forgiving our sins—those sins that we can't seem to master or turn away from? What if He were to reach a point where He decided to mete out exactly what we deserve as punishment for our sins, our faithlessness, our self-centered ways? Of course that turn of events would violate His own gospel: "For God so loved the world that He gave His only begotten Son, that whoever believes in Him should not perish but have everlasting life" (John 3:16). But if God's mercy were to expire, we would perish.

"Oh, give thanks to the God of heaven! For His mercy endures forever" (Psalm 136:26).

"Come and See"

Nathanael said to him, "Can anything good come out of Nazareth?" Philip said to him, "Come and see."

JOHN 1:46

It's not enough to know what the Scriptures say about Jesus, study the doctrines concerning Him, or ponder His teaching. There's only one way to really know Jesus: we must follow Philip's advice and experience Jesus for ourselves.

That's because Christianity is essentially a relationship with a Person. What we experience as we follow Jesus inspires us to love Him, share His truth, and continue following Him.

John told of a blind man healed by Jesus—on the Sabbath. The Jews, outraged that Jesus would violate the law and commit such a flagrant sin, confronted the man about who Jesus was. The man's answer was straightforward: "Whether He is a sinner or not I do not know. One thing I know: that though I was blind, now I see" (9:25). The healed man did not have all of the doctrinal answers. But one thing he did have was a life-changing encounter with Jesus.

We may not be able to respond to all the critics or answer the cynics' every question about our Lord. But we can, like the man Jesus healed, proclaim with confidence that "though I was blind, now I see." Our relationship with Jesus has indeed changed our lives forever.

Lessons from Israel

I wholly followed the LORD my God.

JOSHUA 14:8

Learn the following lessons from Israel, and you may be able to join Joshua in his confident declaration.

- Pray – Joshua prayed and "the sun stood still in the midst of heaven, and did not hasten to go down for about a whole day" (10:13). Prayer is primarily designed to change us. Yet when we pray for God's purposes, nothing is impossible.
- "Wholly follow" God – Wholeheartedly following the Lord calls for focused effort. You cannot seek to please others if you want to follow Him wholly. You cannot protect your interests and guard your comforts and still fervently follow God. It's also impossible to remain proud and humbly follow God.
- Remember – Our generous God expresses His love for us by protecting and providing for us. We must be mindful of all God has given us—we must list our inheritance (15:20)—lest we inadvertently commit the sin of ingratitude.
- Trust – "Not a word failed of any good thing which the LORD had spoken" (21:45) could be the theme of the book of Joshua. After forty years of wandering in the wilderness due to their unbelief, Israel learned that God is always true to His word.

Which lesson on faithfulness will you focus on today?

Giving Thanks

And one of them, when he saw that he was healed,
returned, and with a loud voice glorified God, and fell
down on his face at His feet, giving Him thanks.

LUKE 17:15—16

Consider some amazing facts about our Lord: Jesus' love draws sinners to Him. His righteousness doesn't make us feel condemned . . . The Great Physician welcomes and embraces people in need of healing—spiritual, emotional, or physical . . . Individuals who know rejection and betrayal, who don't feel loved or worthy of love, can find unconditional and unending love in Jesus.

Those of us who truly understand these truths about what God has done for us in Christ cannot thank Him or praise Him enough. Consider the one leper—of the ten whom Jesus healed—who returned to thank Him. This man recognized his unworthiness, and everything within him cried out, "To God be the glory!" May we do the same when we see God at work in our lives and in the lives of people around us.

True disciples of Jesus rejoice and worship God with a grateful heart whenever He does a healing, restorative work in their lives. Grateful people are those who truly understand how amazing it is that almighty God cared enough to become involved in their life. Have you thanked the Lord today for all He has done for you?

Responding to God's Word

[Ezra the priest and later the Levites] read distinctly from the book, in the Law of God; and they gave the sense, and helped [the children of Israel] to understand the reading.

NEHEMIAH 8:8

God's Word is powerful. It can fashion a universe and it can create life. It can transform a life or a nation. It can initiate judgment or it can bring revival. It can transform sinners into saints. Yet often God's people do not clearly understand what Scripture is saying. That is why God gives His people preachers and teachers. In Ezra's time God's people had drifted far from God, so Ezra taught them God's Word. As the people came to understand it, they fell under conviction and turned from their sin. The nation experienced revival because God's Word was taught clearly and accurately. When God's word is clearly understood, it is extremely difficult to remain indifferent to it.

Have you been a careful student of God's Word? Are you currently in a Bible study? Do you listen intently to your minister's sermons? What might happen in you as well as in your life if you better understood God's Word?

Real Love

We have known and believed the love that God
has for us. God is love, and he who abides in
love abides in God, and God in him.

1 JOHN 4:16

Our language needs more words for love. We use the same word to describe our feelings about pizza, our children, soccer, the dog, our spouse, ice cream, our favorite music, weekends, and God! Here we are talking about God's love for you and your love for Him and His people.

First, God doesn't love us because we are of use to Him. What could Almighty God need us to do that He couldn't do (better) on His own? Yes, God chooses to use us, but He doesn't love us just because we serve Him. Instead, God loves us because He places value on us. You are precious to God.

Now consider this: "He who loves God must love his brother also" (v. 21). The clearest evidence that you are a child of God is that you love His people. If you refuse to enter meaningful relationships or are easily offended and angered, you have actually uncovered a problem in your relationship with God. He is love, and He wants to express His love through you. If God loves someone, who are you not to love that person as well? Abide in God, and you will love others.

Devotion, Rebellion, or Something Else?

O LORD . . . You have stricken them,
But they have not grieved . . .
They have made their faces harder than rock;
They have refused to return.

JEREMIAH 5:3

There is—and always has been—a wide range of reactions to God. People may choose heartfelt devotion or total rebellion or, somewhere in the middle, apathy and disregard.

In Jeremiah 5:3, the phrase "faces harder than rock" refers to the deliberate, conscious choice to reject God, His ways, and even His people. Having a face harder than rock comes with the adamant decision to not walk in the ways God has outlined for His people. The inevitable consequence is judgment.

There is also danger in complacency. When the Lord asks later in verse 22, "Do you not fear Me? . . . Will you not tremble at My presence?" He makes clear that He is not a friend to those who regard Him as merely one among many. The one true God whom we come to know through Scripture speaks with a voice that supersedes all else.

You may not be willfully rebelling against God, and you may be committed to not becoming apathetic about your spiritual life. But what specifically will you do today to fuel your devotion and experience more fully the abundant life God wants you to know?

Submit . . . Resist . . . Draw Near . . .

Submit to God. Resist the devil and he will flee from you.
Draw near to God and He will draw near to you.

JAMES 4:7−8

These three sentences are typical James: he offered practical instructions as he exhorted believers to live a righteous life. Look at these points one at a time.

- SUBMIT TO GOD . . . The word *submit* means "to subordinate to, obey, or become subject to another person." When done voluntarily out of love, submission to others is an act of humility and service. It is also recognized as an act of obedience to Christ.
- RESIST THE DEVIL . . . Christians are not commanded to bind Satan, but rather to resist him. Only God can conquer Satan, but every believer can resist him. We can follow Jesus' example in the wilderness (Luke 4:1–13) and respond to Satan's temptation with truth from Scripture.
- DRAW NEAR TO GOD . . . How encouraging to know that when we draw near to God, He immediately comes closer to us! So how do we draw near to God? We repent of our sin, and we purge our lives of unrighteousness.

Like many of God's commands, these are simple to understand but not easy to do. Rely on God's Spirit to help you, one practical step at a time.

Whose Vision Is It?

"Do not listen to the words of the prophets who prophesy to you.
They make you worthless;
They speak a vision of their own heart,
Not from the mouth of the LORD."

JEREMIAH 23:16

The Lord made it clear to me that I should . . ." "I asked the Lord to show me—and look at the verse He gave me . . ." "God told me that you . . ."

A dangerous and far too common occurrence is projecting our own wishes onto God. We conceive a desire in our hearts and convince ourselves—or, as in the case of Jeremiah 23:16, we convince others—that this plan must be God's will.

After all, we Christians know the lingo to make our idea, as well as the process by which we arrived at our conclusion, sound holy. We realize that calling on the Lord's authority makes it difficult for others to disagree with us. We're all good at rationalizing—with or without holy talk—whatever it is we want to do.

So, when an idea comes to you, pray . . . search the Scripture . . . get counsel from other believers you know and trust . . . Ask the Lord to make His will known—and to make it distinct from your own desires if the two don't line up. It is foolhardy to give God credit for your own selfish thinking! Do whatever you must until you are certain that your direction in life is based on a clear word from God.

Living Under His Lordship

"Assuredly, I say to you that tax collectors and harlots enter the kingdom of God before you."

MATTHEW 21:31

The chief priests and elders challenged Jesus: "Who gave You this authority [to teach]?" (v. 23).

Jesus responded not with an answer, but first with a brilliant question that left his critics paralyzed. Then He told a story about a son who initially said no to his father's call to work in the vineyard, but later changed his mind and went. The other son immediately agreed to go and work, but he never did (vv. 28–31). One said the correct things; the other did the right thing. Jesus left no doubt which is more pleasing to God.

Then came Jesus' stinging rebuke (v. 31). He could not have chosen a more socially offensive group than tax gatherers and harlots.

Clearly, Jesus was unimpressed with pious words and hollow orthodoxy; He was looking for action. He pointed out through His parable that actions speak louder than words. Anyone can say the right things about what he will do or what she believes, but God sees what we actually do. To call Jesus Lord is not enough; we must live under His lordship and do what He says.

Why Do You Serve?

"Do you seek great things for yourself? Do not
seek them; for behold, I will bring adversity on all
flesh," says the LORD. "But I will give your life to
you as a prize in all places, wherever you go."

JEREMIAH 45:5

The human heart is not known for its pure motives.

For instance, we make a meal for someone even though we don't especially want to because that's easier than living with the guilt if we don't. Or we serve in the church out of obedience and a genuine love for God, but we don't mind the recognition that may accompany a center-stage role—and might those accolades sometimes even be the reason we serve?

Mixed motives can become full-blown, self-serving ambition, and such personal motivation is foolhardy since it places us out of step with God's activity. Our chief aim ought to be doing God's will, not acting on our own agenda and fulfilling our own dreams. We need to prayerfully determine what God is doing in the world around us, ask Him what role He wants us to play in that activity, and then wholeheartedly obey His instructions.

Dying to self takes many shapes, and one is relinquishing one's own goals when they are not aligned with God's plans. Our supreme ambition ought to be to live our lives daily in the center of God's will.

An Anchor for Life

This hope we have as an anchor of the soul . . .
where the forerunner has entered for us, even
Jesus, having become High Priest forever.

HEBREWS 6:19—20

A glance at the headlines of the daily newspaper . . . A reading of our own emotions . . . A look at our family . . . It doesn't take much in this fast-moving, God-ignoring world to show us that we need an anchor for our lives.

We find that anchor in Jesus. Our hope for this life and for eternity lies not in ourselves but in Christ. He is absolutely faithful to do what He has told us He will do—to forgive our sins, to guide our steps, to be with us always, and so much more. God always fulfills His promises to us. Our confidence in the future is therefore rooted in Him.

In addition to being our anchor in this world, Jesus is also our "forerunner" for the next. *Forerunner* refers to small boats that help larger ships enter a harbor by carrying their anchor into a safe place and thus preparing the way for the larger ship. Jesus Himself precedes us into the harbor of heaven. He carries the anchor of our hope that is His resurrection victory over sin and death, and He makes way for our eternal future. No wonder the Christian is filled with such hope!

From Tears to Joy

Those who sow in tears
Shall reap in joy.
He who continually goes forth weeping . . .
Shall doubtless come again with rejoicing.

PSALM 126:5—6

Aren't these verses encouraging? From tears to joy, from weeping to rejoicing—that's a radical transformation. The almighty God, for whom nothing is impossible; the all-loving God, whose plans for you are plans for good; the all-wise God who knows what is best for each one of His children—our God has the power to bring beauty from ashes. He brings hope in the most difficult circumstances.

The promises found in these verses characterize the Lord and the transforming work He can do in your heart and life. God can transform your tears into joy. Whatever reasons for those tears, we who serve the Lord can always have hope in Him. We know that He can completely transform even the worst situation; we know that His presence can turn tears to joy and sorrow into celebration.

The Crucifixion preceded the resurrection. That was God's power at work. Whatever loss or death, whatever pain or struggle you're dealing with, know that God can bring into your situation new life, genuine joy, and heartfelt rejoicing. That's the God we serve.

Choose Life

"If he has walked in My statutes
And kept My judgments faithfully—
He is just;
He shall surely live!"
says the Lord GOD.

EZEKIEL 18:9

Since the beginning when God spoke face-to-face with Adam and Eve, He has invited His people to choose life rather than death. His law (at first the simple "Of the tree of the knowledge of good and evil you shall not eat" [Genesis 2:17]) has made the choice clear for us: will we obey and thereby choose life?

At the heart of every sin is our fundamental disregard for God's will. Consider your life. Don't the consequences of your sin make it obvious that you should return to God?

As we Christians seek to follow God, we stumble and fall, we ask forgiveness, and—by God's grace—we receive it. Therefore many of us wrongly conclude that judgment is reserved for those who do not belong to Christ. The Bible does indeed teach that the lost are judged for sin because they reject the Savior's redemption (John 3:18). But the saved—you and I—will also be judged according to the way we live our lives (2 Corinthians 5:10).

So choose to follow God—to faithfully keep His ways—and you will please your Lord. That is a life worth living.

Confession of Faith—and Sin

*If you confess with your mouth the Lord Jesus
and believe in your heart that God has raised
Him from the dead, you will be saved.*

ROMANS 10:9

When we hear the word *confess*, we probably think of sin. We know we're to confess our sin so we can be forgiven and enjoy fellowship with a holy God. From Genesis through Revelation, we read about the dreadfulness of sin and the importance of confession.

Notice how *confess* is used in Romans 10:9. The Greek behind this word means "to say the same thing" or "to agree." In the context of acknowledging sin, *confess* means agreeing with God about our sinful condition. In the context of Romans 10:9, *confess* means agreeing with God about the importance of His Son's death and resurrection. The simple but profound phrase "Jesus is Lord" is considered the earliest Christian confession.

Confessions of faith and of sin, however, involve more than intellectual assent; these confessions include the desire to align our lives with God's truth. Confession of sin is perhaps motivated initially by the knowledge of divine judgment and our need for cleansing. But believers whose relationship with Jesus is deepening are moved to confession out of their heart-felt desire to allow nothing in their lives to separate them from their Savior.

Watchful Obedience

As the eyes of servants look to the hand of their masters,
As the eyes of a maid to the hand of her mistress,
So our eyes look to the LORD our God
Until He has mercy on us.

PSALM 123:2

The more attentively he watched the hand of the master—a hand that gestured instructions—the more valuable a servant was. The more carefully she focused on the hand of her mistress, the more effectively the maid could serve.

Similarly, the sharper our focus on the Lord, the more aware we'll be of His presence and His work around us. But if we are to recognize the Spirit's work, we must have spiritual discernment, or else God can be at work all around us and we will miss it. It does not take much for us to be distorted. We can lose focus for just a moment and miss an important message from our Master.

So learn to watch for God at work in the world around you and be prepared to serve your Master with all your heart. If you are preoccupied with your own concerns or pursuing your own goals, God will see that you are not prepared to be involved in His activity—and He will find a servant who is.

Loving Discipline

"I am with you," says the LORD, *"to save you . . .*
I will not make a complete end of you.
But I will correct you in justice,
And will not let you go altogether unpunished."

JEREMIAH 30:11

Once again we see God the Father parenting His wayward people. When discipline is necessary, He will act. He loves us—He loved Israel—too much *not* to act.

God makes it no secret: He will judge sin. He will not look the other way; He will not pretend we didn't stray. Instead—like the perfect Parent that He is—God promises His people that He will discipline us for our sins. The promise doesn't end there, however. God also assures us that He will be with His sinful, disobedient children throughout the process of His chastisement. He will even use His discipline to strengthen our love for Him and faithfulness to Him.

Like a parent who disciplines a child, God—after He disciplines us—always lifts us up in His arms in an act of love and compassion. He shows us that He is ready for a fresh start to His relationship with us.

If God is disciplining you now, be open to His fatherly correction. Receive His discipline—and then receive His embrace. His correction is always intended to enrich our relationship.

A Transformed Life

Peter, an apostle of Jesus Christ . . .

1 PETER 1:1

Peter was a fisherman-disciple of John the Baptist when Jesus called him to be among His twelve disciples.

Peter had a heart of ready obedience (Luke 5:5), a remarkable faith (Matthew 14:28–29), and a depth of spiritual insight beyond that of his contemporaries (16:16), yet Peter was extremely human. For instance, he proudly proclaimed his unwavering allegiance to Christ unto death, yet soon after Jesus' arrest, he denied to a servant girl even knowing Jesus (Luke 22:33–34).

This cowardly act was devastating and humiliating, but Christ shaped the newly humbled Peter into a courageous and compassionate leader of the early church. Peter performed miracles, carried the gospel to the Gentiles, wrote books of the Bible, and eventually died as a martyr in Rome. Legend claims that Peter felt unworthy to be crucified like his Lord and begged his executioner to crucify him upside down. Peter came a long way from his miserable night of failure to his triumphant martyrdom.

Just as Jesus transformed Peter in order to use him to evangelize the world, Jesus can transform you. Peter's life was forever changed after he learned to die to self, be made alive in Christ, and be filled with the Spirit. Yours will be too.

The Law—and Love

Moses began to explain this law.

DEUTERONOMY 1:5

The Hebrew word translated *law* means "teaching" or "instruction." The first five books of the Old Testament are collectively referred to as the "Books of the Law," but Deuteronomy is the clearest exposition of God's Law.

God presented the Law as a guide for His covenant relationship with His people, a relationship He initiated with Abraham four hundred and thirty years earlier. The people of Israel were struggling to uphold their end of the covenant, and God intended the Law to draw them into a deeper relationship with Him.

The basic principle underlying the relationship between God and His people is love. God initiated the covenant relationship with His people out of love, and Deuteronomy challenges believers to follow and obey God not out of a sense of duty or religious ritual, but out of their devotion to Him.

If we love God, we will want to know His laws and commandments so we can obey Him. Just as the Israelites needed to remain close to God and walk in His ways if they were to conquer the Promised Land, we need to do the same if we are to have victory in our lives.

How well do you know what God expects of you? How carefully are you doing what He says?

Building Faith

Jesus made His disciples get into the boat
and go before Him to the other side.

MATTHEW 14:22

Among the twelve disciples were seasoned fishermen and sailors. So the disciples obediently climbed into the boat, and Jesus went off to pray.

When the boat was in the middle of the Sea of Galilee, however, the weather changed—drastically. The wind and waves kicked up, and the boat was tossed violently by the churning water.

However unsettled the rough weather may have been, the disciples were more terrified when they thought they saw a ghost walking toward them on the water. Then the "ghost" spoke: "Be of good cheer! It is I; do not be afraid" (v. 27). An excited and impulsive Peter walked toward Him on the water, sinking only when he took his eyes off his Lord.

Times that deeply challenge your faith will inevitably occur in your life. Eventually a situation will require you to trust God to a greater degree than you have ever had to trust Him before. Don't be shaken. Keep your eyes steadfastly on Jesus. He can see you through any storm. And, when He does, you will have grown to trust Him at a deeper level of faith than you ever have before.

Friend or Foe?

For if by the one man's offense many died, much
more the grace of God and the gift by the grace of
the one Man, Jesus Christ, abounded to many.

ROMANS 5:15

Sin was in the world before the Law of Moses, before there was a clear law to obey or disobey. And sin still resulted in death because all mankind inherited the consequence of Adam's transgression: "by the one man's offense many died." After God gave the Law to Moses, sin meant disobedience, going against the knowledge of God's will.

Into this world of disobedient human beings, God sent His Son to suffer the consequences of our sin and die on the cross on our behalf. Salvation is receiving this gift of Jesus' death in our place. Salvation is not a reward for deeds done. It comes only by grace; it cannot be earned.

When we receive the gift of salvation, we are made righteous before God. But to be made righteous is not a transformation of character. We are made right through the sacrifice of Christ.

Similarly, peace with God is a position before Him, not an emotion. Peace with God means to be in a state of peace as an ally and friend, not in a state of animosity as an enemy of God.

The fruit of Jesus' sacrifice on the cross will be experienced and celebrated by myriads of saints throughout eternity!

"How Long?"

The LORD said to Moses: "How long will these people reject Me? And how long will they not believe Me, with all the signs which I have performed among them?"

NUMBERS 14:11

All I have needed His hand hath provided," the hymnist wrote. Yet still we wonder . . . *How in the world can we afford college? . . . Where will I find a job now that I've been laid off? . . . Will God really help me if I step out in faith?*

How much evidence of God's faithfulness will it take before we learn to trust Him? Refusing to believe God, even though He continues to provide for us, is an affront to our loving God. It reflects an unbelief that hurts the heart of God. If you're a parent, you undoubtedly understand that pain.

God's provision—which is always enough and always on time—is one of His tangible ways of expressing His love for us, His children. Do you recognize the Father's love in all He gives you? Or do you grumble and complain when what you have doesn't satisfy you? Have you learned to expect God's provision whenever you have need? Teach yourself to thankfully receive all that God gives you as evidence of His love and faithfulness, and then you'll find it easier to trust Him next time.

"Love Is of God"

Beloved, let us love one another, for love is of God; and everyone who loves is born of God and knows God.

1 JOHN 4:6

The first epistle of John challenges us in three areas: are we obeying God's law, loving God and His people, and believing correctly about the person of Jesus Christ? John's letter also exposes the falsehood that threatens the church, affirms the reliability of Scripture, and calls believers to pray confidently to God.

Love is a theme that runs throughout 1 John. In fact, John used the word *love* forty-three times. He emphasized that a Christian will take on the nature of the heavenly Father—and that God is love.

Broken relationships with God's people, therefore, are symptomatic of a sin-damaged relationship with God. Our Lord, however, doesn't ask us to cultivate a deeper resolve to put away our sin. Instead He wants us to seek Him with our whole heart so we will not sin. Our efforts are not primarily toward holiness, but toward Him; as we draw near to Him He will sanctify us.

Our love relationship with God determines every other relationship we have. So let your relationship with Him transform your sinful life so you can better love those around you. A pure heart is capable of loving others as God loves them.

Faith for Battle

The LORD our God spoke to us in Horeb, saying:
"You have dwelt long enough at this mountain."

DEUTERONOMY 1:6

We will never be the people God wants us to be if we don't spend time with Him.

Every one of us needs some time on a spiritual mountain with God, but He does not set people free to remain on a mountain. After all, any mountaintop encounter we have with God is not merely for our encouragement; it is also intended to strengthen us for battle. Victories are ultimately not won by extended worship times on the mountaintop, but by going into battle and fulfilling God's purposes for our lives.

Some people are tempted to take up permanent residence on their spiritual mountaintop, but that makes them unavailable for God's service—and they don't experience fresh spiritual victories. Other believers neglect their time with God in order to rush into the next battle for Him. These people inevitably experience humiliating defeat.

During certain seasons throughout our lives and even at occasional points in our week, we need to withdraw from life's battles. At other times we need to leave the mountain and advance on the enemy. God knows which you ought to be doing. Be sure you are seeking His will and obeying His call.

"Open My Eyes!"

Open my eyes, that I may see
Wondrous things from Your law.

PSALM 119:18

The story is told of a prisoner locked away in solitary confinement for thirty-three years with a single book: the Bible. After he died, the people who cleaned out his cell found some interesting sentences etched on the wall:

Psalm 118:8 is the middle verse of the Bible.
Ezra 7:21 contains all the letters of the alphabet except the letter J.
The ninth verse of the eighth chapter of Esther is the longest verse in the Bible.
No word or name in the Bible has more than six syllables.

Clearly, this prisoner was captive to more than a jail. He was constrained by blindness to the relevance and the truth of God's Word. He spent years, even decades, with the Bible and came up with only odd bits of trivia. Tragically, the timeless words of Scripture apparently did not touch his heart.

Even the most brilliant scholars who study God's Word will remain unchanged by its truth apart from the work of the Holy Spirit. God's Word does not simply provide information. It draws us to Him, and He gives us life. God Himself opens our eyes to the truth of His Word and makes the Scriptures come alive to us. Don't settle for information. Strive for transformation!

"No Fool"

*"Behold, I send an Angel before you to keep you in the way
and to bring you into the place which I have prepared."*

EXODUS 23:20

As Jim Eliot prepared to give his life to missions, he earnestly sought God's direction. One day he came upon Exodus 23:20, and instantly he recognized this verse as God's confirmation that he should go to Ecuador to minister to the Auca people. There Eliot would lay his life down for the cause of Christ.

Earlier on Eliot had observed, "He is no fool who gives what he cannot keep, to gain what he cannot lose." This attitude of total surrender to God inspired countless others to seek God's leading for their lives. In fact, Elisabeth Eliot and widows of the other men martyred with her husband returned to the Auca people, and—by God's grace—many of those people chose to surrender their lives to Christ.

Eliot was no fool: he gave up his life for his Lord. Your sacrifice may not be as dramatic as Eliot's, but as you die to self in serving your spouse or family, your community or your nation for God's purposes and kingdom, you are no fool. You are gaining eternal rewards that you cannot lose.

Blessings from God

*Blessed be the God and Father of our Lord Jesus
Christ, who according to His abundant mercy
has begotten us again to a living hope through the
resurrection of Jesus Christ from the dead.*

1 PETER 1:3

Stop for a moment and think about the many ways God has blessed you. Here are some ideas to get you started . . . People to love—and who love you . . . The calling to be His child . . . Freedom to worship Him . . . The Bible . . . The Holy Spirit . . . Forgiveness of your sins . . . Truth . . . Guidance . . . Hope . . . Clothes, food, shelter . . . Health, strength . . . Talents, abilities . . . Opportunities to serve Him . . . Ministries to perform . . .

Current blessings like these—and these are wonderful— are but a foretaste of what is yet to come. Christian rewards have been prepared, but we have not yet fully received them. Our almighty and ever-faithful God promises His people a magnificent inheritance, and that is a hope that will not disappoint those of us born into God's family.

The abundant life that Jesus came to give us starts the moment we accept Him as our Savior and Lord. It lasts throughout eternity, where the blessings of heaven—of living in the presence of God—are glorious beyond description.

Is That Really What You Want?

All the children of Israel complained against Moses and Aaron,
and the whole congregation said to them, "If only we had died
in the land of Egypt! Or if only we had died in this wilderness!"

NUMBERS 14:2

Complaining about our circumstances reveals our refusal to accept God's sovereignty over our affairs. Grumbling is an act of rebellion against His Lordship.

The children of Israel (like us) were a complaining bunch. They criticized the menu, bemoaned their lack of water, and critiqued Moses' leadership. Too many times they cried out, "If only we had died in the land of Egypt!"—conveniently forgetting how difficult the slave labor was, especially when the pharaoh started issuing impossible-to-meet quotas.

One of God's methods of discipline is to give people what they foolishly request. In Numbers 14 God used this method: "The carcasses of you [twenty years old and above] who have complained against Me shall fall in this wilderness" (v. 29). God granted the Israelites their desire to die in the wilderness . . .

At times our greatest folly is getting exactly what we want. So be open with the Lord about your desires, but be just as open to His work in your heart to shape those desires to match His perfect and loving plan for you. And be careful. God might just give you what you are asking for!

Praise—or Pride?

*"Because you have increased in height, and it set its top among
the thick boughs, and its heart was lifted up in its height,
therefore I will deliver it into the hand of the mighty one of
the nations . . . I have driven it out for its wickedness."*

EZEKIEL 31:10–11

Once a powerful nation, Assyria couldn't withstand Babylon's attacks—even with Egypt's help. In reference to this fact, God used the metaphor of a tall tree. Its growth was due to subterranean waters and to the Lord, but the tree did not acknowledge its debt. Instead, it boasted in its height, so the tree—the great Assyria—was chopped down.

In our pride we, too, fail to see our accomplishments as fueled and blessed by God. We fail to give God credit for the ways He enables us to fulfill the tasks He calls us to do. We tend to take credit for our accomplishments instead of acknowledging that our abilities as well as our success are God's gifts.

In light of how God deals with haughtiness (consider Assyria's fall and God's punishment of His own people), we are wise to praise the Lord for the success and victories in our lives and to daily rely on Him for strength.

Pride has brought many a great leader and nation down. We must stay alert for we are not immune to pride's charms.

Hearing—and Responding

All the proud men spoke, saying to Jeremiah, "You speak falsely! The LORD our God has not sent you to say, 'Do not go to Egypt to sojourn there.'"

JEREMIAH 43:2

Well, the Lord did in fact forbid Israel's flight to Egypt— but God's word to us is not always what we want to hear, is it? His word to us, however, *is* always what we need to know. We are wise to obey whatever God says, regardless of what we expected, what we hoped for, or what others think.

We also need to be open to hearing God's message to us. After all, if we are halfhearted in our desire to hear from Him, we will be unprepared to respond to what He says. In fact, there is little point in seeking God's will if there is no determination to follow it. If our response depends upon convenience or favorable answers to our prayers, we are better off not asking.

We need to be aware that it's sometimes easier to discount God's messenger than to heed God's message. Many a pious protest against the words of an emissary are nothing more than the stubborn refusal to heed what God is saying.

What does your present response to God's word to you reveal about your heart?

OCTOBER

The kingdom of God is not in word but in power.

1 Corinthians 4:20

Remembering God

Because you have forgotten the God of your salvation,
And have not been mindful of the Rock of your stronghold . . .
The harvest will be a heap of ruins
In the day of grief and desperate sorrow.

ISAIAH 17:10–11

Forgetting God does not refer merely to an intellectual act. Remembering God or forgetting Him is evidenced in action or lack of action, and both reflect the condition of a person's heart.

Remembering God means putting Him first, making an effort to focus on Him, feeding on His Word, seeking His guidance in daily decisions, and following His ways. Forgetting God is obvious in the absence of such actions.

Easy times bring the temptation to forget our dependence on God. In contrast, times of stress and hardship remind us of our utter reliance on Him. The wise never cease to rely on God in times of prosperity or in times of pain.

Here is a prayer of remembrance . . .

Give us enough trials to keep us strong,
enough tears to keep us tender,
enough hurts to keep us humane,
enough failure to keep us humble,
and enough faith to keep us confident in You,
O Lord, our Rock and our Redeemer.

A Countercultural Way

*Do not swear, either by heaven or by earth or with any other
oath. But let your "Yes" be "Yes," and your "No," "No."*

JAMES 5:12

Christians are to be different from people who don't know
Jesus as their Lord and Savior. Sometimes those differences are obvious, sometimes they're subtle, but they're always
important as we seek to be God's light in our darkened world.

One subtle yet powerful way we can be different from the
world is to simply let our *yes* mean "Yes, we will" and our *no*
mean "No, we won't." In sharp contrast, the world fortifies its
promises with oaths, contracts, and elaborate verbiage.

When we speak straightforwardly, when we offer with integrity a simple yes or no, we reflect the God we love and serve.
After all, when God speaks, what He says is pure truth, and
whatever He promises will transpire. There is perfect consistency between His spoken word and His actions.

As God's people, as His representatives, we should also
speak pure truth. We must follow through on everything we
promise, which also means we should be cautious in making
vows. Always keeping our word ought to be important to us.

*Lord God, help my speech and behavior reflect You and Your
love. May my words bring honor to you.*

Spirit-Powered Victory

*Whatever is born of God overcomes the world. And this
is the victory that has overcome the world—our faith.*

1 JOHN 5:4

We all like to succeed, don't we? And there is no greater triumph than what Jesus accomplished on the cross: His victory over the power of sin and death enables us to be in relationship with God Almighty, our heavenly Father.

The victorious Christian life is lived out day by day, hour by hour, as we—by the power of God's Spirit—break sinful patterns in our lives and obey God. The victorious Christian life is the Spirit's response to our faith.

God gave us the gift of His Holy Spirit, and when we seek to obey God's will, the Spirit's power is released in us. According to Ephesians 1:19–20, that power is the same "mighty power which [God] worked in Christ when He raised Him from the dead and seated Him at His right hand in the heavenly places."

Are you presently overcoming the world, or is the world overcoming you? There is no temptation or persecution at the world's disposal that can defeat Christ in you.

The strength to overcome is a gift of God—and we have a great deal more power than we know. What will you do today to access that power and experience fresh victories in your life?

God's Thoughts

"For my thoughts are not your thoughts,
Nor are your ways My ways," says the LORD.
"For as the heavens are higher than the earth,
So are My ways higher than your ways,
And My thoughts than your thoughts."

ISAIAH 55:8

We don't always understand what God is doing . . . We wonder why He thought His timeframe was better than ours . . . We struggle to understand why He allows tragic things to happen to godly people who have already suffered plenty . . . We speculate about why the unbelievers down the street seem to have such a happy, easy life . . .

God's ways aren't our ways, are they? Neither are His thoughts. But a God we could understand—whose ways we could explain and even predict—wouldn't be very big, very powerful, or very wise. Our omniscient God knows the big picture. He understands how an action today affects eternity, and remembering that fact can be comforting.

The reality that God's thoughts are higher than ours impacts not only our perspective on life but also our approach to the Bible. We should not try to reduce God's Word to a level that makes sense to us. Rather, we should ask God to raise our thinking so we better understand His Word and gain His perspective on the world around us.

Are You Ready?

*"Watch therefore, for you do not know
what hour your Lord is coming."*

MATTHEW 24:42

Jesus' return will come suddenly and unexpectedly, and that truth raises two important issues.

First, do you know whether you are one who will be taken, or are you one who will be left behind? The determining factor is no secret: "Whoever calls on the name of the LORD shall be saved" (Romans 10:13; Joel 2:32). If you have recognized both your status as a sinner and Jesus' status as God's Son, sent to be the perfect Sacrifice for humanity's sin, if you have asked forgiveness for your sin, accepted Jesus as your Savior, and invited Him to be Lord of your life, you will be saved.

A second consideration: if Jesus stepped out of heaven right now, this very moment, to take you home, could you look Him in the eye? Christ's return is certain. And another certainty is that, on that day, we must all give an account of our lives— with no excuses. Are you ready to present your life to Christ and hear His evaluation?

"Watch therefore, for you do not know what hour your Lord is coming," Jesus says to you. Oh that we are ready when He comes!

Choices—and Consequences

We must all appear before the judgment seat of Christ.

2 CORINTHIANS 5:10

U nbelievers are not the only people who will one day give an account of their lives before the judgment seat of Christ. Believers will too, and that ought to make us tremble. It caused even the apostle Paul to tremble when he thought about that coming day (vv. 9–11).

Becoming a child of God does not free us from accountability; instead, that new relationship with Him actually intensifies the matter of accountability. God, whom we now call "Father," is also our Creator and our Judge. We respond to our heavenly Father's infinite love with heartfelt love for Him, but we must never lose our reverence for the Almighty.

Yet almighty God will never force His will on you, but He will always make you give an account for how you responded to Him and to His activity in your life. In this life, we have the freedom to choose our course of action—but we are not free to choose the consequences of our actions. We either receive God's gracious offer of salvation by faith, or we don't—and the eternal consequences of our choice are already set.

The choice is yours; the consequences, determined by God. But one thing is clear: we must all appear before the judgment seat of Christ.

Teaching and Learning

Teach me to do Your will,
For You are my God;
Your Spirit is good.
Lead me in the land of uprightness.

PSALM 143:10

Our ways are not God's ways, and God doesn't keep that fact a secret. His prophet Isaiah spoke on His behalf: "'For My thoughts are not your thoughts, nor are your ways My ways,' says the LORD" (55:8).

God's ways aren't our ways, so He must teach us to do His will. And the fact that He has given us His Word—and His Spirit— reveals His desire to teach us. The issue becomes whether we want to be His students.

Do you want to learn? Do you want to become skilled at living in ways that run counter to your nature? Do you want to do things that the world at large finds laughable? Do you want to live according to values that your society regards as old-fashioned? Do you want to look foolish in the eyes of your neighbors and co-workers, perhaps even your family and your friends?

The choice is yours. It's a choice that affects how you walk through your day. It's a choice that affects eternity. The Lord wants to teach you His ways. The question is, do you want to learn?

A Matter of the Heart

I will put My laws in their mind and write them on their hearts; and I will be their God, and they shall be My people.

HEBREWS 8:10

Here the writer of Hebrews quoted the prophet Jeremiah (31:31–34) as he addressed the covenant that God instituted through Christ. Key to that new covenant is the intimate relationship between God the Father and His sinful but repentant children, a relationship made possible by the cross.

This Old Testament reference underscores the truth that God's offer of salvation through Christ is not to give us a religion to follow. Instead, He wants to be in relationship with us and to make us more like Christ. God is not satisfied with outward religious activity. He wants our hearts and minds to be devoted to Him. He wants us to return the love He showed us in the sacrifice of His Son. We do that by worshiping Him, obeying Him, and walking with Him through life.

The Old Testament law governed God's relationship to Israel and included moral, ceremonial, and civil regulations. This law addressed the people's sins, but it did not change their hearts. On Calvary, our relationship with God became a heart issue.

What has God been writing on your mind and heart lately?

False Prophets

"The prophets prophesy falsely,
And the priests rule by their own power;
And My people love to have it so."

JEREMIAH 5:31

The Hebrew word for prophet is *nabi,* meaning "one who is called." The mark of biblical prophets is that God called them into His service and He gave them—as He gave Jeremiah—a message to deliver (Jeremiah 1:4–5). According to the Law, if the prophecy came to pass, the prophet was authentic. Those individuals exposed as false prophets were to be executed (Deuteronomy 18:20–22).

The twenty-first century has its own version of false prophets: they are people in the pulpit who merely say what people want to hear. Going to church to be entertained—a state of mind characterized by evaluating the performance of the worship band or critiquing the choir's anthem—makes us vulnerable to welcoming a sermon that amuses rather than convicts, to remember the anecdotes rather than listening for God's truth.

Never accept a preacher's words without verifying the message with God's Word. If you leave a service asking yourself what, if anything, you heard from the Lord, and you're not sure, the reason might be your heart as you listened . . . or the prophet as he spoke.

Owning One's Faith

They have walked according to the dictates of their own
hearts and after the Baals, which their fathers taught them.

JEREMIAH 9:14

What did your "fathers" teach you about God—or about other gods? Did your parents instruct you in the ways of the Lord? If so, be thankful. But maybe your family did not know the Lord and could not help you. If that's the case, did other people—who became fathers through the Spirit rather than by blood—teach you about God?

If you're a parent, what are you doing—or what have you done—to teach your children about God? Perhaps your children are being raised in a family that, for generations, has served the Lord, walked in His ways, and known His faithfulness and abundant blessings.

Even so, your children need to—as you did—come to the point of making the family's trust in God their own personal faith. Just as people from a long line of unbelievers must make a personal choice as to whether or not to follow Christ, people descended from many generations of saints must decide as well.

Each one of us is accountable to God for our own choices, regardless of our heritage. Some of us inherit a godly legacy. Others have the privilege of beginning one.

Passing the Tests

You, O LORD, know me;
You have seen me,
And You have tested my heart toward You.

JEREMIAH 12:3

There's nothing quite like a friendship that stands the test of time. Sharing history together, knowing what's not being said between the words, being able to finish each other's sentences, finding silence comfortable—these things characterize a relationship between two people who know each other well.

Such longstanding friendships have undoubtedly withstood other tests as well. Could the thoughtless comment be truly forgiven? Could the forgotten lunch date? Could the betrayal?

Likewise, our relationship with God needs to prove itself steadfast. Will we be faithful even when our prayers seem to go unanswered, when life is unfair, and when the pain we experience is beyond anything we'd ever imagined? Jeremiah knew what it was to have his heart tested by God, and you do too.

Times of God's testing are crucial for His people because they reveal whether or not He can trust us with important matters in His kingdom. Proving faithful in the test gives us confidence because we, too, learn how trustworthy we are.

If you're in a season of testing, let it strengthen your relationship with your God who knows you and loves you.

A Call to Praise

Behold, the Lord GOD shall come with a strong hand,
And His arm shall rule for Him . . . .
He will feed His flock like a shepherd;
He will gather the lambs with His arm,
And carry them in His bosom,
And gently lead those who are with young.

ISAIAH 40:10–11

God keeps the planets in their orbits—yet numbers the hairs on your head.

God is the Author of world history—and the Author of your own personal history.

God has "measured the waters in the hollow of His hand" (v. 12)—and has counted your every tear (38:5).

God's power guides the stars in their orbits—yet He is often portrayed as a gentle shepherd caring for His people.

Both realities in each of these preceding statements characterize your great and loving Lord. Meditate on the wonder of God, of the One whose unlimited strength is guided by His limitless love; of the One whose amazing love is made effective by His perfectly controlled power.

The King of kings is your heavenly Father. The Lord of lords calls you His child. The Alpha and the Omega is your Shepherd.

Yes, your God rules "with a strong hand," yet He tenderly gathers His lambs with that same arm. Worship Him now.

Confidence in the Lord

[Elisha] answered, "Do not fear, for those who are
with us are more than those who are with them."

2 KINGS 6:16

What situation in your life is making you nervous or fearful? In what set of circumstances are you feeling overwhelmed and helpless? Where would you like to see God demonstrate His power in your life?

God's presence in our lives is not merely a doctrine to believe; it's a reality to be lived out. We need to be mindful that every decision we make, every situation we encounter, and every stressful set of circumstances unfolds in the context of Almighty God's presence with us. May that truth give us hope and peace!

When a situation looks bleak, resist the temptation to assume that God must not care. You have no idea how close His answer may be. Don't give up! Today may be the day God does a miracle in your life. Just because you do not yet see the answer does not mean God is not preparing one in His perfect timing.

While you wait, you may find yourself confused, hurting, or worried. Find a friend to pray with you. In times of turmoil there is no better place to be than with someone who trusts in God. So don't be surprised when God places a fellow believer near you.

Infused by the Spirit

*There was a man in Jerusalem whose name was
Simeon, and this man was just and devout . . .
and the Holy Spirit was upon him.*

LUKE 2:25

When God is at work in the lives of believers, His Spirit of wisdom and truth infuses them with insight and understanding that come directly from Him. Simeon is a case in point . . .

The Holy Spirit had revealed to Simeon that "he would not see death before he had seen the Lord's Christ" (v. 26). When the Spirit led Simeon to go to the temple one day, Simeon obeyed—and God fulfilled His promise.

Mary and Joseph arrived with the holy Child, and Simeon was privileged to hold the young Jesus. "My eyes have seen Your salvation," Simeon sang his praises to God (v. 30). The older man blessed the Babe whose life would change the course of history . . .

The longer we serve God—and Simeon had served Him for decades—the more intimately acquainted with Him we become. When God has access to our heart, mind, and soul through years of fellowship and worship, He allows us to see more of His activity and to be more involved in His miraculous work. Stay alert! God is at work all around you!

Wise Words

If any of you lacks wisdom, let him ask of God, who gives to
all liberally and without reproach, and it will be given to him.

JAMES 1:5

In Hebrew thought, wisdom was the ability to apply god-liness to everyday living. Not merely head knowledge, wisdom was the practical ability to do the righteous thing in every situation. This was not an inherent human ability but God's gift. That's why we need to ask for wisdom. It is available to every believer who asks.

James had received God's gift of wisdom, but it did not make him proud. In fact, James described himself as a "bond-servant," meaning a slave or attendant who has given up personal rights to become subservient to another.

This humble and wise servant of God offers an abundance of practical, moral, and ethical instruction. Calling believers to lead righteous lives, James included suggestions on dealing with temptation, curbing the tongue, accessing the power of prayer, and demonstrating one's faith through action and not merely in words. He exhorted us to show compassion, love, and kindness to widows, orphans, and strangers. James taught that God is involved in our day-to-day lives and that He is pleased with even the simplest acts of faith, particularly those that express love practically toward others.

A Blessed Benediction

*Now may the God of peace . . . make you complete in
every good work to do His will, working in you what
is well pleasing in His sight, through Jesus Christ,
to whom be glory forever and ever. Amen.*

HEBREWS 13:20—21

Whatever God commands us to do, He fully equips us to accomplish. That truth is implied in "make you complete," a phrase that means "to equip, to thoroughly complete, to strengthen" and "to repair or mend what was broken." If we are to experience all that God intends for us, we must place our lives completely in His hands.

God knows what your life can become. He understands your potential for serving Him and impacting His kingdom, and He is unwilling to have you settle for less than His best. Nothing in your past or present daunts Him. You may grow discouraged, but He remains faithful. Patient and long-suffering, He will continue His work in your life—and He always completes what He starts.

So wholly submit yourself to God's good work in you until He has fully accomplished all that He wants to do in and through your life. Your Good Shepherd will guide, equip, strengthen, heal, provide for, and love you this day and always.

Fullness of Joy

In Your presence is fullness of joy;
At Your right hand are pleasures forevermore.

PSALM 16:11

I magine standing in the presence of almighty God as He sits upon His heavenly throne. What do you think you'd feel? Awe? Peace? Love? Safety? You would most likely experience all of these sensations. The psalmist David declared that in God's presence is fullness of joy (Psalm 16:11). This joy, emanating from God, results from His absolute power, love, and victory. The joy that radiates from God is powerful, pure, and delightful to those who walk closely with Him. Jesus said that those who truly understand the Christian life experience Christ's joy overflowing within them (John 15:11).

One of the clearest ways to determine how closely you are walking with God is to measure the degree of your joy. That's because abiding closely with God and experiencing joy are synonymous. There isn't one without the other. (Psalm 89:15) Joylessness indicates we have moved away from God and are no longer abiding in His joyful presence.

Many circumstances can draw us away from feelings of joy as well as its Source. Loss, rejection, criticism or hardship. Or the reason may simply be because we haven't spent time in His Word, in worship, and in prayer. There are numerous reasons why we drift away from God, but the result is always the same: less joy.

If you have lost your joy in the Lord, make your way, post haste, back into His presence, and bask in the undiluted, unquenchable, pure, refreshing joy of your Lord and the joy He has for you.

Sin . . . and Defeat

"Israel has sinned, and they have also transgressed
My covenant . . . . Therefore the children of Israel
could not stand before their enemies."

JOSHUA 7:11–12

Even when we are aware of God's presence and He is working mightily in our lives, we can be tempted to disobey Him. Even our smallest sin—as Israel learned—is not ignored however magnificent our previous victories have been . . .

The spies reported to commander Joshua that two or three thousand soldiers would be adequate to defeat Ai. This limited size reflects Israel's total confidence in God, a confidence fueled by their spectacular God-given victory over Jericho. In this battle, however, Israel sustained thirty-six casualties, a relatively small number, but this loss of life represented the people's first defeat under Joshua. If Joshua's forces could be defeated once, perhaps worse things were still to come.

The debacle at Ai also revealed that God's powerful presence will not remain upon a people who embrace sin. God explains, "Neither will I be with you anymore, unless you destroy the accursed from among you" (v. 12). God is not obligated to bless His children regardless of how we live. When we walk faithfully with Him, He defeats our enemies. When we are unfaithful, we suffer defeat.

Are you presently experiencing victory or defeat?

God's Glorious and Terrifying Presence

That all the peoples of the earth may know the
hand of the LORD, that it is mighty, that you
may fear the LORD your God forever.

JOSHUA 4:24

God dried up the Red Sea so that Moses and the children of Israel could escape the army of Egypt . . . God dried up the Jordan River so Joshua and the children of Israel could enter the Promised Land . . . God brought down Jericho's walls in an unforgettable manner. God did these things—as well as the other miracles recorded in the Bible, as well as His mighty work in your life—for His sake, not for Israel's sake and not for yours.

When God works powerfully through us, people around us see His activity, not our ability, and He is glorified and honored. God gives us victory primarily for His sake, not for our sake.

The people inhabiting the Promised Land saw God's powerful work, and they were terrified. God's servants are seldom impressive in their own right (and Israel was no exception); but God Himself is magnificent. Christianity's success through the centuries has not rested upon extraordinarily gifted followers but on God's all-powerful nature. It is still God who inspires people's awe.

What is God currently doing in your life that is bringing Him glory?

Isaiah's Example

Here am I! Send me.

ISAIAH 6:8

The prophet Isaiah saw the Lord enthroned in all His glory with seraphim surrounding Him and singing His praises: "Holy, holy, holy is the LORD of hosts" (v. 3).

Isaiah's response is an example to us: "Woe is me, for I am undone! Because I am a man of unclean lips . . ." (v. 5). People who see God as He truly is can only respond with heartfelt humility. After all, an encounter with our holy God immediately confronts us with our sinfulness.

One of the seraphim acted to purify Isaiah's mouth. Using tongs, he took a coal from the altar fire, touched the soon-to-be prophet's mouth, and announced, "Your iniquity is taken away, and your sin purged" (v. 7).

Cleansed from sin, Isaiah heard the voice of God—"Whom shall I send?" (v. 8)—and responded, "Send me." Thus began Isaiah's faithful response to God's call. He would be a mouthpiece for the Lord. Then, like now, when people encountered God's Word, they either yielded to God's will or their hearts grew hard.

Now consider God's call on your life. Are you following Isaiah's example and keeping your eyes on your King . . . allowing Him to cleanse you from sin . . . and remaining faithful despite people's response? Do you need a fresh glimpse of God upon His throne?

Too Much Like Judas

As soon as [Jesus] had come, immediately [Judas] went up to Him and said to Him, "Rabbi, Rabbi!" and kissed Him. Then they laid their hands on Him and took Him.

MARK 14:45—46

I t came as no surprise to Jesus, but it occurred so heart-lessly . . .

- The chief priests, scribes, and elders arrived in the dark of night to arrest One who was daily in the temple.
- The mob showed up armed to seize the Teacher who was unarmed except for His faith in His Father's perfect plan.
- Judas addressed Jesus as "Rabbi," an expression of respect, and kissed Jesus, an indication of affection—both of which must have pierced our Lord's heart like a sword.

Furthermore, when Judas made his treacherous plans, he asked the chief Jewish priests, "What are you willing to give me if I deliver Him to you?" (Matthew 26:15). Judas received thirty pieces of silver—the price of a common slave.

What a wrenching collection of cold-blooded details—but is Judas so different from us? What wrong deeds do we do in the dark of night? When do we feign affection but wound our Lord's heart? When have we spoken respectfully about and even to Jesus, but acted disrespectfully toward Him who is the Son of God? We might not be as different from Judas as we would like to think.

The Torn Veil

Jesus cried out with a loud voice, and breathed His last. Then the veil of the temple was torn in two from top to bottom.

MARK 15:37—38

The veil separated the people from the temple's Most Holy Place, and it had done so for centuries.

According to tradition, the veil—a handbreadth in thickness—was woven of seventy-two twisted plaits, each plait consisting of twenty-four threads. The veil was apparently sixty feet long and thirty feet wide. The fact that it was torn apart from the top down indicated that the tearing was an irrevocable act of God in heaven that gave people access to Him.

This tearing reflected the rending of Christ's body on the cross. He had just breathed His last. Death by suffocation, death on the cross—it was finished.

Yet it was also the beginning—the commencement of a new kind of intimate relationship between God and His people. Christ's death on the cross removed every obstacle that has separated—and could ever separate—people from God. Our Most Holy God is now accessible to everyone through Jesus Christ. It is we ourselves who erect any barriers that exist between God and us.

What barriers are you choosing to let stand? Jesus died to bring them down.

The Miracle Worker

"Having eyes, do you not see? And having ears, do you not hear? And do you not remember?"

MARK 8:18

God is doing miracles around us all the time.

Consider some of the wonders of your life. The fact that God got your attention and you responded by naming His Son your Savior and Lord . . . The miracle of a fresh start after a sin you long struggled to forgive yourself for . . . The miracle of hope in a world with new reports that strike terror . . . Take time to add to this list some more of the miracles God has done in your life.

Do you realize that God's activity—the miraculous work in your life that you just identified—is an expression of His character? The miracles He does are not just for our benefit; they are meant to reveal who He is and what He is like. We should always consider carefully what God's work reveals to us about Him.

We'll find it easier to learn from God if we take time to be quiet. When we are in His presence, it is far more important to listen to Him than to tell Him what we think He should do. We cannot hear Christ's voice when we are constantly talking.

It is possible to be in the presence of Christ as He performs miracles and yet be disoriented to what is happening. Keep your spiritual eyes open!

Disbelief and Unbelief

The Pharisees went out and immediately plotted with the Herodians against [Jesus], how they might destroy Him.

MARK 3:6

Jesus asked the man to hold out his withered hand. As he did so, "his hand was restored as whole as the other" (v. 5). As a result, the Pharisees wanted to kill Jesus . . . because this radical Rabbi had violated their law of the Sabbath.

Of course there was more going on than that. But why would anyone refuse to believe after seeing God perform a miracle? Because some people—like the privileged Pharisees—find God's existence and His power more of a threat than a blessing. Jesus challenges their lifestyle. They won't believe because they don't want to believe.

In contrast to this *dis*belief is the honest *un*belief of the father whose son was sick. Jesus told him, "If you can believe, all things are possible to him who believes" (9:23)—and the father immediately said, "Lord, I believe; help my unbelief" (v. 24). The father wanted to believe at a higher level.

This honest father shows us exactly where we should go when we have doubts: to Christ. After all, He alone can help our unbelief and strengthen our faith.

Disbelief—not wanting to believe. Unbelief—wanting help to believe. God will respond to both.

Called . . . to Stay?

Then [Jesus] appointed twelve, that they might be with Him and that He might send them out to preach.

MARK 3:14

Before Christ will send you out, He will draw you in. Notice that Jesus' call to His disciples—the Twelve then and us now—is twofold. It is primarily an invitation to spend time nurturing an intimate relationship with Him. But Jesus also wants us to venture out to spread His truth. Both aspects of the call are important because the power to go comes from having first spent time with Him.

That time with the Lord is crucial because His kingdom does not expand due to our human strength and wisdom. God's kingdom grows because His Spirit works in people's hearts. Any of our efforts to enlarge the kingdom are in vain without the empowering presence of God to lead us and to guide us.

Time spent with Christ is never wasted. As we learn His thoughts and His heart, we come to know and love Him more. Then when Christ knows we are ready, He will send us out. However, our success on the field will be determined not by our effort, but by the quality of time we spend with Him. Never be in such a hurry to go that you neglect to adequately draw near.

Amazing Attention

I am poor and needy;
Yet the LORD thinks upon me.

PSALM 40:17

He is the Creator of the universe and the Designer of the human body. He is the Author of salvation history and the Sovereign over world history. He sits enthroned as the ultimate Victor over sin, death, and pain. He keeps planets in their orbits . . . and your heart beating.

Yet the psalmist portrayed this almighty God, enthroned in the heavens, as bending down to listen to the entreaty of one of His children. It's amazing that our almighty God has any thoughts at all toward His creatures. But hear what the psalmist said: "Your thoughts toward us cannot be recounted to You in order; if I would declare and speak of them, they are more than can be numbered" (v. 5). The fact that God's thoughts toward us are innumerable is more than we can fathom.

God sits exalted above the universe. We are weak and needy creatures. Yet the Lord thinks of us, hears our cries, brings us up out of horrible places, sets our feet on rock, and puts a song of praise in our mouths (vv. 1–3). He is our Help and our Deliverer. Go to Him now with praise . . . as well as with requests for deliverance and His holy help.

We are all poor and needy. Only some of us recognize that fact.

Encountering Truth

*The natural man does not receive the things of the Spirit
of God, for they are foolishness to him; nor can he
know them, because they are spiritually discerned.*

1 CORINTHIANS 2:14

Without the aid of God's Spirit, the brightest human mind will never understand the simplest spiritual truth. That kind of truth is revealed only by a divine encounter, not through study, for Truth is a Person. Jesus is Truth.

The Spirit of God brings us to Christ and then unlocks the door to our understanding of spiritual realities. People who are unwilling to accept that Jesus is who He says He is can do nothing but follow a lie. People who accept Jesus as God's Son—and who welcome Him into their lives as Savior and Lord—continue to receive the Holy Spirit's help in understanding God's truth.

Consider, for instance, that God chose the way of the cross for salvation of sinful humanity. Its raw agony, the public humiliation, and the excruciatingly painful death were extreme measures reflecting our intense need for liberation from sin. No one could have predicted the cross, and "Christ crucified . . . [was] foolishness" to the Greeks (1:23)—and it still is to many today.

But an encounter with Truth plus a Holy Spirit-empowered understanding results in faith—and keeps our faith growing.

True Faith

The kingdom of God is not in word but in power.

1 CORINTHIANS 4:20

When Paul referred to the kingdom of God here, he meant the reign of Christ in the hearts of His people. Christ's reign in one's life is ultimately not verified by words or action—as important as those are. The evidence of genuine faith in Christ is His power at work in and through you.

The Holy Spirit is God's gift to empower us for life. This power is real in your life, for instance, when you witness God doing things that can only be explained by His awesome presence in you. God's power is real when He changes people's lives through you and when people glorify God because of what He did through you. When we take a step of faith, we experience in a real way the power of the Spirit working in us. Not surprisingly, we are more aware of God's power in us when we put ourselves in a position where we need that power.

Don't be satisfied with a Christianity of mere words. The kingdom of God advances by the power of the Spirit as He works through the living faith of believers. Don't be satisfied with powerless living. Seek to live each day of your life in the awesome power of almighty God.

Suffering for Righteousness

If anyone suffers as a Christian, let him not be
ashamed, but let him glorify God in this matter.

1 PETER 4:16

The Greek word translated "to suffer" originally meant "to experience something from the outside," whether good or bad. But over time the word lost the positive meaning. It came to be used solely for unpleasant experiences, for unjust punishment, abuse, threats, insults, or discrimination. The word is used forty-two times in the New Testament, mostly to describe Jesus' suffering on the cross and the persecution of His followers. Interestingly, Paul only used it seven times in all of his New Testament writings, while Peter used it eight times in 1 Peter alone.

The apostle Peter suggested that to endure unjust suffering for the sake of Christ is to follow His perfect example. It is not something for which Christians should feel ashamed. While unbelievers may experience good fortune on earth, they will ultimately suffer for eternity. Believers, however, may face adversity on earth, but their reward will be everlasting life.

Suffering is common to all people. We have the choice of suffering as a result of our sin and rebellion, or suffering as a result of righteousness. The former is *at* the hand of God, and the latter is *in* the hand of God.

"Add to Your Faith . . ."

*Add to your faith virtue, to virtue knowledge, to
knowledge self-control, to self-control perseverance,
to perseverance godliness, to godliness brotherly
kindness, and to brotherly kindness love.*

2 PETER 1:5–7

That's quite a list, isn't it? We're to "add" all these things to
the gift of faith in God which our heavenly Father gave
us when He called us into His family. The verb *add* suggests
there are steps we can take and efforts we can make to develop
these godly traits.

But, like every command in the Bible, God does not call us
to do something without enabling us to fulfill His command.

After all, knowledge, self-control, perseverance, godliness,
brotherly kindness, and love do not come naturally or even
easily to us. We need to be willing to work with God as He,
through His Spirit, develops these characteristics in us—
which He will do because He loves us.

Christians are to be content with their circumstances, but
not with their character. Until we are like Christ, we ought to
hunger for God to do more in our lives. Here Peter promises
that the Spirit will keep adding Christ-like qualities into our
lives—until we are just like Jesus.

Teaching That Refreshes

*[False teachers] are wells without water, clouds carried by a
tempest, for whom is reserved the blackness of darkness forever.*

2 PETER 2:17

In 2 Peter 2, the apostle warned believers about false teachers, pronounced doom against those who lead God's people
astray, and exposed their immorality and empty teaching.

Peter talked about false teachers being like wells without
water and clouds without rain. Such teachers are worse than
useless because they promise something they can not deliver
and deceive those who long for refreshment.

Peter went on to say in verse 21 that "it would have been
better for [these false teachers] not to have known the way of
righteousness, than having known it, to turn from the holy
commandment delivered to them." God's revelation of His will
is nothing less than an act of divine grace. We either receive
God's gift and enjoy His blessings, or we reject His grace and
suffer the consequences of life apart from God.

Having received God's grace, are you enjoying His blessings? And are you being careful to receive the life-giving,
faith-sustaining refreshment He provides through teachers
who are faithful to His Word? Stay clear of false teachers! They
will leave your soul spiritually parched.

NOVEMBER

I will praise the LORD with my whole heart.

PSALM 111:1

Be Ready to Speak

Sanctify the Lord God in your hearts, and always
be ready to give a defense to everyone who asks
you a reason for the hope that is in you.

1 PETER 3:15

The Christian life is a different life. It runs completely contrary to the way the world generally thinks and operates. Rather than glorifying God, the world rejects God and His standards. Yet Christians exalt the Lord and strive to obey His commands.

Furthermore, the world has no hope, no remedy for evil. Society cannot transform a sinner into a saint. And despite all of its feigned optimism and confidence in itself, the world is limited, finite, and spiraling downward. Death is as comprehensive as it is unavoidable.

Because the world has no hope—and because the world is bewildered by those of us who do—we must be prepared to provide explanations for our confidence and joy. Why do you treat Christ so reverently? Why do you have hope in the face of such despair? You are confusing to this world! Are you prepared to live a life that stands out in our fallen world? Are you ready to answer its questions?

Society's Norm—or Sin?

We have spent enough of our past lifetime in doing the will of the Gentiles—when we walked in lewdness, lusts, drunkenness, revelries, drinking parties, and abominable idolatries.

1 PETER 4:3

Maybe your walk of faith—the story of your conversion—doesn't involve a radical contrast between the "before" and the "after," but it does make God's grace no less remarkable. Even though your life may have seemed relatively devoid of sin, God helped you recognize your transgressions; He enabled you to see that you need a Savior. And He saved you! That is amazing grace.

Some people's coming to faith in Jesus, however, means a marked change in lifestyle. In Peter's words, they "walked in lewdness, lusts, drunkenness, revelries, drinking parties, and abominable idolatries" (1 Peter 4:3). Interestingly, nothing on Peter's list of ungodly behavior was considered particularly immoral in the Greco-Roman world of the time. When Christians chose not to participate in such activity, they were simply labeled antisocial.

Similarly, many ungodly behaviors today are accepted by society as perfectly normal. And modern society still has its idols. Drunkenness, lust, extramarital sex, greed, profanity, and other sins are generally accepted as the norm. Strenuously avoid these sins—despite how accepted they are all around you—and live as God's light. Don't let an evil world dull your sensitivity to God's presence and His will. Let your salvation continue to be a wonderful testimony to those around you of God's grace.

Join in Prayer

*Daniel went to his house, and made the decision known
to . . . his companions, that they might seek mercies
from the God of heaven concerning this secret.*

DANIEL 2:17–18

Nebuchadnezzar, king of Babylon, summoned the wise men of the land. He wanted them not only to interpret a dream he had but also to tell him what that dream was. The king was not merely looking for people's advice but for someone who heard from God. Should no one be able to discover the dream and its meaning, every wise man in the land would be killed.

That royal decree sent Daniel to his fellow believers—just as tough times should send us to fellow Christians to enlist their prayers and support. We don't have to face life's challenges alone; we can join our hearts in prayer with other believers to seek God's intervention, guidance, power, and hope.

So, if you are in a precarious situation, look first to God. Then see whom He has placed alongside you to intercede in prayer and to help you carry the burden. Ask your heavenly Father to show you who can walk beside you, extending their prayers and support—and then invite those folks to journey with you. All of you will be blessed.

No problem is too difficult when God's people unite together before God's throne.

From Slaves to Sons

*God sent forth His Son . . . to redeem those who were under
the law, that we might receive the adoption as sons.*

GALATIANS 4:4—5

"To redeem" means, literally, "to buy from the slave market." By His death on the cross, Jesus did just that for us: He bought us out of our bondage to sin.

After God redeemed us, He adopted us as His children and heirs. In Rome, adopted children had the right to be legal heirs as long as their adoption was performed in the presence of witnesses. The witness to our adoption into God's family is the Holy Spirit. The Spirit also joins us as family to Christ and to other Christians.

Furthermore, we are reborn as divine royalty, receiving a new nature through the Spirit.

Finally, we are privileged to call the almighty God "Abba," an intimate term for a father that was rarely, if ever, used in Judaism to address God.

Are you living this blessed reality? Are you enjoying the freedom of forgiveness, of having been bought out of your slavery to sin? Are you thriving in your Christian family? Are you calling out to Abba as a loving and loved child? Never lose the wonder that comes with knowing that you can call out to the Creator of the universe—and call Him Father!

Faith Alone

O foolish Galatians! Who has bewitched you that you
should not obey the truth, before whose eyes Jesus Christ
was clearly portrayed among you as crucified?

GALATIANS 3:1

The Galatians had knowledge: they knew that God, in His grace, had received them as His children simply because they expressed faith in Jesus as being both God's Son and the perfect sacrifice for their sin.

But the "foolish Galatians" didn't have wisdom: they were listening to legalistic Jewish teachers who insisted that new believers be circumcised as a means to salvation. Paul argued that such an act would be tantamount to falling away from salvation by grace and to trusting in human effort for salvation, yet the Galatians were easily swayed by confident-sounding Bible-quoting legalists.

Seeking salvation by works is pure folly. It's also flirting with the peril of straying from God's grace and into the bondage of legalism. That's a very real danger because no one is saved by the Law or by good deeds; salvation is by faith in Jesus Christ alone (2:16).

Every age has its imposters and heretics. They can appear confident that they have all the answers. Yet be careful. If you believe them you will shipwreck your faith. Don't be foolish!

Free to Serve

Stand fast therefore in the liberty by which Christ has made us free, and do not be entangled again with a yoke of bondage.

GALATIANS 5:1

People understand and love their liberty, their freedoms *from* as well as their freedoms *to*. Freedom from taxation without representation . . . Freedom to pursue one's dreams . . . Freedom from a forced religion . . . Freedom to live according to our beliefs.

The New Testament, however, presents true liberty as serving Christ and argues that we can be free only as we voluntarily give ourselves to another (Romans 6:18). In Christ—and because He broke the chains of sin on the cross—we have been liberated from sin, from the law, and from death. This freedom is not license to do as we wish, but to do as God wills. We are to exercise this liberty in love and service to God's family. Freedom from sin comes when we live with Christ as Lord over our lives.

But be alert! The world is filled with people, causes, and beliefs that will place you in bondage once more. This enslavement cannot be forced on you, but you can foolishly embrace it without thinking. Jealously guard the freedom that Christ has purchased for you.

"Come Near . . . to Hear"

Come near, you nations, to hear;
And heed, you people!
Let the earth hear.

ISAIAH 34:1

God invites you to draw near to Him so you can hear what He has to say to you. You won't hear His voice if you don't walk closely with Him. So draw near today and listen carefully.

Remember the first step on the pathway to God is holiness (35:8). We are not free to enter His presence any way we choose. We approach Him on His terms. We must be sanctified if we are to enjoy fellowship with Him. Key to being near enough to God to hear His voice is confessing your sin and receiving the forgiveness God offers. Then, cleansed from your sin, you are free to approach the throne of grace for guidance and comfort, for hope and instruction, for anything and everything you need.

However, listening to what God has to say is one thing; receiving it is another. When God speaks, His voice deserves our full attention and our immediate response. Don't skip this step!

Cleansing, hearing, and receiving—those three go together if we are to understand what God wants for our lives and then live our lives in such a way that we receive all that He offers to us.

A Matter of Perspective

You will keep him in perfect peace,
Whose mind is stayed on You,
Because he trusts in You.
Trust in the LORD forever,
For in YAH, the LORD, is everlasting strength.

ISAIAH 26:3—4

Hear the confidence in these joyful words. This worshiper has experienced God's deliverance and provision; this person's faith has been strengthened and trust in the Lord has grown. But that doesn't mean life is easy . . .

A sense of peace is not determined by your circumstances but by your state of mind. When you focus on God, His majesty, and His love for you, what is happening around you matters less. Pondering the character of the good and holy God you serve, remembering His faithfulness to His people through the millennia and to you personally, and standing strong in the truth and the promises of His Word—this kind of focus gives you a different perspective on what is going on in the world around you. You are mindful of who is in control and whose plan is unfolding.

Consider this analogy: A woman can brave labor pains because of the joy of receiving a child. Likewise, God's people can endure suffering because they know God will deliver them. Seeing your situation from the perspective of this truth brings peace. Keep your mind fixed on Christ, regardless of what is happening all around you.

God's Sustaining Word

Because you have made the LORD, who is my refuge,
Even the Most High, your dwelling place,
No evil shall befall you.

PSALM 91:9—10

During the early years of Charles Spurgeon's ministry in London, the city was swept by a deadly cholera epidemic. Over two thousand people died in just the first week.

Spurgeon exhausted himself tending to the sick and the dying, as well as performing the funerals of those who succumbed to the illness. Fatigue and the constant specter of death took their toll on the young pastor, sinking him into a state of depression.

While returning home from a funeral, the disconsolate minister passed an apothecary shop. In its window was printed Psalm 91:9. Spurgeon immediately grasped the truth of this verse, and he felt the dark cloud of depression lifted from his soul.

When has the Lord used a word from Scripture to speak directly to you at just the right time? Thank Him for doing so. Praise Him for His living and active and life-giving Word. Make time each day to sink your roots down into the nourishment that Scripture offers you. Like Charles Spurgeon, you will find the Lord meeting you in a personal and powerful way through His Word that will set you free.

Vengeance Is Whose?

In return for my love they are my accusers,
But I give myself to prayer.

PSALM 109:4

Have you ever been falsely accused of wrongdoing? Think back to the storm of feelings that threatened to swallow you up—or, if you've never had this experience, imagine the outrage, the anger, and the frustration you would feel in response to the lies about what you did and, by extension, about your character.

David knew what it was like to be maligned, but his response was neither revenge nor retaliation. His hope for vindication and justice remained in the Lord: "I give myself to prayer," he said. What a model for us!

Yet, as he prayed, David was extremely human and candid: he asked God to see that his enemy reaped what he sowed (v. 17 and Galatians 6:7). Still, throughout the psalm—and despite his difficult circumstances—David chose to praise God. He knew that God "shall stand at the right hand of the poor, to save him from those who condemn him" (Psalm 109:31).

Whatever the persecution, whatever the accusations, know that God stands with you. He will not let you face any problem alone. Vengeance *is* His.

Relentless and Ruthless

I will set nothing wicked before my eyes . . .
I will not know wickedness.

PSALM 101:3—4

As God's chosen people, we are to be relentless and ruthless in our avoidance of sin. Every one of us who is privileged to be called a child of God should be passionate about avoiding evil. After all, God is holy, and if we are to honor Him, we must actively pursue holiness. Both the pursuit of holiness and the avoidance of sin require determined effort—a striving fueled by the Holy Spirit, not by mere human willpower.

Refusing to "know wickedness" means we will not fill our minds with sin or take it in with our eyes. Yet our society—the supplier of many things that can fill our mind or that we can take in with our eyes—has a far different, far more lax standard for wicked than holy God does!

Rejecting wickedness therefore requires diligence on our part. We must be preemptive and proactive, or we will find ourselves beset by wickedness. We cannot trust others to protect what we see or watch. That's our responsibility.

Ask the Lord to make you sensitive to His holy standards and discerning in your choices. His Holy Spirit can and will help you scrupulously avoid evil.

Wholehearted Praise

I will praise the LORD with my whole heart.

PSALM 111:1

The writer of the old hymn got it right: "My heart is prone to wandering." If only that weren't so true . . .

Our hearts do wander . . . because our attentions are divided. Genuine praise—as Psalm 111 suggests—is *whole*hearted. A distracted mind and a divided heart are incapable of worshiping God as He deserves. But what can we do about our divided heart? We need wisdom to answer that question.

Thankfully, as the psalm goes on to say—"The fear of the LORD is the beginning of wisdom" (v. 10). Our fear of God—our awareness of His infinite love and mercy, His immeasurable grace and faithfulness, His unlimited power and goodness—brings humility. It reminds us that God deserves everything we have and not our careless, halfhearted praise. After all, God has adopted us as His children and given us the priceless gift of eternal salvation. How could we be stingy in our praise and worship of Him? How could we withhold even a small fraction of our hearts from Him?

Furthermore, God's Spirit is seeking to give us a new, transformed heart . . . an undivided heart. Focusing on our glorious God will not only prompt sincere praise but enable *wholehearted* worship. Make time to enter His presence and stand silently in awe.

A Family Resemblance?

Those who make [the idols] are like them;
So is everyone who trusts in them.

PSALM 115:8

B e careful about what you choose to worship because, Scripture warns, we will become like that which we worship. Whatever you spend time with will rub off on you. Just as spending time with wise people will make you wise (Proverbs 13:20), choosing to spend your time with worldly and wicked things will cause you to gradually adopt worldly and wicked values.

Furthermore, realize that whatever you instinctively turn to in times of trouble is an idol. The idols of the psalmist's day were powerless and unable to provide practical assistance (119: 5). Likewise, many modern idols appear to offer strength and joy, but those who trust in them soon discover that the idol's image of strength is merely a facade.

So where do you instinctively turn for help? What do you value and admire? To what are you giving your discretionary time? What do you turn to in times of crisis? What does that say about you?

The person each one of us is today reflects what has been most important to us. If you're worshiping your heavenly Father, there should be a distinct family resemblance.

To God Be the Glory

"I acted for My name's sake, that it should not be profaned before the Gentiles among whom they were, in whose sight I had made Myself known to them, to bring them out of the land of Egypt."

EZEKIEL 20:9

The reason God did not completely destroy Israel was not last-minute pity for His chronically disloyal people. Nor did these stubborn people finally realize their need for God's forgiveness and repent. The Lord did not totally wipe out Israel because of . . . His own reputation.

After all, God's unique relationship with Israel was not a secret. The children of Israel were living among pagan nations, and the Almighty had openly demonstrated His covenant relationship with them by delivering them from Egypt. He spared them for His own name's sake.

So, when the children of Israel built the golden calf and God's anger flared at them, Moses called on Him to once again spare the people for His name's sake (Exodus 32). After all, Moses reasoned, what would the watching Egyptians think if Israel's God delivered them from slavery only to annihilate them?

God knows that people are watching Him care for us, His children. And the glory is His when He chooses to show mercy by delivering us. We might not always be concerned with God's reputation, but God is!

Standing in the Gap

"So I sought for a man among them who would . . .
stand in the gap before Me on behalf of the land,
that I should not destroy it; but I found no one."

EZEKIEL 22:30

The people of Israel turned away from God—and so did their leaders . . .

God is constantly looking for intercessors. Even as God prepares to pour out His righteous wrath upon sin and rebellion, God graciously looks for one righteous person who will stand before Him on behalf of someone else. That was the case in Ezekiel's day: holy God was perfectly justified in punishing evil, yet, out of His grace, He looked for someone, anyone, who would stand in the gap to represent the people. Incredibly, He found no one. How utterly tragic. Not one person was available; not one person cared enough to intercede for those who were most in need of His redemption. Perhaps the righteous were busy, juggling many good and even godly commitments. Maybe they had full schedules. Whatever the reason, nothing is more important than interceding before God on behalf of others.

Whom are you currently interceding for? Whom are you praying for and pleading with God to do a redemptive work?

God hasn't changed His plan for reaching ungodly people—saved or unsaved. So Look around at the depravation and brokenness in your world. Ask God to use you to "stand in the gap" on behalf of a reckless, desperate, and sinful society.

Loving God's People

*We then who are strong ought to bear with the
scruples of the weak, and not to please ourselves.*

ROMANS 15:1

The Greek word *bastaz-o*, translated "to bear" in the verse
above, means "to lift up, pick up, sustain." God's command here is for believers to carry—to bear—the burdens of
those who are weak in order to build up the body of Christ.

This can happen because Christian love is unselfish
love. Believers share their strengths with those who are less
established in their faith, and those who are weaker humbly
receive help from those who are stronger. Knowing that Christ
bore their weaknesses, God's people support one another. In
this way God's entire body is fortified.

Christian love is unselfish because, as we are conformed
to the image of Christ, we become fulfilled with the love of
Christ. We begin to see people as God views them. We begin
to love them as Christ loves them. Jesus surrendered His life
in order to bring people into a relationship with the heavenly
Father. Christlike love therefore willingly lays aside liberty—
just as Jesus sacrificed His life—and puts others first.

Said differently, godly people love God's people. They seek
unity through the bond of peace, they serve one another, they
forgive those who wrong them, they build up those who are
weak, and they seek to edify the body of Christ. Whose life are
you presently undergirding?

Fearful But Trusting

"Do not be afraid of the king of Babylon, of whom you are afraid; do not be afraid of him," says the LORD, "for I am with you, to save you and deliver you from his hand."

JEREMIAH 42:11

B e honest with yourself. Who or what are you afraid of?

We live in a dangerous and frightening world, and even though we know from the book of Revelation that God wins in the end, the enemy's efforts to defeat God's kingdom and destroy His people—combined with the fallen world in which we live—give us plenty of events and people to be wary of. Some of us might even be afraid of what God will call us to do to serve Him.

Of course God's people do well to pray about the events and people that cause them trepidation. But sometimes God's answers to our prayers require us to act despite our fears—to go exactly where we fear and do exactly what we dread—and submit ourselves in complete dependence on our all-good, all-powerful, all-loving God. Simply put, sometimes God's answers call for brave steps of faith.

Choosing to believe that God is greater than what we fear is the first step toward victory over that which frightens us. At times the greatest act of faith and courage we can make is to take that first step of obedience in the direction God is calling us.

Foundation for Faith

Faith comes by hearing, and hearing by the word of God.

ROMANS 10:17

When did you first hear the Bible with your heart, not just with your head?

Our postmodern, post-Christian culture doesn't value the Bible the way earlier generations did. But believers know that all God's Word "is profitable for doctrine, for reproof, for correction, for instruction in righteousness" (2 Timothy 3:16). We also understand that Scripture outlines the story of God's love for us from Eden through the New Jerusalem . . . via Calvary. How could people not respond to this amazing love story of redemption and grace?

People can only respond to what they know, and many don't know what God's Word reveals about Himself or His righteousness. Many people today don't understand that Christian faith is not a leap in the dark or a step of ignorance. A person's step of faith is based upon knowledge of what God has said in His Word. When you share the gospel, you're doing your part. You're giving people the opportunity to hear God's Word, and the Holy Spirit will work to confirm it as the truth and to call for a response of faith.

As you continue your personal study of God's Word, you'll see your love for the Lord growing—and your faith in Him along with it. Fill your heart and mind with God's Word, and watch your faith grow.

Oh, the Depths!

*Oh, the depths of the riches both of the wisdom
and knowledge of God! How unsearchable are His
judgments and His ways past finding out!*

ROMANS 11:33

We cannot imagine the magnitude of God's love for us. Neither can we plumb the depths of His wisdom and knowledge. Consider these statements:

*The law of the LORD is perfect . . . The statutes of the LORD
are right . . . The judgments of the LORD are true and righteous
altogether . . .* (PSALM 19:7–9)

Give me wisdom and knowledge, that I may go out and come in before this people; for who can judge this great people of Yours? (2 CHRONICLES 1:10)

*For the LORD gives wisdom;
From His mouth come knowledge and understanding.*
(PROVERBS 2:6)

*"For My thoughts are not your thoughts, nor are your ways My ways,"
says the LORD. "For as the heavens are higher than the earth, so are
My ways higher than your ways, and My thoughts than your thoughts."*
(ISAIAH 55:8–9)

The Lord can teach us so much, yet we are often content with only a shallow relationship and a superficial understanding of Him. It is tragic to be satisfied with so little when so much is available to us.

A Living Sacrifice

I beseech you therefore, brethren, by the mercies of God,
that you present your bodies a living sacrifice, holy,
acceptable to God, which is your reasonable service.

ROMANS 12:1

Too often Christians have abused and neglected their physical bodies while they've diligently cared for their souls. God wants us to do better than that.

Among the issues that were especially dear to the apostle Paul was what believers did with their bodies. Paul begged Christians to present their bodies to Christ as a living sacrifice that would be holy and acceptable to Him. (Romans 12:1)

This means that our physical condition matters to God. In fact, our bodies reflect our reverence of and our submission to Christ. Our mastery over our physical condition is evidence of Christ's control over us. Our bodies ought to reflect the strength Christ brings us, strength that keeps us from being overpowered by sensual pleasures. When we abuse or neglect our body, it indicates we are not good stewards of what God has given us. It reveals that we have been disobedient to God's clear commands. It also indicates we are not prepared for what God might have us do next. God calls us to maintain our bodies so they honor Him and so that we are fully able to accomplish whatever kingdom assignment God gives us.

Does the current condition of your physical body bring glory and honor to God?

Hardened Hearts

"I will put a new spirit within them, and take the stony heart out of their flesh, and give them a heart of flesh . . . and they shall be My people, and I will be their God."

EZEKIEL 11:19—20

If you've raised children, you know about selective hearing. Whisper something about them while they're watching TV, and they perk up immediately. Ask them about their homework in a normal tone of voice, and they somehow don't hear . . .

God's Word is God's Word whether we accept it or reject it. In our most rebellious times, we—like the people Ezekiel was addressing—may not hear, but we can't say that God does not speak to us. The truth is that we simply do not want to listen. Ezekiel's audience had the ability to hear God's warnings, but their sin desensitized them to God's words. The same thing happens to us.

Repeatedly disobeying God leads to a hardening of the heart until we are impervious to the Holy Spirit's conviction. Nevertheless, God offers to replace our "stony heart" with a heart of flesh that is soft and tender toward Him. If you have developed a hard heart, turn to God, repent, and receive a heart of flesh. Then you will find yourself seeking His promises and desiring His way. You will begin to regularly hear His voice and find delight once more in spending time with Him.

Broken Fellowship

The glory of the LORD departed from
the threshold of the temple.

EZEKIEL 10:18

B reaking God's law—sin—has been defined as missing the mark, falling short of His standards, and transgressing His covenant. However you define sin and whether you sin in thought, word, or deed, it is a rejection of God's love and an insult to His holiness. Sin leads to separation from God. It's no surprise, then, that He doesn't ignore sin or let it continue unchecked. Oh, God will not forsake us, but by our own willful rebellion we can choose to sever fellowship with Him. The loss is ours, and it is enormous.

In Ezekiel's day God's people had forsaken Him, so His glory departed from the temple. He would not remain where He was not wanted. It was a devastating time for the people of God.

Never take God's presence—in your life, in the church, or in our nation—for granted. He will not allow Himself to be dishonored. He will not be neglected. If you don't treat God with all due respect, you may awaken one day to the startling reality that the glory of God has departed.

Two Sides of Compassion

While [angel army was] killing [the rebellious Hebrews],
I was left alone; and I fell on my face and cried out, and
said, "Ah Lord GOD! Will You destroy all the remnant
of Israel in pouring out Your fury on Jerusalem?"

EZEKIEL 9:8

This is one of the few times that the prophet Ezekiel questioned God. The stark reality of his dying countrymen prompted him to cry out to the Lord with pleas for His mercy and compassion.

Empathy for people undergoing judgment is an appropriate and even godly response. We Christians should never take delight in the suffering of others regardless of how much their punishment is warranted. When we see other people's distress, our reaction should be marked by compassionate love and the heartfelt prayer that those who are suffering may be brought to repentance and be saved.

But don't let a sympathetic heart keep you from speaking the truth that needs to be uttered. There is always a temptation to say what people *want* to hear rather than what they *need* to be told.

When God's Spirit is convicting someone of sin, don't let your commiseration cause you to give poor counsel. Don't be too quick to rescue people from God's discipline. In our misguided zeal to ease people's heartache and pain, we may inadvertently interfere with God's redemptive work in their lives. Trust in God's love and wisdom and then stand ready for whatever role God might have for you as He deals with others.

A Divine Example

*"I have raised you up, that I may show My power in you,
and that My name may be declared in all the earth."*

EXODUS 9:16

The nations of the earth love to strut across the world stage and flaunt their power and wealth. World leaders make bold pronouncements and jealously guard their power. At times dictators and world leaders can appear invincible. But of course they are not.

Pharaoh, for instance, led the most exalted monarchy of his day, and the people of Egypt treated him like a god. Yet God was unimpressed. Soon this proud man would be stripped of his nation's wealth, its means of production, its army, and its reputation. Pharaoh's downfall would be as spectacular as it was thorough. Because Pharaoh would not submit to God's will, God chose to make him a public example of the cost of such proud defiance. Thousands of years later, people continue to be awed by how completely almighty God humbled this overconfident leader

Are you concerned about what ungodly rulers are doing in the world today? Remember that those who stand at the center of the world stage today can be humiliated in a moment by almighty God. So place your fear, reverence, awe, and trust in the only One who truly deserves it.

The Passover Blood

*"Now the blood shall be a sign for you on the houses where
you are. And when I see the blood, I will pass over you;
and the plague shall not be on you to destroy you."*

EXODUS 12:13

The Hebrew word *pesah* means "to pass over," "to spare,"
"to show mercy." It also suggests protection.

God established the annual Passover Feast to commemorate His protecting the Israelites from the last plague and their ultimate emancipation from slavery. This deliverance signified their adoption by God, and it laid the foundation of their national identity. More than a remembrance, though, Passover also pointed prophetically to the sacrificial Lamb of God, Jesus Christ. John the Baptist announced at Jesus' baptism, "Behold! The Lamb of God who takes away the sin of the world!" (John 1:29). Whereas the blood of the lamb saved the Israelites from physical death, the blood of Jesus saves those who believe in Him from spiritual death.

Are you protected by Jesus' blood? All people sin, and all sin has consequences. If God does not see the atoning blood of Jesus Christ covering your life, you will face His judgment. God gives mercy on His terms—through the sacrificial Lamb of God. Where there is the blood of Christ, there is life and salvation. Have you received that gift?

Sojourns

*Now the sojourn of the children of Israel who lived
in Egypt was four hundred and thirty years.*

EXODUS 12:40

The Israelite people lived in Egypt for over four centuries. During that time several generations had the opportunity to consider their sin, cry out to God, and finally see His power as He delivered them.

Moses, the man God called to lead Israel out of slavery, spent his own sojourn preparing for that role. After killing an Egyptian who had assaulted a Hebrew, Moses fled to Midian, where he spent forty years as a shepherd. During that time God developed Moses into a person who could lead His people.

God knows where He ultimately wants to take us, but often along the way He has us abide in a difficult place, a place we would never choose for ourselves. Before we are ready to serve in the way He wants us to, we must first let Him build our character. Then, in His perfect timing, God will lead us forward.

When has a time of sojourn in your life prepared you for kingdom work later? No season of life is wasted if you spend it right where God wants you to be.

If God currently has you waiting on Him, what might He be planning for you? Are you using your time wisely? Faithfully? Expectantly?

Daily Bread

So they gathered [manna] every morning,
every man according to his need.

EXODUS 16:21

Manna was round, sweet, and nutritious: "it was like white coriander seed, and the taste of it was like wafers made with honey" (v. 31). God supplied this flaky bread every morning except the Sabbath. Manna collected the day before the Sabbath lasted two days. Every other gleaning would spoil after one day—and the supply stopped when the Israelites entered the Promised Land (Joshua 5:12).

God certainly could have provided weekly or even monthly amounts of manna. Then the Israelites could have saved time and energy by collecting it less often. But God chose to supply the food daily, with the single exception of the Sabbath so that His people could know a day of rest.

God's provision—now as then—is daily so we constantly remember our dependence on Him. Every day we must rely on Him to meet our needs, physical and spiritual, large and small. We cannot relive yesterday's divine encounter. God's provision for us yesterday won't be adequate to sustain us today. We must regularly seek provision from God who perfectly provides for our needs each day. You cannot hoard God's provision. He insists that we receive it from Him daily.

Supportive Friends

*Moses' hands became heavy; so they took a stone and
put it under him, and he sat on it. And Aaron and Hur
supported his hands, one on one side, and the other on the
other side; and his hands were steady until the going down
of the sun. So Joshua defeated Amalek and his people.*

EXODUS 17:12

As long as Moses held up his hands in intercession, Israel's army prevailed over the Amalekite enemy. When Moses let down his hands, Amalekites began to prevail. Clearly, Joshua, the leader of Israel's army, needed Moses to help him succeed. And Moses needed Aaron and Hur to fulfill his key role in the battle.

God made us, His children, to need one another. Even though God is with us, He often undergirds us through the instrument of human encouragement and assistance. That's one reason why Jesus sent His disciples out two by two. That's why God calls us to be part of a community of believers. We aren't made to walk the journey of Christian faith on our own; nor are we meant to stand alone against the enemies we encounter along the way. Modern society often celebrates autonomy and independence. But God does not. He created us to need one another.

Thank God for people who have come alongside you—and ask Him to whom He wants you to offer support and encouragement. You'll be blessed as you are a blessing to those people!

"A Jealous God"

*"You shall have no other gods before Me . . . . For
I, the LORD your God, am a jealous God."*

EXODUS 20:3, 5

God is admittedly a jealous God. He cherishes His
people's affections and will tolerate no rivals. He is not
content to be *a* priority in your life; He wants to be *the* priority. God demands your exclusive devotion. He does not abide
unfaithfulness or attitudes and habits that threaten His central place in your heart.

Take a quick inventory. What is competing for God's foremost position in your life? Look at your calendar . . . Mentally
review your financial commitments . . . What do you see about
yourself and about the priority God is in your everyday life?
In what ways are you investing in your relationship with the
Lord? Or are you busying yourself in inconsequential activities and earthly pursuits?

Now consider the objects of your devotion. Has your love
for someone made that person an idol? Are you longing for
riches or the success and security that the world offers? What
keeps you from loving God with all your heart, soul, mind, and
strength?

God is a jealous God: He wants your devotion. His Spirit
can grow that kind of love in your heart. Why not lay your bad
attitudes, destructive habits, and false gods at His feet today?

Holy . . . and Humble

For thus says the High and Lofty One
Who inhabits eternity, whose name is Holy:
"I dwell in the high and holy place,
With him who has a contrite and humble spirit,
To revive the spirit of the humble,
And to revive the heart of the contrite ones."

ISAIAH 57:15

It's the miracle of the Incarnation! Our holy God took on human flesh in the form of Jesus to pay the price for our sin. So perhaps it's no surprise to read here in Isaiah that God reaches down from His throne to people who are humble in heart.

The almighty God reigns supreme in the universe. He judges humanity with fairness and mercy. He is exalted and righteous above all powers—natural as well as supernatural. He alone is worthy of worship. No wonder He dwells in "the high and holy place."

But that holy place—that place set apart for a special purpose—is not in a heavenly, celestial palace. That holy place where Almighty God chooses to dwell is in the contrite and humble heart of a believer.

Do you want almighty God, your Creator, to come and fellowship with you? Then humble yourself and develop the kind of temple in which your Sovereign Lord delights to inhabit.

DECEMBER

For with God nothing will be impossible.

LUKE 1:37

The Lord's Delight

You shall no longer be termed Forsaken,
Nor shall your land any more be termed Desolate . . .
For the LORD delights in you.

ISAIAH 62:4

We all know—to one degree or another—what it is to be forsaken and alone. You may be in such a place right now—but even if you're not, hear the good news that the prophet Isaiah has for you.

- ALMIGHTY GOD TAKES PLEASURE IN YOU. The holy, infinitely loving, all-powerful God takes pleasure in you, one of His less-than-holy, inconsistently loving, and weak creatures. Despite the quantum differences between you and your heavenly Father, He delights in *you*.

- GOD ENJOYS HIS FELLOWSHIP WITH YOU. God communes with the angels and the saints already in heaven—yet finds joy in relating to you!

- GOD DELIGHTS IN THE GLORY YOU BRING HIM. You bring Him glory when you share His love, worship Him, repent, serve . . . the list goes on.

- Although God needs nothing, HE IS PLEASED TO RECEIVE YOUR OBEDIENCE, WORSHIP, AND PRAISE. In what ways is God receiving your obedience? His Spirit will show you . . . What worship and praise can you offer Him this day . . . this minute even?

Spend time with the One who delights in you.

God the Father

Doubtless You are our Father . . . .
You, O LORD, are our Father;
Our Redeemer from Everlasting is Your name.

ISAIAH 63:16

When people hear the word *father*, many different images, memories, and feelings immediately occur. For some, thoughts of a father connote feelings of love, affirmation, guidance, and provision. For others, feelings of rejection, criticism, and abandonment come to the surface. In Old Testament times God's chosen people generally understood that He was Father to them. This verse from Isaiah, however, is one of the few direct Old Testament references to God as a Father.

In the New Testament, Jesus addresses the almighty God as "Abba" or "Daddy" (Mark 14:36). The apostle Paul adds that, by the power of the Holy Spirit, we believers are privileged to cry, "Abba, Father" as well (Romans 8:15). The term reflects a healthy tension between respect and intimacy, a tension you may or may not have known with your earthly father.

Our view of God our Father must come from Scripture, not from our childhood experience. The Bible clearly teaches that our heavenly Father guides His children, enjoys fellowship with them, and is glorified through them (v. 14). Allow your heavenly Father to develop the loving, fatherly relationship with you that He is seeking, and enjoy it for all eternity.

Judged and Restored

*"I will save My flock, and they shall no longer be a
prey; and I will judge between sheep and sheep."*

EZEKIEL 34:22

The prophet Ezekiel confronted the people of Israel—and
he confronts us—with the reality of sin's devastating
power. But he also offers words of hope about the restoration
God will bring to those who experience His judgment. After
all, God does not hold a grudge or punish unfairly. God is just
and will deal with sin, but He also provides the opportunity for
every person to repent and find life. Once God has addressed
your sin, He will act as your Advocate and Protector.

That's what we read about in Ezekiel 34:22. God will hold
us accountable for our sin, but He will also bless and protect
us. Just as a shepherd evaluates his sheep and judges which to
breed, sell, or butcher, the Lord will determine those who are
His and which sheep need care, judgment, or blessing.

We like to think of ourselves as more noble than mere
sheep. But that's what we are. We are vulnerable and easily led
astray. Thankfully we have a Good Shepherd who knows how
to safely guide us.

Learning—and Teaching—about God

Then Pharoah's daughter said to her, "Take this child
away and nurse him for me, and I will give you your
wages." So the woman took the child and nursed him.

EXODUS 2:9

God chose Moses to lead His people out of bondage and establish a new nation under God's rule. God gave the Law through Moses, establishing a covenant that would characterize His relationship with the Israelites. Clearly, Moses had a special relationship with God and experienced many significant face-to-face encounters with the Almighty.

Yet Moses may not have been such a servant of God had he not been nursed by a Hebrew woman who was his mother. In fact, the phrase "your wages" in the verse above would have made the Hebrew listeners smile. Imagine, Moses' mother Jochebed was paid by the Egyptians to nurse her own son! God's deeper purpose, however, was that Moses would learn from his faithful mother about the God of his fathers (3:15); young Moses received important instruction from her about the promises God had given to his ancestors.

Looking back, you may recall people God placed in your life who led you to know Him. They were ordinary people in ordinary settings, yet joining in God's plan for you to one day walk with Him.

God Remembers

Then God remembered Rachel, and God
listened to her and opened her womb.

GENESIS 30:22

Maybe you know the heartache of infertility . . . of a way-ward child . . . of an unfaithful spouse. Or perhaps you know the pain of being abandoned as a child, the pressures of never measuring up at the office, the struggle with ongoing, even terminal health issues. You may be dealing with financial difficulties, estranged family members, and loneliness despite all the people in your life. In any of these situations and count-less others, we can wonder if God has forgotten us.

Rachel may have entertained that same thought as she watched her sister bear son after son—a total of six—plus a daughter. For years Rachel longed for a child, yet she remained barren.

Then, we read, "God remembered Rachel"—and God remembers us as well. He knows our troubles just as He knew Rachel's heartache. God does not hesitate to address those troubles, but He does so in His own way and in His own time in order to accomplish His will and glorify Himself in the pro-cess. His help may not come as soon as we would like, but it does come when it is best.

Take heart! God remembers you.

Taking Matters into Our Hands

*Esau hated Jacob because of the blessing with which his father
blessed him, and Esau said in his heart, "The days of mourning
for my father are at hand; then I will kill my brother Jacob."*

GENESIS 27:41

As Isaac approached the end of his life, he requested his
favorite meal before he blessed his older son and died.
Isaac's desire to fulfill his physical appetites gave his younger
son Jacob an opportunity for deceit.

With his mother's help, Jacob prepared the stew, disguised
himself as Esau, and received the blessing that was rightfully
his brother's. As soon as Isaac pronounced the blessing, a
hungry Esau returned from his hunting, made the meal his
father had requested, and learned that his father had given his
blessing to his brother.

Throughout Esau's life he chose to do things his way. He
lived how he chose. He married a woman his parents opposed.
He ignored God's call. But it cost him. When we look at Esau's
plans, we see a man who chose far less than God would have
given him. He rejected God to gain his independence, but it was
a sorry exchange indeed.

God's Word Challenged

Sarai said to Abram, "See now, the LORD has restrained me from bearing children. Please, go in to my maid; perhaps I shall obtain children by her." And Abram heeded the voice of Sarai.

GENESIS 16:2

Sarai had an idea. Since she couldn't bear children, maybe God intended for Abram—in line with the custom of the day—to take a concubine. Maybe God needed that kind of help from Sarai and Abram . . . or maybe not!

Counsel contrary to God's instructions is often plentiful. Human thinking and advice from others may appear quite reasonable, but those suggestions must never supersede God's clear directions. Accept His guidance and let His methods stretch your faith.

When Abram acted outside of God's instruction and went to Hagar, we see that even people of great faith—people who have trusted God in difficult circumstances before—can suffer lapses that cost them dearly. After all, sin has both immediate and lasting consequences. The results of some sins linger for many generations. In fact, Muslim Arabs today claim their descent from Ishmael, Abram and Hagar's son.

So when you hear God's clear instruction, don't try to improve upon His plan. Have faith and obey—and be willing to wait for Him to act. When she ultimately bore Isaac, Sarai realized that God can indeed be trusted.

Impossible Promises

"Is anything too hard for the LORD? At the appointed time . . . and Sarah shall have a son."

GENESIS 18:14

Sarah became a mom at the age of ninety, and Abraham was one hundred years old when God blessed him with Isaac, the son God promised them many years earlier. In His perfect timing and in His own divine way, God answered their prayers and kept His promise.

But imagine what this season of waiting had involved. Agony and heartache as time passed . . . Skepticism and doubt and perhaps hopelessness and despair . . . Questioning their memories of the promise and undoubtedly forgetting God's great faithfulness to them in the past . . .

Are you in a season of waiting? Have you felt the heartache and perhaps some despair? Have you forgotten God's great faithfulness to you in the past? Are you wondering if God will even come through? Are you afraid it's too late?

God *will* come through on His promises to you, and He has promised you many things such as protection, provision, and His presence. In fact, God promises things that only He can accomplish, so that the world may see Him work in our lives. Though we may doubt and others may scoff and some time may pass, nothing is impossible for God. You can trust Him.

Consult God

Now Abraham said of Sarah his wife, "She is my sister."
And Abimelech king of Gerar sent and took Sarah.

GENESIS 20:2

It's easy to see why Abraham said what he did. He didn't want King Abimelech to have him killed. Even though God had promised to give him and Sarah an heir (obviously Abram's death would make it hard for God to keep His promise), Abram did what he could to protect himself from the powerful ruler.

Abraham failed to consult God in this time of crisis; he took matters into his own hands. Doing so put him and those he loved in danger. Like Abraham, we can be guilty of not trusting God in difficult situations. God uses such blunders to show us our limitations and our need for Him.

But perhaps Abraham's lying words—like some of your decisions—were an unthinking reaction to the dangerous situation he found himself in. And perhaps you can remember less-than-honest, less-than-godly responses to circumstances in your life. May you reach the point where you are so close to God that your automatic reaction is to consult Him!

Then, when God does offer His guidance, trust Him and obey regardless of whether His direction makes perfect sense to you. He knows what He is doing!

Praise His Names!

Abraham planted a tamarisk tree in Beersheba, and there
called on the name of the LORD, the Everlasting God.

GENESIS 21:33

El olam means "Everlasting God."
El Elyon, "God Most High" (14:18)
El Roi, "The God who sees me" (16:13)
El Shaddai, "God Almighty" (17:1)

Through this series of names, God revealed aspects of His nature to the patriarchs—and to us.

- As God made promises to Abraham, what an assurance for this man of faith to know that the God who would fulfill them is eternal.
- As Abraham was learning to follow God more faithfully, what a gift to hear that he had chosen to follow the King of kings!
- After Abraham and Sarah sent Hagar away, what comfort for Hagar to realize that God saw her in her distress.
- When God renewed His covenant with Abraham, He introduced Himself as "God Almighty." What a comforting thought!

In light of your current circumstances, what does it mean to you that God is everlasting? that He is the Most High? the Almighty? What does it mean to you that God sees you?

Find comfort, hope, and reason to praise God as you learn His names and hear in them reasons to trust Him and draw closer to Him.

Consecrating the Priests

"You shall kill the ram, and take some of its blood and put it on the tip of the right ear of Aaron and on the tip of the right ear of his sons, on the thumb of their right hand and on the big toe of their right foot."

EXODUS 29:20

God gave these instructions to Aaron and his sons, the line of Israel that would serve as priests for the nation. Their role was to go before God on behalf of the people. Entering into the presence of Holy God requires purification. Sprinkling blood on the ear, thumb, and big toe was an act of consecrating one's ears to hear the Word of God, one's hands to perform sacrifices, and one's feet to lead the people to worship.

We New Testament believers are also priests (1 Peter 2:9), and our consecration is necessary. What are you doing—what are you avoiding—in order to have an ear that is sensitive to the Word of God and not deafened by the noise of the sinful, fallen world? What do you do—and what do you avoid—in order to keep your hands clean and ready to serve? And where do you go—and what places do you avoid—in order to lead people to worship God? God has made clear provision and instruction so you can serve Him honorably. Are you?

Forgetting the Lord

When the people saw that Moses delayed coming down from
the mountain, the people gathered together to Aaron, and
said to him, "Come, make us gods that shall go before us."

EXODUS 32:1

God had just delivered these people from slavery in Egypt. He had worked amazing wonders as He sent the plagues, parted the sea, and destroyed the Egyptian army. But when Moses was delayed in his conference with the Lord, the people panicked and demanded a new god to worship. As unbelievable as we may find their change of heart, we are not that different from them.

Despite God's miraculous intervention in our lives, our memories of His power and deliverance, of His presence and provision, of His goodness and grace are remarkably short. We too easily trade our loyalty to the true and living God for a passing whim or fancy. What's the newest quick-fix or self-help solution being preached by the world? Could it be a possible solution to that problem we've been praying about for months or even years? How easily we walk away from the almighty, all-sufficient God! Our memories are too short.

Take some time today to put down in writing a record of God's faithfulness to you. Be specific—and keep the list updated so you aren't tempted to forsake your Lord.

Intercession and Sacrifice

*Moses said to the people, "You have committed
a great sin. So now I will go up to the LORD;
perhaps I can make atonement for your sin."*

EXODUS 32:30

The people of Israel built the golden calf while Moses was meeting with God. When he returned, he threw down the tablets on which God's Law had been inscribed. Shattering the tablets demonstrated more than Moses' anger. It also symbolized that the people had broken their covenant with God. Their relationship with Him was fractured and would remain so unless they repented.

As the appointed mediator between unfaithful Israel and Holy God, Moses went before Him as an intercessor. Perhaps his urgent pleas on their behalf would compel the Lord to have mercy on these sinful, disloyal people. Moses even offered his life in exchange for theirs (v. 32). Godly leaders like Moses empathize with their people and intercede with God on their behalf.

People today are still in need of an intercessor. People have forsaken God. They have rejected His Word and are paying the price.

Will you, like Moses, plead with God on their behalf? Will you do everything in your power to bring people back to God?

Servants

*Bezalel the son of Uri, the son of Hur, of the tribe of
Judah, made all that the LORD had commanded Moses.*

EXODUS 38:22

Construction of the tabernacle was underway. Offerings
for the materials, the worship ceremonies, and the
priests' clothes had flowed in. And here we read that Bezaleel
"made all that the LORD had commanded Moses." Just as God
had provided the material resources through His grateful
people, He also raised up workers.

For every need in His kingdom, the Lord has prepared someone to serve. Our God-given skills and gifts are not merely for
us; they are God's provision for His people by which He fulfills
His sovereign purposes.

Think about the purpose of your church home. Whom has
God raised up to lead? What gifts are clearly evident in those
people? Thank God for equipping those leaders—and for their
willingness to use their God-given skills for the Lord.

Now think about your own role in your church. What need
in God's kingdom might He want you to meet? In what specific
ways has He equipped you to serve? Ask for God's direction
and then serve where He calls. The role He has for you may
surprise you, but know that there's nothing more satisfying
than being used in God's kingdom for His eternal purposes.
Let God impact eternity with your life.

He Is God

[God] says to Moses, "I will have mercy on whomever
I will have mercy, and I will have compassion
on whomever I will have compassion."

ROMANS 9:15

Theologians love to speculate about what God will and won't do. Huge theological debates surround the issue of whom God will save and whom He will not save. Some of those self-appointed critics complain that God is not being fair or just in His dealing with people, speaking as if God is somehow accountable to us for His actions. While it is true that God remains consistent with Himself and that He has set forth His standards and expectations in Scripture, we are foolish to think that we can evaluate, much less judge, what He chooses to do. Ultimately God will save whom He will save and judge those He chooses to judge . . . because He is God! He is sovereign! He is not answerable to us. He is also infinitely wise. He knows every person's heart and motive. He is not fooled by appearances. God is perfectly, infinitely just. We don't need to try to understand all of God's actions. It is enough to know that everything He does is just, loving, and good.

God Wins!

The Revelation of Jesus Christ, which God
gave Him to show His servants.

REVELATION 1:1

Revelation comes from the Greek word *apokalupsis,* meaning "to uncover" as well as "appearing," signifying "the coming of Christ." In Revelation 1:1, it refers to the unveiling of truth that has long been hidden.

God reveals truth so that it can change lives, and He expects us to faithfully and accurately share His truth with others. Believers don't always understand the truths found in the book of Revelation, but "blessed is he who reads [it]" (v. 3). After all, one purpose of the book is to exalt Christ. In these pages, we see Jesus not as the humble servant, but as the glorious King of kings, the Alpha and the Omega, and the Mighty Warrior who thoroughly conquers all His enemies. The persecuted people for whom John wrote this book needed a word of hope, so the apostle assured them that God always rewards faithfulness and that His justice always triumphs over evil.

Revelation has continued to offer Christians great hope and inspiration for remaining faithful to Jesus to the end. The reward for perseverance will be wonderful beyond description. We who name Jesus as our Savior and Lord can look forward to being in His presence, worshiping Him face-to-face together with all the faithful, and experiencing God in ever new and magnificent ways. Rest in knowing that God will ultimately triumph and keep every promise He has ever made. The last days are already planned. They will occur exactly as God intends.

The Heart Behind the Works

*"I know your works, that you have a name
that you are alive, but you are dead."*

REVELATION 3:1

The Greek behind the word *hypocrisy* means "the act of playing a part on the stage." It refers to wearing masks, to not being whom you appear to be . . .

Our Lord sees past our facades even when fellow believers don't. We live under Christ's watchful eye. He isn't looking to be sure we are busy, but to see that we are obedient. He watches not just what we are doing, but, looking at our hearts, why we are doing it.

But with our religious activity—teaching a Bible study, serving on a church committee, tithing, being an usher, visiting shut-ins, working at the soup kitchen—we can fool even ourselves into assuming we are spiritually vibrant and growing . . . when in fact we have no vitality at all. An industrious church is not necessarily a spiritual church. What indicates our spiritual vitality is our obedience and love for Christ.

Are you busy with what God wants you to be doing? Are you serving with the heart He wants you to have? Never be content with the appearance of spiritual vibrancy. Be sure your works flow from a genuine love for Christ.

It matters not what your reputation is with others. What's crucial is your reputation with God.

Not Invited

*"Behold, I stand at the door and knock. If anyone
hears My voice and opens the door, I will come in
to him and dine with him, and he with Me."*

REVELATION 3:20

We all know what it's like to not be invited to a party. It
can be heartbreakingly lonely to not be included in the
festivities—and that's the sad picture of Revelation 3:20.

Jesus Christ is standing outside of the very church for whom
He suffered an excruciating death. He is trying to gain the
attention of the very people for whom He spilled His blood.
He wants to gain admission into the fellowship of His own
people, the ones He purchased with His death.

The people at the party are lukewarm followers—"neither
cold nor hot" (v. 15). And they're unaware of just how
"wretched, miserable, poor, blind, and naked" they are (v. 17).
It doesn't sound as if Jesus is missing much of an event, but
because they are His people, He wants to be with them. He
wants them to experience the healing and the renewal, the
riches and the joy that He alone offers.

A church without Christ is not a church at all. It is a religious organization. Is your church talking about Christ but
not actually communing with Him? Is it serving God without
enjoying Him? Behold, Jesus is knocking . . .

A Song of Praise

Holy, holy, holy
Lord God Almighty,
Who was and is and is to come!

REVELATION 4:8

This heavenly song of worship is being sung to the enthroned God by the four living creatures. Extremely aware of whose presence they are in, these four can't help but praise Him.

These creatures were awesome. One angel could obliterate an enormous earthly army. Yet, when these heavenly beings gazed upon almighty God, they felt overwhelmed, for His mighty and power dwarfed theirs by comparison. Likewise, the mightiest earthly kings will be as nothing when they stand before our heavenly King. Earthly rulers used to adulation and deference during their life will recognize how puny they are in contrast to the Creator of the universe. And when you and I find ourselves in the presence of the risen Christ, no other response will do but absolute surrender. No words can describe the unimaginable awe we will experience as we stand before our glorious Lord.

"Holy" is our Lord's name, and holiness is the identifying quality of His kingdom. Everyone who stands in God's presence acknowledges His holiness. Everything God does, whether punitive or redemptive, is a function of His undefiled—His holy—character.

The world often tries to minimize God. But one day, all will see Him as He is. For in that day, we will see what the heavenly creatures experience constantly. We will then understand why they continually cry out "Holy!"

The Day of Wrath

The great day of His wrath has come, and who is able to stand?

REVELATION 6:17

The creatures of heaven understand the significance of Christ's sacrifice for humanity, and they can't cease from shouting praises. But then comes a much more somber scene . . .

God has foretold a day of judgment when He will call into account every soul on earth. People who exalted themselves will be brought low, and those who humbled themselves before Christ will be raised up. On that day everyone will bow before Jesus and acknowledge that He is Lord. On that awesome day, holy God will pour out His wrath on those who have defied, rejected, or rebelled against Him.

Before that day comes, we do well to remember that salvation is available to everyone. God's kingdom is open to anyone who will accept His gift of salvation. In fact, Revelation speaks of "a great multitude which no one could number, of all nations, tribes, peoples, and tongues . . . saying, 'Salvation belongs to our God who sits on the throne, and to the Lamb!'" (7:9–10).

Many Christians prefer to ponder what it will be like to walk the streets of gold and to enjoy fellowship with the saints throughout history. But we must also consider the sobering truth that a day of wrath is looming. On that day neighbors, friends, and family members will have to give an account of their lives to almighty God. Such a reality ought to compel us to urge everyone we know to be prepared for that day.

The Shepherd-King's Heart

The Lamb who is in the midst of the throne will shepherd them and lead them to living fountains of waters. And God will wipe away every tear from their eyes.

REVELATION 7:17

In the pages of Revelation, we see Jesus as the risen and glorious Christ. He has left behind His broken and wounded earthly body, and He sits on His heavenly throne clothed in splendor. But we see a mighty seraphim crying out "Holy! Holy! Holy!" We also see the triumphant and sovereign Ruler still has a tender heart of compassion for His people.

Yes, Jesus is Almighty God, Creator, and Redeemer—but He is also kind, merciful, gentle, and sympathetic to the hurts of His people. His eternal care and comfort await His followers, our pain and suffering will be cast away forever, and God will wipe away our tears. What a humbling and tender picture of intimacy and affection! It's amazing to be loved like that by the Holy One. It is amazing to contemplate that almighty God is aware of every tear that has been shed.

As we imagine one day looking into our Good Shepherd's eyes, how can we not be moved to express our gratitude?

"We give You thanks, O Lord God Almighty, the One who is and who was and who is to come, because you have taken Your great power and reigned" (11:17).

"The Lamb Will Overcome"

These [enemies of God] will make war with the
Lamb, and the Lamb will overcome them, for
He is Lord of lords and King of kings.

REVELATION 17:14

Christ's true followers are not the ones who loudly profess allegiance to Him in the comfort of the church. His true followers are those who persevere despite the fiercest tribulations. Menacing trials have already come, and they will continue . . .

This world is dangerously deceptive and openly hostile toward God. The Almighty's enemies are vicious and relentless, but even the most satanic, ruthless, powerful, and determined foes cannot withstand God's awesome might. No enemy is so powerful that God cannot utterly destroy it. The fact that Satan must be released from the bottomless pit (20:3) indicates that his every move is—and will continue to be—under God's sovereign control.

Even in history's darkest moments, God's purposes prevail, and His people are empowered to remain faithful. Though Satan's forces rage, God's chosen stand firm. The day is coming when the loyalty of God's true followers will be revealed and their suffering will be rewarded.

God's people may find themselves surrounded by forces hostile to God, yet the world's despots and earthly powers do not determine the victory. God does that. The Lamb will overcome. Praise God!

All Things New

I saw a new heaven and a new earth, for the first
heaven and the first earth had passed away.

REVELATION 21:1

Our earth is perishing . . . We who dwell here suffer from illness, natural catastrophes, and evil . . . Even the righteous grow weary of living in a place so contrary to their values . . . But the day is coming when God will create a new heaven and earth, and His creation won't simply be a newer model. God will not merely *re*form our present situation; He will *trans*form it. His new heaven and new earth will be qualitatively different:

- There will be no more tears (v. 4). Sorrow, pain, and suffering shall be forgotten, and unimaginable joy will be our constant experience.
- The New Jerusalem will be a perfect place to dwell (v. 16).
- The wall, over two hundred feet thick, will be crystal clear, indicating the city's purity (v. 18).
- Only one street is mentioned, and it is pure gold (v. 21).
- Jesus came as the Light of this world, so we should not be surprised that the glory of God and of the Lamb will provide the illumination in the New Jerusalem (v. 23).
- The city gates are not closed because there will no longer be any enemies (v. 25).

And He shall reign forever and ever!

Nothing Is Impossible

"For with God nothing will be impossible."

LUKE 1:37

She was probably thirteen or fourteen . . . The angel's visit had been more than a bit of a surprise—and his announcement more than a little unbelievable . . . No one could blame Mary for having a question or two. *How could I have a child,* she wondered, *when I have known no man?*

Her question, though, reflected her confidence that God would perform the miracle. Mary didn't ask for a sign. She was enquiring *how*—not *if*—God was going to perform this miraculous work.

The angel explained that the "Holy Spirit will come upon you" (v. 35) and also told Mary that her relative Elizabeth would be giving birth to a son despite her old age (v. 36). "For with God nothing will be impossible," said the angel in closing.

Mary humbly replied, "Behold the maidservant of the Lord! Let it be to me according to your word" (v. 38).

God's purposes for us far exceed our human abilities to accomplish them. Our efforts can't succeed apart from Him, and that's exactly how God intends it to be.

What is God presently asking you to do? Is it difficult? Does it seem impossible? Are their critics? Trust Him—and remember, with God, *nothing* is impossible!

"Prince of Peace"

For unto us a Child is born,
Unto us a Son is given;
And the government will be upon His shoulder.
And His name will be called
Wonderful, Counselor, Mighty God,
Everlasting Father, Prince of Peace.

ISAIAH 9:6

Many of us find it hard to read those words without hearing Handel's *Messiah* in our mind. That magnificent music beautifully captures the glorious promise and rich truth of these ancient words.

Israel hoped for, longed for, waited for a messiah who would prove victorious over her military oppressors. Israel anticipated a messiah who would bring peace on earth.

God's Messiah—Jesus, His Son—would prove victorious over a greater enemy: sin. God's Messiah would also bring a much greater peace: reconciliation between God and man.

Christ can indeed bring peace to any situation. The most difficult circumstance, the most ruthless enemy, the deepest pain—none of these is beyond Christ's reach. He can calm your heart and mind. No one brings peace like Jesus.

What do you need from the Messiah right now? A counselor? A mighty God? A Prince of peace? The Messiah will be all those in your life and much more. He is God's answer to every need in your life.

The Promise of His Presence

"Therefore the Lord Himself will give you a sign:
Behold, the virgin shall conceive and bear a
Son, and shall call His name Immanuel."

ISAIAH 7:14

Sometimes in the face of the grief and tragedy inevitable in life, there just aren't words to say . . .

That's not always easy to remember when a friend is in pain. We so often want to do or say something that will make the situation better and the heartache go away. But we can't . . .

When the pain is ours, though, we know that genuine comfort can come simply from another's presence. We know how superfluous—and perhaps even annoying—words can be. We just want someone to be with us in our pain. Answers, solutions, problem-solving ideas, even words intended to bring comfort—none of these can be as helpful as warm, silent presence.

It's no wonder, then, that the greatest gift God gives is His presence. His name is Immanuel—"God with us."

For God to be with us indicates that He has dealt with our sin. Experiencing His divine presence also means that, no matter who is against us, every resource of heaven is at our disposal. Knowing that He is with us is testimony to His tender love—and nothing can separate us from that love.

Immanuel—God is with you. Whether you go to church, to work, to the hospital, God will always be with you!

Getting Our Attention

[Jerusalem's] adversaries have become the master,
Her enemies prosper;
For the LORD has afflicted her
Because of the multitude of her transgressions.
Her children have gone into captivity before the enemy.

LAMENTATIONS 1:5

The writer of Lamentations saw the city of Jerusalem destroyed in 587 BC. He expressed the anguish of seeing God's judgment enacted, and he addressed the reality that, when His people forsook Him, God abandoned them and even allowed His holy temple to be looted and destroyed.

The Hebrew people had believed that God would never allow pagans to capture the holy city or enter the Most Holy Place. They mistakenly assumed that, regardless of their disloyalty, God would protect them from their enemies. The book of Lamentations clearly reveals that God will not tolerate forever His people's infidelity. God will allow His wayward people to suffer because He knows that it may require hardship to draw them back to Him.

One way God allows hardship and gets our attention is by removing His protection from us. So, if everything seems to be going against us and we're experiencing continual defeat, we must consider whether we are dealing with consequences of our sin. It is futile to ask for God's protection when we should be pleading for His forgiveness.

First Love, Last Breath

"I have this against you, that you have left your first love."

REVELATION 2:4

D o you remember the first time you fell in love? How you couldn't spend enough time with him? How the hours you were with her seemed like minutes? Perhaps you had a similar experience when you first recognized Christ's amazing love for you and your heart was filled with love for Him.

As we busily serve the Lord, though, we can too easily lose the joy we knew when we first loved Him. The service that began as a response of deep affection for the Lord can deteriorate into acting merely out of a sense of duty; our Christian life can become routine, even drudgery. We must never allow religion to overtake our love relationship with God.

In the second century, Polycarp—who trained for ministry under the apostle John—served as a pastor. When a great persecution of Christians under Roman emperor Antonius Pius began, Polycarp was arrested. Ordered to renounce Christ, Polycarp boldly proclaimed: "I have served Him for eighty-six years, and He has done me no wrong. Can I revile my King who saved me?"

Polycarp was burned alive at the stake for a love that lasted almost nine decades. How has your love for Christ grown over the years?

"What Is Man?"

LORD, what is man, that You take knowledge of him?
Or the son of man, that You are mindful of him?
Man is like a breath;
His days are like a passing shadow.

PSALM 144:3—4

The almighty Designer and Creator of the universe keeps the planets in their orbits and holds the stars in their places—and He numbers the hairs on your head.

The One who crafted the mountains and carved out the seas knit you together in your mother's womb.

The Author of history and the Sovereign over the world's governments knows you by name.

It is incomprehensible that God concerns Himself with us, isn't it? In truth, we are nothing compared to Him, yet He loves us and cares about the smallest details of our existence.

Think about that: God loves you; God knows you; God is "mindful" of you. Yet what is man? A wayward, capricious creature. What is man? A creator of idols, a worshiper of the world's gods, a persistent rebel. What is man? Finite and limited, longing to be independent, made of dust. And yet God loves us.

No wonder the psalmist sang praises to the Lord! Join your voice with his today and marvel with the songwriter that God cares about you.

"The Fragrance of Christ"

We are to God the fragrance of Christ among those who
are being saved and among those who are perishing.
To the one we are the aroma of death leading to death,
and to the other the aroma of life leading to life.

2 CORINTHIANS 2:15–16

The Romans celebrated their military victories with a parade. During these triumphant processions, priests would burn incense. After the priests came officers and soldiers leading captives to either slavery or execution. As the parade wound its way through the streets, the aroma of the incense would spread, declaring the victory to everyone around.

When Christ resides in the hearts of believers, we become living evidence of His victory over sin. God puts us on display as trophies of His grace, and we disseminate the sweet and distinctive essence of Christ.

As a believer, you know the ultimate victory over sin and death that Jesus achieved on Calvary. What mastery over specific sins in your life has He helped you achieve—and what battle is He helping you fight now?

Know that God will place in your life people who are being defeated by sin so they can see the contrast between their situation and that of people who have been captured by Christ. What aroma is your life dispensing to those around you?

Our Interceding Savior

*We have such a High Priest, who is seated at the right
hand of the throne of the Majesty in the heavens.*

HEBREWS 8:1

The Jewish priests daily entered the sanctuary to burn incense and trim the lamps. Once a week they replaced the showbread. Once a year, on the Day of Atonement, the high priest entered God's presence. Clearly, the old covenant did not provide for full fellowship between God and His people.

The blood of Christ changed that, though. His death on the cross was the perfect and complete sacrifice for humanity's sins. In fact, no sin or offense is so great that Jesus' atonement cannot make you clean and holy.

In addition to offering this forgiveness and cleansing from sin, Jesus is also our Advocate. Seated at the right hand of God—a sign that His sacrificial work is finished—Jesus has constant access to His Father, and He receives everything He asks for on our behalf.

We will face temptations and difficult circumstances. At times our strength may fail and our faith may waiver, but we have this hope: Christ our High Priest forever intercedes for us with the Father. He is victorious over death and sin, and He will bring us victory as well. The risen Christ watches our life with great interest and is determined that we ultimately triumph.

About the Authors

Popular author and speaker Dr. Henry Blackaby is best known for writing *Experiencing God: Knowing and Doing the Will of God*, which has sold over six million copies and been translated into sixty-four languages. Henry is married to Marilynn, and all of their five children are serving in full-time Christian ministry. Dr. Blackaby has spoken in two hundred countries, contributed to the *Blackaby Study Bible*, and written dozens of books, including the Legacy Series studies of Abraham, Samuel, Joshua, Paul, and Mary. He is the founder of Blackaby Ministries International (www.blackaby.org).

Dr. Richard Blackaby, Henry's oldest son, currently serves as the president of Blackaby Ministries International. He has co-authored numerous books with his father, including: *Experiencing God* (Revised Edition), *Spiritual Leadership*, *Experiencing God: Day by Day*, *Blackaby Study Bible*, *Hearing God's Voice*, and *Called to Be God's Leader: Studies in the Life of Joshua*. He has also written *The Seasons of God* and *The Inspired Leader*. Dr. Blackaby is married to Lisa, and they have three children: Mike, Daniel, and Carrie. He speaks internationally on living the Christian life.

NOTES

Notes